REASON TO READ

THINKING STRATEGIES FOR LIFE THROUGH LITERATURE

■ VOLUME ONE ■

CATHY COLLINS BLOCK
TEXAS CHRISTIAN UNIVERSITY

JOHN N. MANGIERI
ARKANSAS STATE UNIVERSITY

INNOVATIVE LEARNING PUBLICATIONS

ADDISON-WESLEY PUBLISHING COMPANY

MENLO PARK, CALIFORNIA ■ READING, MASSACHUSETTS ■ NEW YORK ■ DON MILLS, ONTARIO
WOKINGHAM, ENGLAND ■ AMSTERDAM ■ BONN ■ PARIS ■ MILAN ■ MADRID
SYDNEY ■ SINGAPORE ■ TOKYO ■ SEOUL ■ TAIPEI ■ MEXICO CITY ■ SAN JUAN

To our students, colleagues, mentors, and families—
your encouragement is such a special gift. Thank you.

ABOUT THE AUTHORS

Dr. Cathy Collins Block is a professor of the School of Education at Texas Christian University, where her research focuses on advancing higher-level thinking, language learning, and increasing teachers' ability to extend students' learning. She is a prolific author of books and articles in *The School Administrator, The Reading Teacher, Journal of Reading,* and *Reading Today* and has appeared on a nationally televised (ABC) broadcast on creativity in United States schools. She serves on the Editorial Board for *The Reading Teacher* and *National Reading Conference Yearbook.* In 1992 she was chosen as a USA Citizen Ambassador to Russia and Hungary.

Dr. John N. Mangieri is currently president of Arkansas State University. He has been a Fulbright Scholar, Dean of the School of Education at Texas Christian University, has served as consultant to school districts and colleges, and has had published numerous books and articles in reading and education journals. He has served on HEW's National Task Force on Urban Education, as a representative at the Institute for Educational Management at Harvard University, and is a member of the Board of Directors for the Eisenhower Center.

This book is published by Innovative Learning Publications™, an imprint of the Alternative Publishing Group of Addison-Wesley Publishing Company.

Senior Editor: **Lois Fowkes**

Project Editor: **Rachel Farber**

Design Manager: **Jeff Kelly**

Production Director: **Janet Yearian**

Production Coordinator: **Claire Flaherty**

Design and Production: **Graham Metcalfe, Paula Shuhert**

Illustrations: **Joel Snyder, Carl Yoshihara**

Cover Design and Illustration: **Rachel Gage**

ISBN 0-201-49047-1

1 2 3 4 5 6 7 8 9 10–ML–98 97 96 95 94

CONTENTS

Contents

Contents

ACKNOWLEDGMENTS

We would like to express our deep appreciation to the following school districts and educators who participated in the field-tests of lessons in *Reason to Read*.

Saint Andrew's Presbyterian School, Fort Worth, TX

Fort Worth Independent School District, Fort Worth, TX

Grapevine-Colleyville Independent School District, Grapevine, TX

Fort Worth Country Day School, Fort Worth, TX

Saint Mary of the Mills School, Laurel, MD

Arlington Independent School District, Arlington, TX

Everman Independent School District, Everman, TX

Fort Worth Hebrew Day School, Fort Worth, TX

Fort Worth Christian Academy, Fort Worth, TX

Trinity Valley, Fort Worth, TX

Fort Worth Academy, Fort Worth, TX

Arlington, Virginia Public Schools, Arlington, VA

Hurst-Euless-Bedford Independent School District, Hurst, TX

Saint Andrew's Episcopal Private School, Fort Worth, TX

Grand Prairie Independent School District, Grand Prairie, TX

We wish to extend our deep gratitude for the critiques and instruction the following teachers provided for *Reason to Read*. We also express our appreciation for all the students in their classes who wrote individual evaluations of the lessons they were taught. These teachers and students worked diligently to improve the quality of the instruction in this reading program. The teachers and administrators included were: Jodi Baker, Jan Bauer, Cindy Blevins, Kirsten Borchert, Donna Brown, Paul Burrer, Meg Capaioli, Elizabeth Carey, Lisa Clark, Laura Dapra, Sarah Depee, Laura DeLong, Debbie Dickinson, Gail Donahue, Aimee Elwell, Diane Evans-Gayer, Carol Gerrick, Juliana Glover, Mary Graham, Mary Grassl, Angela Griffith, Patricia Gutierrez, Sally Hampton, Tory Hess, Susan Hodgkins, Valerie Hoffman, Laura Jaynes, Beverly Juster, Marilyn Kellough, Many Kuehl, Julie Kulp, Laura Lane, Billie Latimer, Sarah Layne, Laura Liggett, Kathryn Luton, Cindy Mayes, Danielle McDonald, Branda McFarlane, Jennifer McKenna, Kelley McLain, Kathy Miller, Martha Murdoch, Lanita Nickerson, Sharon Nolan, Pat O'Connor, Kathryn Oglesby, Linda Pawley, Jennifer Pearson, Katherine Preissinger, Sheila Pryor, Linda Ramos, Anna-Margaret Ray, Matthew Ripley-Moffitt, Loretta Ross, Carl Scherrieb, Dorothy Scott, Judy Siebenberg, Jo Shaffer, Michelle Smith, Elizabeth Sparks, Susan Steinberg, Angela Stephenson, Connie Swinden, Michael Taranto, Nancy Thomas, Cindy Walling, Heather Westfall, Laura Young, and Julie Zobal.

PREFACE

Reason to Read is a three-volume reading program that has been designed to strengthen students' decoding, comprehension, metacognition, and thinking competencies. Volume One contains sixteen lessons that develop 79 reading, writing, speaking, and listening competencies, as well as fifteen higher- level comprehension, metacognitive, and thinking abilities. Students learn to self-initiate many strategies that enhance decision making, conflict resolution, problem solving, creativity, cooperative group work, and abilities to work effectively alone.

All lessons in *Reason to Read* assist students to think for themselves, not merely to recite strategies or to repeat what other people have thought. Students implement these higher-level decoding, comprehension, metacognitive, and cognitive processes with literature and activities they select as they work with content area problems and conflicts that occur out of school. During instruction students reference "thinking guides," graphic depictions and verbal explanations of individual strategic processes. "Think alouds" and teacher modeling have proven to be highly effective instructional devices and are used in this program.

Reason to Read began to take shape as we conducted research to identify characteristics of highest-achieving readers and thinkers, analyzed characteristics of highly

successful schools, and researched the effects of *Reason to Read*'s lessons on student achievement. This work verified that although good and poor comprehenders use similar strategies to understand, only the best readers consistently and persistently use a variety of strategies and transfer them to unique situations without instruction. This behavior contrasts to that of poorer readers who have not learned the strategies in this series. These poorer readers will reuse a limited set of reading/thinking strategies throughout their lives and will more likely give up after their first decoding, comprehension, or thinking strategy is unsuccessful (Block, 1993a; Kletzien, 1991; Zabrucky and Ratner, 1989). The implementation of these and other research findings makes *Reason to Read* unique in many respects.

Reason to Read is the only literacy program in which comprehension strategies, higher-level thinking abilities, and metacognition are developed as specific objectives in each lesson. While many basal reading and whole-language programs teach the names and ask questions about a few of the strategies developed in this program, *Reason to Read* is the only program that equips students with the abilities to initiate their use unprompted. *Reason to Read* develops these abilities by infusing strategy instruction in a process, literature-based program. In field tests, this combination significantly increased the achievement of more than 2,000 students from the southwestern, northeastern, and eastern sections of the United States. Specifically, students who were taught using *Reason to Read* lessons significantly outperformed control subjects on standardized tests of decoding, vocabulary, comprehension, self-esteem, critical thinking, and creative reasoning. They also significantly outperformed untrained peers in their abilities to solve problems, reflect, appreciate multiple genres, work cooperatively in groups, and use several higher-order strategies interactively as they read, wrote, spoke, listened, and thought.

We wrote *Reason to Read* to make such growth accessible to as many teachers and students as possible. Because literature substitution is possible in every lesson, Volume One can be used at a variety of grade levels. If lessons are used as written, however, they are most appropriate for students whose interests and readability levels range from the third to fifth grades. Among *Reason to Read*'s special features are that it:

■ contains lessons that develop students' multiple intelligences: verbal/linguistic, logical/mathematical, musical/rhythmical, bodily/kinesthetic, visual/spatial, interpersonal, and intrapersonal (Gardner and Hatch, 1989; Sternberg, 1985)

■ can be used as a stand-alone reading program or as a companion to basal and whole-language reading programs

■ includes multiple opportunities to integrate reading, writing, speaking, listening, and thinking strategies with content areas and current events

■ includes thirty-three genres so as to develop students' breadth of literary knowledge and appreciation

■ includes strategies for less able and advanced readers in every lesson, as well as literature and experiences that build multicultural understanding

■ employs lessons that are easily teachable without prior training

■ provides options to meet the needs of varied classroom groups

■ enables teachers to extend some parts of individual lessons and eliminate others, based on students' special needs

■ has been extensively field-tested

■ has three or more experiences in each lesson in which students can work independently; these provide extended practice for early finishers or homework learning experiences and allow teachers to meet with individual students

■ contains lessons that provide direct explanation, modeling, and graphic depictions of strategic processes and enable students to choose and enjoy literature and activities as they meet their own strategic goals

■ uses literature already available in individual classrooms and schools, eliminating the expense of purchasing multiple copies of specific selections

■ includes at least two student self-assessments in each lesson and numerous opportunities for teachers to document students' competencies

■ includes 22 different types of performance-based assessments for whole-class and individual student evaluations (see pages 191–216)

INTRODUCTION

HOW TO TEACH <u>REASON TO READ</u>

The principal goal of education is to create [people] who are capable of doing new things, not simply of repeating what other generations have done—[people] who are creative, inventive discoverers. The second goal of education is to form minds which can be critical, can verify, and not accept everything they are offered.

—*Jean Piaget*

After reading the three parts of this section you will be able to implement *Reason to Read* without additional instructions. Part I describes the learning principles and rationale upon which *Reason to Read* is based. Part II describes ways this program addresses current issues in education. Part III suggests multiple plans for implementing the series in your classroom.

PART 1

WHY <u>REASON TO READ</u> WORKS

ON WHAT LEARNING PRINCIPLES IS <u>REASON TO READ</u> BUILT?

Reason to Read contains many learning principles that support teacher instruction and bolster students' chances for success. Presently many American students exert little or no effort to learn because our schools are not addressing their cognitive and affective needs. "The old theory that 'We can make 'em work; all we have to do is get tough' has never produced intellectual effort in the history of the world," says William Glaser as interviewed in *Phi Delta Kappan* (Gough, 1987, p. 605). Instead we need to enable students to satisfy their needs for power, caring, sharing, creating, and cooperating as they reach goals they set for themselves. As an educator, you know students can easily repeat what you tell them, guess at answers to comprehension questions, memorize information, move their eyes across text as their minds wander, copy from the board, and think what you want them to think. This book is designed to assist you in teaching them to do more.

You are also probably aware that most of your students do their highest levels of thinking outside the classroom. As they conduct the inescapable, personal affairs of everyday life, students are forced, and often flounder as they try, to think. Such unassisted, trial-and-error thinking will no longer be necessary for your students. *Reason to Read* enables you to teach students how to initiate their own higher-level thinking strategies, enact their own initiatives, speak up, listen actively, read purposefully, write original syntheses, and modify strategic processes as they construct ideas throughout their lives.

Moreover, these lessons promote students' positive attitudes toward reading and thinking and develop high levels of self-esteem because they contain the following instructional principles:

- multiple opportunities for teacher/student selection or material and activities
- flexibility in the difficulty of lesson content
- rewards for partially correct answers
- encouragement to ask questions
- adequate pupil response time[1]

In addition, these lessons explicitly model and instruct "sense making," metacognition, higher-level comprehension and thinking, decision making, problem solving, group work skills, and reflectivity (Porter and Brophy, 1988; Block, 1993a). Students complete authentic and intrinsically motivating activities. Students become engaged in real-life experiences and are more likely to retain the lessons they learn. (Pau, 1989). Assessments are made during, rather than after instruction to document how well students read and think while they are involved in the processes.

WHY DO WE NEED TO BUILD THINKING ABILITIES DURING READING INSTRUCTION?

First, students must reach responsible decisions earlier in contemporary society than in the past. Today's youth, often by the ages of ten to fifteen, "have their last best chance to choose a path toward productive and fulfilled lives." (Carnegie, 1989, p. 20) Many students live in neighborhoods where they are afraid to walk to school. Many students are tempted or pressured to experiment with drugs and alcohol at a young age. Without sound thinking strategies, surrounded by equally confused peers, many children will make poor choices with harmful consequences. As Hahn, Dansberger, and Lefkowitz (1987) found, significant correlations exist between students' inability to think on

---

[1] Based on research by Borick, 1979; Brophy and Evertson, 1974; and Collins and Mangieri, 1992

higher levels and their use of destructive means to fulfill a need for power and importance. Moreover, research demonstrates that without instruction, the patterns of thinking developed during childhood will not change in adulthood (Eichorn, 1989).

Second, students in North America did not perform as well on measures of higher-level thinking as students in other countries (Kutscher, 1989). We contend that if our students are to continue to rise to international leadership positions, we must begin to teach them how to (1) use thinking strategies, (2) employ fair-minded flexibility in groups, (3) create ideas cooperatively, (4) encourage multiple options, and (5) select among equally attractive alternatives. To help students develop these abilities, we need to devote more time during reading instruction to the development of critical thinking about printed materials, which is the goal of *Reason to Read*. As Beck (1989) stated, "Reading and language arts are the perfect vehicle for developing higher-order thinking because literature—perhaps more than any other source of information—provides powerful models of problem-solving processes. It is full of characters who engage in effective and ineffective attempts at solving problems, who use incisive or fuzzy reasoning, and who rely on adequate or inadequate evidence....What is needed is to move the activities that involve higher-order thinking into the core of our lessons, to move our concern toward developing higher-level thinking into the mainstream of instruction." (pages 680, 682)

Third, educators now realize that language abilities and thinking competencies shape each other, and that both are of equal intensity in fostering learning. For example, through the power of reading development, the quantity and quality of student thought improves. Likewise, by improving thinking strategies, the transitory thoughts that occur in the process of reading, writing, and interacting with others can be transformed into lasting principles. These transformations occur because new ideas enter the mind as cognitive entries, and readers use cognitive strategies to bond these ideas with previously collected categories of thoughts. In turn, the combinations of categorical thoughts that strategic processes enable are stored as dense cognitive structures (called schema), the collections of

learning, experiences, emotions, and values one has about a topic. Subsequently, the nerve endings, or dendrites, in schema, expand in length and breadth as students discuss and learn new thinking strategies and concepts. This depth and breadth forces more and more dendrites to intertwine, which increases students' reflection and thoughtfulness (Rosenblatt, 1978; Smith, 1978). Thus, as students learn the thinking strategies in this series, they will regularly and continuously ignite concept attainments and strengthen or modify the understandings that already exist.

Fourth, prior to the twentieth century, after-school apprenticeships performed the role of developing strategic processes and higher-level thinking abilities. Every day children worked with adults. They observed and questioned mentors about work skills and world events. In addition, students enjoyed the stories their parents and grandparents told and often read in common rooms at the end of the day. Elders often explained the strategies and higher-level thinking processes they used in their lives. The popularity of television and the increasingly busy pace of contemporary society has greatly decreased the oral interaction between children and adults. Through the instruction in this book, however, you can recreate these thinking and communication opportunities for your students.

Fifth, knowledge in contemporary society is increasing at a rate of more than fifteen percent per year. Many jobs that students will hold in the twenty-first century have not yet been invented, and today's required technological competencies are only ten percent of what present kindergarten students will need when they become adults (Duffy, 1992). Contemporary literacy requires that students independently validate spoken and written statements and solve problems using incomplete data. They must also discern thought patterns among disparate sources of information. Therefore, while much of the content and information in the reading instruction your students receive will likely become obsolete by the time they become adults, the thinking competencies you assist them to develop today will retain their value.

Sixth, through the lessons in this series, you will promote students' creativity, an important tool in building original ideas and becoming successful in professional pursuits. Creativity will not develop naturally to its fullest extent without instruction. For example, in a longitudinal study of kindergarten students, eighty-four percent of all kindergartners ranked high in aptitude for creative thinking. By the end of second grade, however, without instruction, only ten percent sustained even a significant level of inventive capacity (Block, 1993). Without assistance, most students will stop their exploratory thinking processes as soon as they state their first answer and, through their school experiences, will come to erroneously accept that *there is only one right answer and that it is very easy to be wrong.*

Creativity also enhances students' abilities to resolve conflicts and solve complex problems in life. Unless you assist students to recognize the complexities and relationships between seemingly disparate ideas, many forces outside of school will convince them that answers to problems should be simple and that problems do not demand deep, creative reflection. For example, students see on television that "all you need is one grand shoot-out at the O. K. Corral at high noon and all this complex fuss that they have watched for three hours will be over" [and so too should all problems in their lives be instantly and simply solved] (Stuart and Graves, 1987, p. 23). Furthermore, developing students' creativity strengthens qualities that lead to students' success outside of school. Specifically, research indicates that creative people maintain high standards, accept confusing uncertainties, and view the higher risks of failure as part of a process for monumental accomplishments. Such highly creative and reflective individuals also approach what they perceive to be important aspects of their work with considerably more intensity than students who use fewer creative and critical-thinking strategies. Creative people also exhibit an internalized license to challenge the conventional and to express their own insights frequently and fervently.

Finally, perhaps the greatest strength of this series' thinking-strategies approach to reading comprehension is its direct and constant connection to literature and the opportunities it provides for students to choose the literature and activities relevant to their own lives. A significant corollary to this feature is the program's strong metacognitive component—making students aware of what they are doing as they are doing it.

PART 2

WAYS <u>REASON TO READ</u> ADDRESSES CURRENT ISSUES IN EDUCATION

WHY DOES <u>REASON TO READ</u> USE INDIVIDUAL LITERATURE TITLES AS THE BASIS FOR INSTRUCTION?

Many researchers have documented that reading and sharing a wide variety of literature motivates students to (1) read more frequently; (2) read voluntarily and show increased interest in books; (3) achieve higher scores on standardized tests; and (4) achieve higher levels of comprehension and vocabulary knowledge because these students read significantly more words than students in classrooms where short-story selections are read (Anderson, Hiebert, Scott, and Wilkinson, 1985; Morrow, 1987; and Mervar and Hiebert, 1989). To realize these achievements for your students, *Reason to Read* uses more than 300 selections of literature appropriate for young people. You may work with the titles suggested for each lesson and/or substitute other books students wish to read.

WHY DOES <u>REASON TO READ</u> INTEGRATE READING INSTRUCTION WITH CONTENT–AREA DISCIPLINES?

Part 3 of each lesson enables students to use the strategies in this series to increase comprehension in their content area courses. Our research demonstrates that through this critical reading instruction, students learn to emulate thinking patterns employed by scientists, mathematicians, artists, historians, and public speakers. In doing so, students assess their aptitudes and interests in these professions in a more realistic fashion.

Moreover, the integrated approach in Part 3 of each lesson provides such intense engagement with a topic that students generate denser background knowledge, stimulate multisensory

experiences, and strengthen schema. This process in turn enables students to more easily retain and transfer the new information to their lives (Norton, 1990; Beck and Dole, 1992). Students also read and think using more references and contrast several perspectives and thinking strategies. Such comparisons tend to become habitual patterns of thought for students due to the repeated emphasis that the integrated lessons in this series provide. Also, as students integrate reading and thinking strategies with content area knowledge, their creative thinking expands. They exercise options, examine issues with differing ideas, and practice flexibility. Students need instructional guidance, however, before they can consistently use these creative-thinking strategies to make a variety of new connections in real-world situations. *Reason to Read* enables you to support students as they make such discoveries.

In summary, through your instruction with *Reason to Read*, students learn to appreciate the strengths and limitations of their own knowledge, the methods and fallibility of rationality, and the universality or specificity of reading materials or spoken information (Block, 1993b).

WHY DOES PART 4 OF EACH LESSON ADDRESS STUDENTS' SPECIAL NEEDS?

In the past, educators believed that instruction for students who have special needs should be the same as that for students without special reading/thinking difficulties, only slower and less demanding. We now realize that students with special needs require more complex and intense instruction. In Part 4 of each lesson, you can reinforce what students have learned through previous exposure to the strategy in Parts 1 through 3. In omitting such direct instruction, many teachers unknowingly place a distance between themselves and less able students. They give students less time to answer questions, call upon them less often during discussions, sit them near the back of the room, or demand less from them (Willinsky, 1990). *Reason to Read* assists you in providing supports less able students need because students are given the opportunity to meet with you for special activities in each lesson of this series.

Similarly, while gifted students have advanced reading abilities, develop extensive vocabularies, and sprinkle complex sentences and complicated syntactical forms with accurate and creative expression, they need special activities to increase their capabilities (Bonds and Bonds, 1984). Gifted students need to learn to perceive relationships, solve problems, and grasp abstract ideas. Such students do not learn as well unaided as they will through the lessons in this series. Among the types of assistance *Reason to Read* provides are the freedom to (1) learn at a more rapid pace, (2) engage in hypothetical reasoning, (3) make higher-order inferences, (4) create interdisciplinary projects, and (5) prepare in-depth studies using thinking strategies they have learned in areas of talent and interest.

Second-language learners also benefit from *Reason to Read*. Research documents that second-language and culturally diverse students benefit from reading activities that are not language dependent but are performance based. Lessons in *Reason to Read* provide such learning opportunities by placing second-language learners in group leadership roles and enabling them to report their learning through recounts of important events in their lives.

Your special students will profit from the instruction in *Reason to Read* because it bolsters their talents and maximizes the strengths they possess. Such students can use the strategies, lessons, and instructional assistance of *Reason to Read* in furthering their reading/thinking development. Such repeated guidance will assist them in reaching their potential.

WHY DOES <u>REASON TO READ</u> INCLUDE MULTIPLE FORMS OF ASSESSMENT?

This series contains more authentic, performance-based achievement measures than other reading programs. The goals of these assessments are to assess students as they (a) internalize high standards and develop valid criteria for judging the quality of their work, (b) recognize their own potential, and (c) articulate their goals for upcoming projects and learning activities. Students will develop these evaluative thinking processes through the practice *Reason to Read* provides in producing original conversations, products, and writings for assessment and through the repair and modifications of strategies that the program's performance assessments encourage. Such disciplined self-inquiry is a result of three features: students (1) self-select their own knowledge base, (2) prepare their own in-depth demonstrations of knowledge gained (as opposed to reacting to superficial rote application of strategies), and (3) produce new understandings and uses of the strategies in integrated forms that have intrinsic value to the students themselves. Many of the assessments afford opportunities for students to ask and depend on the help of peers in collaborative evaluations, a process which will occur more frequently as they enter their adult lives. In addition, the assessments (see pages 191–216) enable you to evaluate students' growth over time, as students express strategic knowledge through conversations, performances, and/or products they use in their lives outside of school. For example, the Classroom Assessment Monitor enables you to evaluate several weeks after instruction students' impromptu insights, transfers of previous instruction to novel events, and demonstrations of unprompted strategy use.

These assessments measure a wider range of intelligences than possible through other reading programs. Specifically, other assessments measure almost exclusively the language and thinking abilities that occur in the prefrontal cortex: students' verbal/ linguistic knowledge and their abilities to be logical with and manipulate printed words. In the evaluations in *Reason to Read*, students have the opportunity to use logical/mathematical, verbal/linguistic , bodily/kinesthetic, intrapersonal, interpersonal, musical/rhythmical, and visual/spatial intelligences to demonstrate their strategic knowledge and comprehension.

Reason to Read's assessment exercises enable you and your students to engage in collaborative reflections and student self-assessments and to include parents in some instances. Such experiences enable students to gain long-lasting confidence through successful experiences of evaluating themselves.

In summation, this program addresses a whole-language, literature-based philosophy while incorporating a thinking-strategies approach to learning. The program builds on the strengths of both these philosophies by:

- enabling the use of multiple intelligences/ learning styles to succeed

- adapting lessons to meet special students' needs

- providing readings and inputs from diverse cultural backgrounds

- involving parents in their children's learning and achievements assesses knowledge in authentic ways, with students knowing in advance the criteria upon which they and others can judge their work

- introducing students to thirty-three genres to further their literary appreciation and understanding

This new instructional approach—strategy instruction in a student-centered curriculum—combines explicit strategic instruction with students' choice of objectives, activities, and literature. This method aids students in valuing reading and thinking as self-initiated, personalized problem-solving and information-gathering processes.

HOW TO USE THIS PROGRAM IN THE CLASSROOM

HOW TO INITIATE THE PROGRAM

You can teach lessons in the order in which they appear in the series or you can present them according to students' needs. For example, if lessons are taught in their chronological order, the more basic, cognitive processes in the first lessons can assist students as they learn the more advanced strategies. For example, recognizing different points of view (Lesson 3) enhances students' abilities to recognize varied persuasive, propaganda devices (Lesson 6). Teaching individual lessons when students demonstrate a need for a specific strategy or have an upcoming event in which adeptness in a particular strategy would be advantageous is equally effective. For example, in one classroom, students could not establish effective interpersonal relationships and quarreled each time they engaged in group work. Therefore, during the first week of school, their teacher taught Lessons 13 and 14 ("Working Cooperatively in Groups"). Because students learned these strategies first, they developed productive group-work skills, established a positive classroom climate, and learned the remainder of their lessons more rapidly and effectively.

TIME SCHEDULE OPTIONS

Reason to Read, Volume One, can be used as the complete reading curriculum for one school year by allocating two to two-and-one-half weeks per lesson in Lessons 1 through 15, and one to four days instruction for Lesson 16, the final review. Using this schedule, students will learn all the thinking and reading/language arts competencies and have opportunities to apply them in depth.

Reason to Read can also be used as only one component of a reading program. If used in this manner, individual lessons can be modified so as to require less than two weeks of instruction.

You can alter a lesson by combining activities in Parts 3 and 4 and reducing the length of time in which students engage in each learning opportunity for all parts of each lesson. Alternatively, many teachers have used the lessons for more than one period in a day, instructing activities from Parts 3 and 4 in their afternoon social studies, science, and mathematics programs. This schedule intensifies students' initial exposure to strategies and provides more concentrated learning experiences.

FORMAT OF EACH LESSON

Each lesson is based on four premises. First, research has demonstrated that if students use strategic processes *consistently and reflectively* as they read, they comprehend more. Second, students who have trouble comprehending have shown a need for new reading/thinking strategies before they can be successful readers because such students' thinking processes appear to be underdeveloped, leaving them without the strategic knowledge to effectively and simultaneously decode and comprehend. Therefore, as lessons in *Reason to Read* strengthen students' thinking processes, their reading problems are reduced. Third, students who become confused about important concepts, inferences, and relationships in a text appear to experience these difficulties because past experiences have not exposed them to the inductive or deductive reasoning pattern the author used to create that text. Such readers do not understand the connections between pieces of information. However, students who learned the inductive and deductive thinking strategies in *Reason to Read* comprehended authors' thought patterns better. Finally, students can learn to solve their own decoding and comprehension problems independently if they use the variety of thinking and problem-solving processes contained in this series.

Each lesson is divided into four parts. Part 1 provides an introduction to a strategy. In Part 1, you describe to students the strategy, the goals for the day's work, methods students will use to apply the strategy, and how they will know they have learned to use the strategy effectively. You also dispel any misconceptions students may hold about a particular strategy, eliminate their inaccurate prior knowledge, and discuss students' successful or unsuccessful attempts to think strategically in the past. Immediately following this introduction, you give students a Thinking Guide, which is a one-page diagram of a strategic process. Thinking Guides are designed to make the information more vivid and memorable for students.

Prior to the first use of a strategy, however, you and students generate several examples of how they can use the strategy in their lives and during the subsequent reading in Part 2 of the lesson. In essence, Part 1 contains the following components that can be instructed in one class period: (1) a statement of student objectives; (2) a listing of the reading and language arts competencies addressed in the lesson; (3) an explanation and modeling of the thinking strategy in the "Exploring The Strategy" section; (4) an opportunity for students to view and use a one-page graphic depiction of the strategy on a Thinking Guide and as they complete the "Using The Thinking Guide" section of the lesson; (5) an activity in which you and your students use the thinking guide while reading from a selection of children's literature, in the section entitled "Applying The Thinking Guide to Literature"; and (6) a list of assessment options.

Part 2 of the lesson enables students to choose an activity in which they can employ the strategy as they read. Such choices enable students to regulate their depth of thinking while they read and establish their own purposes for reading. Moreover, when students select a strategy and goal before reading in Parts 2 through 4 of the lesson, their lessons simulate how thinking and reading occur in the real world. This simulation makes transfer of instruction easier (J. Mangieri, August 30, 1991). Part 2 begins when students engage in a reading activity of their choice that can be completed alone, with a friend, or in a small group. Students place their

Thinking Guides on their desks beside the material they chose to read. This method enables easy reference and reflection and encourages application of the strategy. After completing their reading, students can self-assess or you can evaluate how much they have learned through several options, such as (a) answering the question, "What have I learned from this lesson that I will use later in life?"; (b) generating and reporting new uses of the strategy; (c) discussing what they have learned with a peer and preparing a report of their joint work; and (d) presenting a summary to you or the class.

Part 2 can be completed in one to four days by increasing the time students read from their selection of children's literature. This reading activity can become the second through the fifth day of the first week's work with each lesson. For example, on day two of the lesson, students can set their own objectives, select their reading material, and begin reading and applying the strategy introduced on the previous day in Part 1 of the lesson. On days three and four students complete their readings and plan their self-assessments and demonstrations of what they have learned. On day five, students can write and/or perform their demonstrations.

In essence, Part 2 of each lesson contains: (1) a review of the Thinking Guide and description of literature that students may wish to consider as they use the strategy, in a section entitled "Applying The Strategy Themselves"; (2) a section entitled "Using The Thinking Guide in Part 2" whereby students select from several activities or design their own in which they apply the strategy to an area of their interest. (Activities in this section provide opportunities for students to elect to work alone, with a friend, in a small group, or with you; and (3) student self-assessments and teacher assessments in which several evaluation options are suggested.

Part 3 of each lesson enables students to use the strategy across several curricular areas. You may use as many activities in this section as you deem appropriate to meet students' needs. Activities are designed for all areas of the curriculum, including fine arts, physical education, social studies, history, mathematics, and science. Part 3 is designed to build students' automaticity. The goal is for students to use thinking strategies without being prompted to do so. Activities in Part 3 can be completed in one day or extended for one week's duration.

Part 4 facilitates your ability to meet individual students' needs and gives students extended opportunities to apply the strategy to their lives. Activities in this part of the lesson are designed to provide opportunities for (1) less able readers to elect to meet with you; (2) more gifted readers to learn advanced applications of the strategy; (3) students of multicultural backgrounds to interpret their understandings through avenues that reflect their respective cultures; (4) individual students to develop reflectivity as they work alone to apply the strategy to personal incidents in their lives; and (5) groups of students to develop a deeper understanding of themselves and others, as they use the strategy to solve a difficult situation that frequently occurs in life. The goal of Part 4 is to provide new methods of learning the strategy and to extend the strategy to new situations in life.

LESSON 1

ASKING QUESTIONS WHILE READING, THINKING, AND LISTENING

STUDENT OBJECTIVES

In Part 1, students will learn to ask effective questions of themselves and others as they read historical fiction or other types of literature. In Parts 2 through 4, they will identify questions fictional characters and famous people asked to clarify their thinking.

READING AND LANGUAGE ARTS CONNECTIONS

- introducing eight word-recognition strategies
- appreciating, recognizing, and responding to historical fiction for personal enjoyment
- strengthening interpretive comprehension
- strengthening literal comprehension
- practicing phonetic analysis and comparing word families
- practicing structural analysis
- using semantic context clues
- using syntactic context clues
- practicing dictionary skills
- recognizing appropriate incidents for skipping words
- asking for word meanings

EXPLORING THE STRATEGY

INTRODUCING THE LESSON

To introduce Lesson 1, share with students that researchers have discovered a common element among successful people in a variety of fields. These people ask questions of themselves and others when they become confused or want to understand something more completely. Add that students can also learn to ask good questions, and doing so will increase their understanding of themselves and the world around them. Tell students they will know they have improved their abilities when they notice they are asking more questions of themselves and others and when they feel as if others understand them better. Explain that these changes will likely occur within two weeks of practicing the strategy introduced in this lesson.

USING THE THINKING GUIDE

To introduce the Thinking Guide "Asking Questions to Clarify" (Blackline Master 1), ask students to think of times they benefited from asking someone else a question. List students' situations and the specific questions they asked on the board. Then have students explain how the questions they asked were helpful. Distribute the Thinking Guide. As you read aloud each question on the guide, ask students to think of examples of literary characters who ask questions to help clarify something, or share examples from your own life when asking questions listed on the guide helped you. Finally, ask students to place a checkmark in front of three questions they will try to ask in the coming week.

You may want to close this introduction to the Thinking Guide by sharing comments other students have made about the benefits they have received from learning to use the question-asking strategy.

Keri said,	"I am now able to ask questions of anyone and not feel stupid doing it."
Natasha said,	"I want to be more specific when asking questions."
Steven said,	"When I asked a question, the teacher gave me ideas about it. I wasn't confused for the rest of the period. I was able to keep up with what the class was thinking. It felt good to be with everyone else."
Nic said,	"The harder my problem, the better questions I will have to ask. You definitely need to ask questions to be a good thinker."

APPLYING THE THINKING GUIDE TO LITERATURE

In the next activity, students will read or listen to you read the story on Blackline Master 2. Before you begin, explain that the story is about President Franklin Roosevelt and a newspaper reporter. You may want to clarify that the story is historical fiction, which means it is based on real people and events, but some parts may be fiction. Tell students they will have a chance to ask questions as they read. Ask students to pretend they are the reporter in the story. Tell them they will read with you to a certain point in the story and ask themselves what they would have done had they been the reporter. Distribute Blackline Master 2 and read the story orally or ask students to read it silently.

When students have reached the stopping place and written their answers, ask several students to share their answers and why they would have done what they decided. Then distribute Blackline Master 3. Ask students to return to the story and compare what they wrote to what actually occurred. Tell them to notice the reporter will use a strategy used by other successful people. After students read what actually occurred, ask them to explain whether they would change their answers now that they know how the newspaper reporter responded. Confirm for students that just as learning to ask questions helped this reporter to better understand President Roosevelt, asking questions to gain more information will help them as well.

ASSESSMENT OF PART 1

If you wish to assess or have students self-assess how much they have learned at this point in the lesson, ask them to do the following:

- Answer the question, "What have you learned from this lesson that you will use later in life?"

- Generate new uses for the strategy.

- Discuss and write with a partner about what they have learned.

- Share insights with the class orally or in writing.

APPLYING THE STRATEGY

RECOGNIZING EFFECTS OF QUESTION-ASKING IN LITERATURE: HISTORICAL FICTION

You may use historical fiction readings for this lesson, other fiction, or short stories from basal readers or literature anthologies in which characters ask questions to gain new information and solve difficulties. If you select historical fiction, define the genre for students before they select the book they wish to read. Help them understand that historical fiction is about real or fictional people at a specific period in time engaged in events that could have but may not have occurred. You may want to refer students to any historical fiction in the library or make a selection available in your classroom. The following books are widely available:

High Interest/Low Vocabulary

Fritz, J. *Can't You Make Them Behave, King George?* New York: Coward McCann, 1977.

Greene, Carol. *Martin Luther King, Jr.: A Man Who Changed Things.* Chicago: Children's Press, 1991.

Greene, Carol. *Thurgood Marshall: First Afro-American Supreme Court Justice.* Chicago: Children's Press, 1991.

Jakoubek, Robert E. *Harriet Beecher Stowe: Author and Abolitionist.* New York: Chelsea House Publications, 1989.

Lawson, R. *Mr. Revere and I.* Boston: Little, Brown, 1953.

Lundgren, Hal. *Mary Lou Retton: Gold Medal Olympist.* Chicago: Children's Press, 1985.

Monjo, F. N. *King George's Head Was Made of Lead.* New York: Coward McCann, 1974.

Levels 4–6

Fleischmon, P. *The Borning Room.* New York: HarperCollins, 1991.

Forbes, E. *Johnny Tremain.* Boston: Houghton Mifflin, 1943.

Fritz, J. *The Double Life of Pocahontas.* New York: G. P. Putnam's Sons, 1983.

Ho, M. *The Clay Marble.* New York: Farrar, Straus & Giroux, 1991.

Kallen, Stuart. *The Civil Rights Movement.* Edina, MI: ABDO and Daughters, 1990.

Levine, E. *Freedom's Children.* New York: Viking, 1991.

O'Dell, S. *Island of the Blue Dolphins.* Boston: Houghton Mifflin, 1960.

Wilder, L. I. *Little House on the Prairie.* New York: Harper & Row, 1935 and 1953.

Levels 7–8

Hart, Michael H. *The 100: A Ranking of the Most Influential Persons In History.* New York: Hart, 1978.

Myers, Walter Dean. *Malcolm X: By Any Means Necessary.* New York: Scholastic, 1993.

APPLYING THE THINKING GUIDE TO EVERYDAY LIFE EVENTS

To help students practice using their Thinking Guides and asking questions to clarify, have them select one of the following activities or allow them to suggest an alternative. Review the Thinking Guide with the class before students select their activities.

Collaborative Thinking Have students choose to read a historical nonfiction or fiction book of which you have multiple copies. Ask students to form small reading response groups in which all group members read the same book. Before they begin to read, have students write specific questions on their Thinking Guides that they want Chapter l to answer.

After twenty minutes of silent reading, ask students to return to their questions, write the answers they found, and write about the benefits of asking themselves questions before and during reading. Then have all students share what they wrote and compare the types of questions they asked as they read.

Students on Their Own Have students select and read a book, write on their Thinking Guides the questions the main characters asked, and describe the effects on the plot of asking such questions. After a twenty-minute silent working period, ask students to discuss their analyses. This discussion will be valuable for all students, as those students who were unable to identify any questions asked by the main characters will hear their peers' results. After this discussion, ask students to identify characteristics of more and less effective communicators in their books and why they judged each character as they did.

Thinking with a Friend Pairs of students can skim two favorite books they have read prior to this lesson. As they skim, have students note on the Thinking Guides incidents in which characters do or do not ask questions and the effect of having done so or not upon the characters and the plot. After twenty minutes have elapsed, ask students to report their results to the class.

Dramatic Thinking Have students create a humorous or dramatic role-play of a scene from one of the books they have read prior to this lesson. Stipulate that each drama must include five questions of clarification in the plot. Allow students to practice their role-plays and present them to you in a dress rehearsal before they deliver them to the class. After each role-play ask the audience to identify the questions asked and the benefits they created. Alternatively, students may stage a panel discussion in which they become famous historical figures who respond to questions from their classmates.

STUDENT SELF-ASSESSMENT

At the end of any activity in Part 2, have students report what they learned about the value of asking questions.

or

Students may keep a diary or tally of the questions they ask over a two–week period.

or

Students may interview a person they admire and write a description of the types of questions this person asks most frequently.

TEACHER ASSESSMENT

Review students' written and oral presentations. To evaluate how much students have learned, tally the number of questions students ask over a two-week period and present your findings to students. Then ask them to suggest ways their individual question-asking skills can be improved and to recommend ways the question-and-answer periods in class can be improved.

PART 3

APPLYING THE STRATEGY ACROSS THE CURRICULUM

The following activities are designed to teach students to ask questions in several different areas of the curriculum. You may want to review the Thinking Guide before students begin.

History Have students think of a current political event and write questions that might clarify the issues involved in the event. Alternatively, students can read another book about President Roosevelt or another former United States President. Have students analyze how skillful they were in using the question-asking strategy as they listened and read.

Language Arts Have students select and read a biography or autobiography about a famous person, with no two students reading about the same person. Ask students to prepare a three-to-five-minute videotaped speech in which they pretend they are the person about whom they read. Encourage students to dress as the person might have dressed and to use props to enhance

the speech. Have classmates use the Thinking Guide to ask questions of the speakers. Have students critique their videos either in private or with you. During the critique you and/or the student can use the question-asking strategy to suggest improvements for the content and style of students' presentations.

Science, Mathematics, and Social Studies Invite students to practice asking questions in small group discussions of content topics for one or two days a week for a six-week period. At each meeting, ask students to study a content chapter and appoint a different student to be the "questioner," asking questions from the Thinking Guide as the group discusses and works together. As questions are asked, the answer is recorded on the "questioners'" Thinking Guide. At the close of each meeting, have students describe how these questions aided their group work.

PART 4

MEETING INDIVIDUAL NEEDS

STRATEGIES FOR LESS ABLE READERS

Review the Thinking Guide with students who wish to meet with you individually or in small groups. Have students practice asking questions using the Thinking Guide "When I Don't Know A Word" (Blackline Master 4) by either distributing the Thinking Guide to each student or making it into a classroom chart. Ask students to read each strategy and to ask questions about each one. Teach students each decoding strategy on the guide, explaining the following:

1. As a general rule, frequently occurring words should be memorized. Therefore, when students see words that appear often they should ask themselves: "What clues about that word can help me memorize its pronunciation and meaning?" Help students understand that memorization should be the first decoding strategy they use with such sight words, because it will enable them to recognize such words very rapidly.

2. As a general rule, words with familiar spelling patterns should be analyzed phonetically, comparing and contrasting word parts.

3. As a general rule, long words should be decoded through structural analysis. Locating sections of the word students can pronounce and for which they know the meaning often will be the key to understanding the full word's meaning.

Next demonstrate how students should ask themselves the following questions when they come to a word they do not know:

1. What type of word is this? (e.g., It is a long word.)

2. Which strategy should I try first to decode this word? (e.g., If it's a long word, I know I should first try the structural analysis decoding strategy.)

Once students understand the decoding strategies, have them practice with a partner. Have pairs select a book to read. One student reads orally as the second follows along silently. When students come to a word they don't know, they should see if their partner knows it or ask themselves orally the above questions. Together the pair can reference the Thinking Guide "When I Don't Know a Word" to decode each unknown word. As students read, move from pair to pair to assess their decoding ability and answer any questions. After ten minutes, ask partners to switch roles and continue the activity.

Close this activity by asking for volunteers to meet with a small group of younger schoolmates to teach them how to ask questions and select appropriate decoding strategies. Share with students that such teaching will increase their self-initiated use of both the question-asking strategy and the decoding strategies they have learned.

STRATEGIES FOR BETTER READERS

Ask students to conduct their own research on a chosen topic. As they work, have students reference the Thinking Guide and keep a learning log. In this log, have students record the questions they ask themselves as they research. Before they begin, tell students to establish a goal of asking themselves at least five different questions as they work. Afterwards have them report how these questions improved their research project.

UNDERSTANDING SELF

To assist students in transferring the question-asking strategy to their personal lives, tell them they can understand more about how they learn when they think about why one activity is more appealing to them than others and by trying to use things they enjoy to improve less appealing tasks. To begin, explain to students they can identify qualities in tasks they enjoy by choosing the task they would most like to do from the list you will read to them. As you read, have students write the task they select on a sheet of paper. Read the following tasks to students:

■ Write a question-answer book about a historical time period, and then quiz peers who have studied the same time period.

■ With a partner, create the front page of a newspaper that reflects a time period of your choice.

■ Write and illustrate a picture book for younger students about a specific period in United States history. Read this book to younger children and ask them whether they have any questions about the events described in the book.

■ Keep a diary or write letters in the voice of a famous historical figure.

■ In a small group, create a television program of historical fiction or nonfiction.

■ Read historical fiction about a particular time period and write five questions you want to answer by reading historical nonfiction.

After you have read the list and students have chosen the task they would prefer, ask them to share the reasons they think the activity would increase their learning more than the other activities. When students have heard the rationale behind different peer selections, they can make their final choices, complete the activity, and ask themselves whether they learned as much as they expected to learn.

ASSESSMENT OF PARTS 3 AND 4

Ask students to recall, summarize, and give insights into the strategy of asking questions for clarification. Then complete one or more of the assessments:

■ Class Monitoring Record, Blackline Master 62, to record students' ability to ask effective questions

■ Attitude/Interest Inventory, Blackline Master 68, as a pretest of attitudes and interests in literacy and thinking development (A posttest will be given in Lesson 16 so students' growth can be assessed.)

■ Reading Wheel, Blackline Masters 69 and 70, which can be administered in two ways; as a book record in which students record titles and responses to books read during each lesson or as an end-of-year assessment of students' knowledge of genres

■ Oral-Language Needs Monitor, Blackline Master 71, speech critique or informal checklist for usage if students conducted interviews at the end of Part 2 or made the videotaped speech in the Language Arts activity in Part 3

■ Student Self-Assessment of Thinking Abilities, Blackline Master 79, to evaluate students' growth in thinking ability

■ Associative Word Test of Creative Thinking, Blackline Master 83, to pretest students' creativity (This test will be given at the end of Lesson 12 to assess students' growth.)

LESSON 2

COMPARING AND CONTRASTING (AFTER ASKING QUESTIONS) TO OVERCOME CONFUSION

STUDENT OBJECTIVES

In Part l, students will learn to compare and contrast when they become confused as they read, listen, and think. In Parts 2 through 4, students will practice the strategy by comparing and contrasting folktales from various countries. They will also learn to use comparative thinking to understand perplexing topics in their personal lives and in content area disciplines.

READING AND LANGUAGE ARTS CONNECTIONS

- understanding authors' and speakers' use of comparisons and contrasts to inform, persuade, entertain, and clarify ideas
- recognizing sequential words that signal comparative and contrastive statements
- strengthening interpretative and inferential comprehension of complex concepts through the use of comparative and contrastive thinking
- appreciating, recognizing, and responding to folktales, myths, and legends for personal enjoyment
- participating in rewriting conferences

EXPLORING THE STRATEGY

INTRODUCING THE LESSON

To introduce Lesson 2, ask students to describe their thinking processes when they are bewildered or do not fully understand something, such as directions for assembling equipment, rules of a game, or a confusing paragraph in a textbook or library book. List the ideas on the board. Next ask students what particular items they find confusing. List these on the board and tell students that a strategy they can use to eliminate confusion is to compare what they know to what they just read. Then help them look for similarities and differences betweeen what they are trying to understand and what they know for each item listed on the board. You may wish to give an example from your own life in which comparative thinking eliminated confusion for you. An example might be the choice between going to the humane society or a pet store to get a pet. Then state that today students will learn that when they face any confusion, they can gain more information by asking questions and comparing the new or difficult information with something they already know. Confirm for students that they will know they have learned to use the comparative thinking strategy when they self-initiate it by either picturing the Thinking Guide in their minds or by consciously linking new information to familiar information when they are confused.

When the discussion is over, have students write in their journals or compose a drawing or diagram about a topic, question, or issue they do not fully understand. They may want to think of new questions, or they may want to use the same question they used in the discussion, if they still find it puzzling. Give students examples of complex topics they are studying in other content areas. Last, share with students that they will have an opportunity to explore and answer the question during this lesson.

USING THE THINKING GUIDE

Have students select a partner. Distribute the Thinking Guide "Comparing and Contrasting" (Blackline Master 5) to each pair. Explain to students that in order to learn how to think when they are confused, they are going to answer a question that confuses some people. The question to pose to them is, "A whale lives in the ocean like a fish; what makes it a mammal?" To explore the question, students compare and contrast characteristics of mammals to whales and to fish. You may want to read *The Sierra Club Book of Great Mammals* by Lindsay Knight (New York: Sierra Club, 1993) before you show Blackline Master 6. Place a transparency made from Blackline Master 6 on the overhead projector and describe how each piece of information you knew about whales, mammals, and fish lead you to the answer written in the outer circle. Then ask each pair of students to either select from the two questions they wrote in their journals or to select a new topic about which they will combine their knowledge and comparative thinking strategies to eliminate their confusion. When students have identified their topics, explain that the Thinking Guide can help them compare and contrast their ideas. Tell them to write all similar items on their lists in Section B. Then have them write all the different elements in Sections A and C, using one section for each of the two ideas they are comparing or are confused about. When they have finished, have partners discuss the information in the Thinking Guide and explore how the new and familiar information is similar and different. Then explain that the outer circle contains space for ideas that arise when students are using their comparative-thinking strategies. Such thoughts can help answer the perplexing question and provide new insights.

When students understand how to use the Thinking Guide, tell them they will use it to explore something that confuses them in two folktales, one Native American and the other Romanian.

APPLYING THE THINKING GUIDE TO LITERATURE

Read aloud the two stories on Blackline Masters 7 and 8, or have students read together in small groups. When students have finished reading, ask them to describe something about the stories that confuses them or about which they wonder. Then write their responses on a copy of the Thinking Guide that you have drawn on the overhead or the chalkboard. To stimulate students' thinking, you may ask questions such as the following:

• What makes legends different from fairy tales?

• Why do woodpeckers have long beaks?

• Why do you think the legends were written?

• What might these stories tell you about the similarities and differences between the cultures from which they originate?

After the discussion, write in the outer circle of the Thinking Guide any conclusions about the stories students have reached or other ideas that were expressed during the discussion.

ASSESSMENT OF PART 1

If you wish to end the lesson at this point or to assess how much students have learned, you can use one or more of the assessment options on pages 194–216 or allow students to select the option that enables them to demonstrate what they have learned.

APPLYING THE STRATEGY

RECOGNIZING COMPARATIVE AND CONTRASTIVE THINKING IN LITERATURE: FAIRY TALES AND MYTHS

Review the Thinking Guide. For this section of the lesson, you may use any type of literature selection. However, you may want to use this lesson to introduce the genre of folk literature. If so, ask students what elements folktales, legends, and myths have in common. Help them deduce such stories are part of ancient oral traditions in which stories are told from one generation to the next within a particular culture. Point out that these stories often contain important information for people of the culture. Some may explain natural phenomena, such as the origins of the sun and moon, while others may suggest codes of behavior. For example, the Native American story in Part 1 indicates it is unwise to be stingy. Using the same topic, however, the Romanian tale teaches it is best to mind one's own business. Tell students that reading stories from a culture can help them gain a deeper understanding of the customs and ways of that particular group of people.

Have students choose stories they would like to read. They may be interested in choosing stories that come from their own countries or cultures of origin. While students may select any book in the library, the following is a list of suggested books containing folktales and myths:

High-Interest/Low Vocabulary

Bierhorst. *Doctor Coyote: A Native American Aesop's Fables*. New York: Macmillan, 1987.

Bruchac, J. and London, J. *Thirteen Moons on Turtle's Back: A Native American Year of Moons*. New York: Philomel, 1992.

Coatsworth, E. *The Adventures of Nanabush: Objibway Indian Stories*. New York: Atheneum, 1980.

Goble, Paul. *The Gift of the Sacred Dog*. Scarsdale, NY: Bradbury Press, 1980.

Kendall, R. *Eskimo Boy: Life in an Inupiaq Eskimo Village*. New York: Scholastic, 1992.

Kimmel, Eric A. *The Greatest of All: A Japanese Folktale*. New York: Holiday House, 1991.

Rodanas, K. *Dragonfly's Tale*. New York: Clarion, 1991.

Scieszka, Jon. *The Stinky Cheese Man and Other Fairly Stupid Tales*. New York: Viking, 1992.

Levels 4–6

Baker, Olaf. *Where the Buffaloes Begin*. New York: Puffin Books, 1981.

Baylor, Byrd. *God on Every Mountain*. New York: Scribner, 1981.

Erdoes, Richard and Ortiz, Alfonso. *American Indian Myths and Legends*. Pantheon, 1985.

Grinnell, G. *The Whistling Skeleton: American Indian Tales of the Supernatural*. New York: Four Winds Press, 1982.

Kimmel, Eric A. *Folktales from Foreign Countries: A Russian Folktale*. New York: Holiday House, 1991.

Medearis, Angela S. *Dancing with Indians*. New York: Holiday House, 1992.

Osofsky, A. *Dreamcatcher*. New York: Orchard, 1992.

Potter, Robert and Robinson, Alan. *Myths & Folk Tales Around the World*. New York: Globe Book Company, 1992.

Reeves, James. *Heroes and Monsters of Greek Myth*. London: Piper, 1993.

Taylor, C.J. *How Two-Feather Was Saved From Loneliness: An Abenaki Legend*. Plattsburgh, NY: Tundra, 1990.

Levels 7–8

Weiss, Malcolm E. *Gods, Stars, and Computers: Fact and Fancy in Myth Science*. Garden City, NY: Doubleday, 1980.

APPLYING THE STRATEGY TO EVERYDAY EVENTS

To help students practice using the Thinking Guide "Comparing and Contrasting" and to experience the concepts in this lesson, ask them to choose from the activities below or to use their own topics about which they are confused.

Students on Their Own Have students read the question they wrote in their journals in Part 1 of this lesson. Then ask them to use the Thinking Guide to read, compare, and contrast new information to what they already know about that question. For example, remind students of the example you gave earlier about being confused as to why a whale is a mammal because it lives in the ocean as fish do. Using the Thinking Guide, students should begin by listing what they know about a topic in Section A and then listing the features of the topic about which they read in Section B. When students compare the two, they will find important similarities, such as that breathing air and being warm-blooded are important in classifying animals. Finally, have students write an answer to their question and any other insights they have in the outer circle of the Thinking Guide.

Thinking with a Friend Have students work in pairs and choose two myths, folktales, or fairy tales to read that are about a similar subject. See Blackline Master 9 for suggestions. When students have finished reading, ask them to compare the stories by listing on the Thinking Guide similarities and differences they find. Next have students write in the outer circle any ideas they discover about each story and its culture of origin. When students are finished, have them write in their journals how using the Thinking Guide helped them to gain a deeper understanding of the moral each author was trying to convey.

Collaborative Thinking Students can apply the thinking strategy to an aspect of their lives. Have them think of a problem they are having with another person. Then ask them to list each side of the conflict in Sections A and C of the Thinking Guide and points of agreement in Section B. Allow students to work for approximately thirty minutes. When they have completed these sections, ask them to think of a possible solution to the conflict and to write it in the outer circle. Have them discuss with partners what they discovered by comparing and contrasting two points of view and to write similarities/differences among their discoveries on the back of the Thinking Guides. Last, ask them to list other ways they can use the comparative thinking strategy in their lives.

STUDENT SELF-ASSESSMENT

At the end of any activity in Part 2, ask students to write, diagram, or illustrate how using the comparative thinking strategy has helped them understand new or perplexing information more clearly. Then have them relay what they have learned about thinking that will help them in the future.

or

Have students list situations in which they imagine comparing and contrasting might be most useful and give examples.

or

Have students keep a learning log for a week. Note or ask them to note how many times they report overcoming puzzlements through comparative thinking.

TEACHER ASSESSMENT

To assess how well students have learned to think through puzzlements, you may evaluate whether students:

- use the comparative and contrastive words on Blackline Master 10 more frequently in their speaking and writing than in the past

- exhibit less frustration in content area studies when they become confused

- draw the Thinking Guide "Comparing and Contrasting" without prompting while they are trying to work through confusing situations or learn new information during small group assignments

- describe orally or in writing the thought processes they use to overcome confusion

APPLYING THE STRATEGY ACROSS THE CURRICULUM

The following activities are designed to give students the opportunity to use comparative and contrastive thinking in several areas of the curriculum. Review the Thinking Guide before students engage in their activities.

Science   Have students use the Thinking Guide to understand a science concept that confuses them, such as what makes reptiles different from fish or amphibians or what makes the seasons change. First ask students what the first step should be when they begin to wonder (they should use the comparative-thinking strategy). Then suggest students work with objects and concepts with which they are familiar to answer their questions, such as comparing the earth and sun to a lightbulb and ball. They may alternatively choose two examples (e.g., animals from different species) to compare and contrast by listing dissimilar characteristics of each animal on Sections A and C of the Thinking Guide. When students have finished, have them write the similarities in Section B. Finally, ask students to write or discuss how using the Thinking Guide helped them come to a conclusion. This lesson can take one or two class periods.

Social Studies   Have students work in small groups and discuss a conflict in history they have recently studied or that presently exists in the world. Ask them to use Sections A and C of the Thinking Guide to state the position of each side in the conflict and to use Section B to show whether there are any areas of agreement between the two sides. Then ask students to write ideas they have about the conflict in the outer circle. Encourage them to suggest ways the two sides might have worked out their differences based on the information they have written. At the end of the class period, ask students to share their work with the class.

Drama   Have students work in small groups or as a class to act out two folktales of their choice. Before they begin, demonstrate how actors study many sources before portraying a character, and explain how they use comparative thinking to identify key mannerisms they will convey. First, have students read the story and choose characters to portray. Encourage students to use the Thinking Guide when planning how to portray the characters, pointing out that by comparing characters in a story they will learn about elements that distinguish each character from the others. Share Blackline Master 11 as an example of one group's work.

Allow each group time to prepare for their performance. As an alternative, students may wish to present two dramatic readings or an actual play about the topic. After performances are complete, have students compare them, using the Thinking Guide.

Language Arts   Have students write about a complex issue, such as plagiarism or politicians hiring speechwriters rather than writing their own material. Have students use examples and words that evidence their comparative and contrastive thinking. When they have finished, ask them to exchange papers with a peer and edit each other's work, using the checklist provided on Blackline Master 12. Have partners exchange papers, revise their writing, and explain how the use of comparison and contrast in their writing can clarify meaning.

MEETING INDIVIDUAL NEEDS

STRATEGIES FOR LESS ABLE READERS

Review the Thinking Guide with students who choose to meet with you individually or in small groups, and discuss students' questions. Explain that some authors use words to help readers know when to use comparative thinking. Show samples of the words authors use on Blackline Master 10. Explain that authors use these words to signal comparative and contrasting thinking when they write and speak. Demonstrate how recognizing these words can help readers know when authors are comparing and contrasting items by reading a passage from one of the books listed in this lesson and performing a think-aloud. To demonstrate the think-aloud for students, share the thoughts you have as you compare and contrast events in the book. Then ask students to choose a book of their own and read until they find a sentence that uses comparative and contrasting words. Have students raise their hands when they identify such sentences, then go to their desks, and have them quietly explain to you the meaning of the sentence. Once a student has explained a sentence orally, she or he should write five other comparative sentences related to the sentence as you continue to move to other students who orally describe to you a sentence's meaning. Continue until you have heard at least one oral explanation and receive five written explanations from each student in the group.

STRATEGIES FOR BETTER READERS

Ask students to create a contemporary story that explains why a particular animal looks like it does. They can refer to Blackline Masters 7 and 8 and use the woodpecker or another animal. Before they begin, have students use the Thinking Guide to compare the animal they have chosen to other birds or animals. Students can research in trade books, textbooks, an encyclopedia, or books such as the following High Interest/Low Vocabulary books:

Van Allsburg, Chris. *Jumanji.* Boston: Houghton Mifflin, 1981.

Van Allsburg, Chris. *The Wreck of the Zephyr.* Boston: Houghton Mifflin, 1983.

Encourage students to write their stories in settings with which they are familiar. You might suggest they include characters from their own lives or that they compare the animals to people they know. When students have finished writing, have them illustrate their stories and share them in small groups.

UNDERSTANDING OTHERS

Have students use the comparative thinking strategy to determine how they know who "villains" and "heroes" are in books. They can elect to analyze differences and similarities between villains or heroes in myths or to compare and contrast qualities of villains or heroes in their favorite selections of children's literature. For example, they can analyze why foxes and wolves are used as villains in so many fables and fairy tales. They can also analyze characteristics of the fox in "The Amazing Bone" by William Steig; the donkey in "Sylvester and the Magic Pebble"; and the wolf in "The Three Little Pigs" stories listed on Blackline Master 9 and in "The Little Red Riding Hood" stories listed on Blackline Master 9. Ask students to use the Thinking Guide "Comparing and Contrasting" to make these comparisons, and then have them write what this analysis of villains taught them about detecting possible sources of sorrow, distress, or harm in their lives.

MULTICULTURAL CONNECTIONS

Ask students to find two or three folktales from their families' cultures or countries of origin or from the ones listed on Blackline Master 9. After students have found their stories, have them work in small groups and use the Thinking Guide to compare the stories they read in the group. Then have them discuss how the stories were similar and different and what they discovered about each culture from the stories they have read.

ASSESSMENT OF PARTS 3 AND 4

Ask students to recall, summarize, give insights, and ask questions to extend what they learned in this lesson. Then complete the class and indi-vidual students' assessment records you have selected from pages 194–216. You may want to use one or more of the following:

- Class Monitoring Record, Blackline Master 62

- Reading Wheel, Blackline Masters 69 and 70

- Editing Checklist, Blackline Master 75

- Writing Overview, Blackline Master 76

- Assessing Thinking Abilities, Blackline Master 78, to assess students' growth in "basic thinking abilities," Division 1

- Student Self-Assessment of Thinking Abilities, Blackline Master 79

- Portfolio Assessment, Blackline Master 84, to complete the first evaluations of student portfolios

LESSON 3

RECOGNIZING PATTERNS TO INCREASE RETENTION

STUDENT OBJECTIVES

In Part l, students will learn four patterns authors and speakers use to communicate their ideas. In Parts 2 through 4, they will use these patterns to follow speakers' and authors' ideas and to comprehend more when they read by using nonfiction books and different content area materials.

READING AND LANGUAGE ARTS CONNECTIONS

- using semantic mapping to increase vocabulary and comprehension
- recognizing paragraph structure
- relating supporting sentences to main topic sentences
- appreciating, recognizing, and responding to nonfiction and fiction for personal enjoyment
- increasing literal comprehension so as to organize information
- strengthening reading and listening retention
- comparing information on charts, graphs, tables, and lists
- developing vocabulary
- identifying sequential clue words
- using sequential clue words, chronological and spatial order, and order of importance

EXPLORING THE STRATEGY

INTRODUCING THE LESSON

To introduce Lesson 3, ask students to define patterns. Help them understand that patterns in writing and speaking create a definite direction, grouping, or organization that assists listeners and readers in predicting upcoming details. Explain that in this lesson students will learn to recognize patterns that people use to organize their thoughts so they can comprehend more about what they read and hear. State that scientists classify species of animals according to common characteristics and patterns of behavior; authors organize their thoughts into recognizable writing patterns so readers can predict where main ideas and details will appear. When students recognize patterns people use, they can more easily understand and remember the ideas being communicated. For example, tell students that they will remember more when they read mathematics and history textbooks if they recognize that mathematicians order elements according to their ranking in increasing or decreasing numerical order; historians order temporally or sequentially in time; and some people organize their conversations by placing the most important, relevant, or special idea first and less important ideas next. Explain to students they will know they have identified a pattern when they can use this pattern to predict an upcoming event, categorize new information, and remember more ideas because of an awareness of their sequence.

At this point, you may wish to outline an easily recognizable pattern on the chalkboard. For example, the circular pattern of the seasons of the year may be illustrated by writing the names of the four seasons within a circle and connecting them with arrows, as shown below. Ask students to discuss how the visual representation of the pattern helps them to understand and remember it.

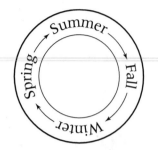

Ask students to share the titles of their favorite books and list the titles on the chalkboard. Tell students you will ask them to describe how the author patterned his or her thoughts to make that book so enjoyable, but first have students listen to the following example as you read three of the opening paragraphs from *Call It Courage*.[1] As you read, ask students to identify how author Armstrong Sperry patterns his ideas; e.g., Where does he place his main ideas? Does he order ideas by placing events in sequential order? Read aloud Blackline Master 13 or duplicate it as an overhead transparency for students to read.

Discuss the patterns students identified in Armstrong Sperry's writing style. Then return to the list of students' favorites, ask if they can identify the types of patterns they enjoy in these books, and have them write their answers next to each title. You may want to provide examples before students think about their responses. For instance, the author clearly moved from event 1 to event 2; the author always stated the main idea in the first sentence of each paragraph; or the author gave lots of details about topics.

---

[1] *Call It Courage* by Armstrong Sperry, New York: Macmillan Publishing Co., 1940. Eighth printing 1979, pp. 7–8.

USING THE THINKING GUIDE

Distribute one pattern at a time from the four-page Thinking Guide "Recognizing Patterns" (Blacklines Masters 14–17) and ask students to look at each illustrated pattern while you explain it:

"Main Idea First" or Concept Pattern explains a topic, concept, or theme by stating the main ideas (represented by the radiating diagonal lines), and elaborating on them with details (represented by the horizontal lines). This pattern is used by many people and can be recognized because the main concept is usually repeated often and emphasized. Ask students to return to one of the paragraphs from *Call It Courage* and diagram on their Thinking Guides the main concept the author was presenting. A sample answer students may create is:

"Plots in Stories" or Problem/Solution Pattern is a pattern that occurs frequently in life and in literature. A problem is presented, described, solved, and often a final action is taken after the solution. Return to the list of books on the chalkboard and ask students to identify one in which the author followed this pattern in the creation of the story. As a class, diagram the events in that book on the Problem/Solution Pattern page of the Thinking Guide (Blackline Master 15). You may want to provide the following example.

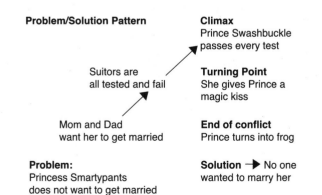

"Telling Both Sides" or Similarity/Difference Pattern defines how things are similar and how they are different. People who think in this way often say "On the other hand," "Sort of...but," and "Consider this." When talking to someone who thinks in this way or when reading a book that has a lot of details about more than one topic, it is easier to keep track of the ideas if a person visualizes the Similarity/Difference Pattern while listening or reading. Ask students if they know of anyone who uses this pattern to organize their ideas or if any of the characters in the books on the chalkboard utilize this pattern. If students can recognize this pattern in either acquaintances or literary figures, have them list a few of the statements that typify their speech. If students cannot recognize this pattern, return to your example from *Call It Courage* on the previous page and pretend you are Tavana Nui, Mafatu's father, using the Similarities/Difference Pattern to explain how his son is brave in other ways than going out to sea.

"Telling Things in Order" or Sequence Pattern uses time relationships as a link between thoughts or events. For example, authors who write how-to guides and cookbooks follow a sequence pattern. Sequence patterns are often easy to recognize because books and people who use this pattern frequently use sequence words such as "first," "then," "next," "after," and "finally." Ask students to return to the list of books on the chalkboard and identify any books utilizing the sequence pattern. Diagram samples of sequential patterning on the Sequence Pattern page of the Thinking Guide. If students cannot identify any books that utilize this pattern, describe how direction-giving usually follows a sequential pattern. Demonstrate by giving a set of directions to a location in the school without telling students what the directions are for. Before you begin the direction, explain that because they know that directions will follow a sequential pattern, students can listen for key sequence words to improve their comprehension. After you give the directions, ask students to tell what location the directions describe and how thinking about the sequence pattern helped them remember the directions better.

To help students practice recognizing how these patterns relate to their personal lives, ask them to suggest games, natural phenomena, or everyday events that follow the patterns on the Thinking Guide or might be explained by them. The chart at the bottom of this page may help you guide student discussion. Students can write each example on the appropriate pattern it represents from the Thinking Guide.

You may wish to point out that the Thinking Guide illustrates only four of the most frequent thought patterns. Students may recognize other patterns as they complete the activities in this lesson. Encourage them to draw diagrams of new patterns on the reverse side of the Thinking Guide. (For example, the Venn diagram in Lesson 4 demonstrates the compare and contrast pattern of thinking; and when main ideas are placed first in a paragraph the pattern of thoughts flows like this:

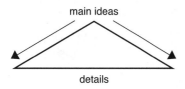

and when main ideas are placed last in a paragraph the pattern of thoughts flows like this:

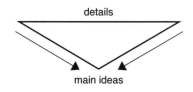

APPLYING THE THINKING GUIDE TO LITERATURE

Continue to read the first chapter of *Call It Courage* or select a textbook chapter that students read silently. Ask students to identify a pattern or patterns from the Thinking Guide that the author follows to organize his or her ideas in that book. Then have students work in small reading response groups to repeat this activity as they do one of the following:

- read a chapter from a textbook
- read a chapter from a nonfiction book
- listen to the order in which you present ideas from another content area during a class period later in the day

	Concept Pattern	Problem/ Solution Pattern	Similarity/ Difference Pattern	Sequence Pattern
Games	■ Charades	■ Football ■ Chess	■ Olympic skating	■ Chutes and Ladders™
Science	■ mental problems	■ surviving in winter	■ animals ■ varieties of insects or animals	■ environment ■ day/night ■ seasons ■ plant/water grow/harvest
Your Life	■ thinking about who you are	■ a problem with your younger sister	■ A conversation about two of your friends	■ getting ready for school ■ getting dressed

 # ASSESSMENT OF PART 1

If you wish to end the lesson at this point or to assess how much students have learned, you can use one or more of the assessment options on page 194–216 or allow students to select the option that enables them to demonstrate what they have learned.

APPLYING THE STRATEGY

RECOGNIZING PATTERNS IN LITERATURE: NONFICTION BOOKS

Review the Thinking Guide Blackline Masters. If you do not want to use nonfiction literature, students may select from any type of literature or read from stories in basal readers and periodicals. If you choose to use nonfiction, you may wish to initiate a discussion about nonfiction by having students discuss nonfiction books they have read. Ask:

- What was the book about?

- What did you learn from reading the book?

- Was there anything about the author's writing or the way the information was presented that helped you to understand it?

Help students understand that nonfiction books contain events, facts, and people that actually exist or existed in the world. As students select nonfiction books from the library or from the reading list provided on page 000, ask them to diagram as many patterns as they recognize and/or to write in their journals about their objectives before choosing their reading material. Students' objectives should include recognizing and comparing patterns. They may also record other personal objectives; for example, learning about something they know nothing about, learning more about a favorite subject, or reading another book by a favorite author.

APPLYING THE STRATEGY TO EVERYDAY EVENTS

To help students practice using the Thinking Guide and to recognize patterns in communication, have them choose from the activities below or design their own learning experiences.

Students on Their Own Have students individually or with partners choose two nonfiction books on the same topic from the reading list or from the school library. Have students use the Thinking Guide to identify the pattern each author uses to present facts. Next ask each student to write a short paragraph comparing the writing patterns in each book and describing why they think the author used a particular pattern. Ask students to describe whether and why it was helpful to identify the authors' thinking patterns.

Collaborative Thinking Have students divide into groups of five and have each student in the group select a different book to read. Allow students to read their chosen books for twenty minutes and then ask them to jot in their journals the patterns they identify. Ask group members to share the patterns they recognized and to identify the most frequently used pattern in the group's selections. At the end of the period, have each group share their findings with the class. You may want to ask each group to create a diagram illustrating the frequency of the patterns in the books.

Thinking with a Friend Have students practice recognizing thinking and speaking patterns with a partner. First students read for twenty minutes to discern the author's writing patterns. Then each partner describes the plot of the book to date and what he or she likes about the book so far. Next students use the Thinking Guide to discover the patterns their partner employs to explain ideas. When partners have decided which patterns are used by the other person, they can write an example of that pattern or complete a new pattern diagram on the back of the Thinking Guide that better depicts the partner's speaking pattern. You can extend this activity as a homework assignment by asking students to use the Thinking Guide to discover the patterns family members and other friends employ.

STUDENT SELF-ASSESSMENT

At the end of any activity in Part 2, ask students to meet in pairs and discuss the patterns they recognized and any new patterns they discovered. Then have students explain how they recognized patterns and which types are easiest and most difficult for them to understand.

or

Ask students to write about the patterns used by their two favorite authors and to identify whether these patterns are part of the reasons why they like these authors so much.

TEACHER ASSESSMENT

To assess students' progress at the end of Part 2, you may ask students to:

- describe the purpose, benefits, and types of patterns they have learned

- cite examples of patterns they have recognized during the course of this lesson

- name patterns from examples you give

- identify their most frequently used thinking, writing, and speaking patterns and how each can be improved so others retain more of the information they give

PART 3

APPLYING THE STRATEGY ACROSS THE CURRICULUM

The following activities are designed to give students the opportunity to apply the strategy in several different areas of the curriculum. Review the Thinking Guide before students engage in their activities.

Language Arts and Social Studies   "Ann Landers to the Rescue": Have students write an advice column for younger students. First invite third-grade students to write anonymous letters asking for solutions to problems they face in their lives. Then have your students divide these letters into groups so similar problems can be researched simultaneously, and let them work in small groups to research the kind of problems they select.

Next tell each group to consult three sources to ask for solutions to the problems and to record the thought pattern followed by each source on the Thinking Guide. For example, a younger student may write that she wants to get her ears pierced and her parents won't let her. In small groups, students may use the following sources: 1) calling a doctor or nurse to learn about ear piercing (diagram the concepts learned on the concept pattern); 2) reading a book about ear piercing (show how the ideas were reported in the sequence pattern); and 3) asking a friend who had the same problem how she was able to either convince her parents to let her pierce her ears or understand that she should wait until she is older (presented in the problem/solution pattern).

As soon as research is complete, have students write responses to the letters that include

specific advice and solutions they found. Instruct students to follow the problem/solution pattern from the Thinking Guide in their columns and to recommend at least one book or article for each younger student to read concerning the problem. Finally, return the letters and responses to the younger students.

Just for Fun   To help students practice their pattern recognition skills, ask them to meet in groups of three to play the pattern game on Blackline Master 18. Each group will need a copy of Blackline Master 18, scissors, and a pencil. Rules for playing and scoring are provided on the page.

All Subject Areas   Use the relevant pages from the Thinking Guide in content areas to introduce patterns authors will follow in the material or chapter students are about to read. After students have read the material, ask them to reexamine the patterns and discuss whether the ones they chose still apply.

Science   Divide the class into small groups and take students outside.

Challenge students to work in their groups to identify as many concept patterns, attribute patterns, sequence patterns or problem-solution patterns in nature as possible in a specified amount of time. When students return to the classroom, ask representatives from each group to compare what they observed.

PART 4

MEETING INDIVIDUAL NEEDS

STRATEGIES FOR LESS ABLE READERS

Review the Thinking Guide with students who wish to meet with you individually or in small groups. Teach semantic webbing before students read a book and ask them if they recognize the pattern that semantic webbing represents. (It is a type of concept pattern.) Then ask students to skim a chapter or preview a portion of the material that will be used in a content area class later in the day and make a new semantic web about the topic. After the semantic web is completed, have students read for fifteen minutes from a portion of the material they diagrammed. When fifteen minutes have elapsed, ask whether and how the semantic web increased students' comprehension of that material. At the end of the day, ask students to report whether the semantic map and pattern recognition strategy increased their comprehension and retention when they studied the material.

To assess students' understanding of semantic webs and the concept pattern, on the following day ask students to draw a web that depicts themselves, like the one shown below. Ask them to write their name. Then have them write simple categories that describe themselves under each section of the web. Students may want to web facts about where they live, names of friends or family members, likes and dislikes, favorite foods and hobbies, special talents or traits, and so forth.

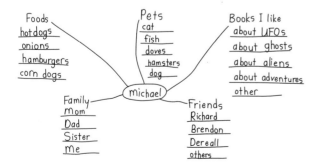

STRATEGIES FOR BETTER READERS

Have students diagram patterns followed by the authors of a content area textbook. Ask them to share their diagrams with the class and give suggestions as to ways of using these thinking patterns to remember more from these books. Before they begin, you may want to share the following examples of different ways patterns can be depicted:

- Descriptions can be conveyed through pictures, diagrams, maps, plans, drawings and tables.

- Sequences and processes can be conveyed through timelines, flowcharts, and cycle graphs.

- Choice patterns can be conveyed through weighted matrices, decision trees, figures, and branching flow charts.

- Classifications can be conveyed through webbings and trees.

- Principles can be conveyed through line graphs, Venn diagrams, and outlines.

- Evaluations can be conveyed through grids, rating charts, and benchmarks.

Students can share their work at the end of the period or at the beginning of the next day.

UNDERSTANDING SELF

Distribute Blackline Master 19 and have students talk to a friend about something that is important to them. As they talk, the friend is to identify the pattern being used to organize the oral presentation and place information being given at appropriate points on the concept map. After five minutes, ask students to exchange roles and repeat the activity. Then have students discuss the patterns they identified and how they can improve the way they organize their speech.

ASSESSMENT OF PARTS 3 AND 4

Ask students to recall, summarize, and give insights about what they have learned in this lesson. Then complete the class and Individual Student Assessment Records you have selected from pages 194–216. You may want to use:

- Class Monitoring Record, Blackline Master 62

- Journal Writing Assessment: Student Self-Evaluation, Blackline Master 64

- Journal Writing Assessment: Teacher Evaluation, Blackline Master 65

- Reading Wheel, Blackline Masters 69 and 70

- Oral-Language Needs Monitor, Blackline Master 71

- Clues to Improving Handwriting, Blackline Master 77 (especially if students complete drafts and final copies in the "Ann Landers To The Rescue" Activity in Part 3)

- Student Self-Assessment of Thinking Abilities, Blackline Master 79

UNDERSTANDING DIFFERENT POINTS OF VIEW

STUDENT OBJECTIVES

In Part l, students will learn how to acknowledge, understand, and accept other people's points of view and to recognize points of view in literature and conversation. In Parts 2 through 4, students will learn to appreciate different points of view in real-life situations and in various content areas of the curriculum.

READING AND LANGUAGE ARTS CONNECTIONS

- strengthening reading and listening retention
- explaining and relating to the feelings and emotions of characters
- recognizing differences in first-, second-, and third-person points of view

EXPLORING THE STRATEGY

INTRODUCING THE LESSON

To introduce Lesson 4, ask students to think of someone who thinks differently from themselves and who is sometimes difficult for them to understand. Then have students share why they have difficulty understanding these people's points of view and list their reasons on the board; for example: haven't done the same things they do; have different interests; have different senses of humor. Then explain that looking at different points of view is important in daily life and reading because it enables people to accept others' points of view and it increases understanding. Tell students they will have an opportunity to practice understanding others' points of view, and they will know they have learned to recognize different points of view when they can outline specific differences between a character's point of view and their own. Conclude this introduction by stating you would like to know what they already know about points of view so you can focus teaching what they do not yet know. To stimulate their thinking, list students' answers on the board to questions such as:

■ What characterizes a book written from the first-person point of view? What characterizes a book written from the second-person point of view? What characterizes a book written from the third-person point of view?

■ Have you ever tried to change your point of view when you were involved in a discussion? How did you do so? How did it feel? What did another person say that caused you to change your point of view?

■ What causes authors to write and people to talk from a specific point of view?

USING THE THINKING GUIDE

Distribute the Thinking Guide "Looking at Different Points of View" (Blackline Master 20), explain each step on the Thinking Guide, and ask students to cite examples of each step. The following are descriptions you can use:

Step 1. *Another's shoes:* When a perspective is difficult to understand, put yourself in that character's or person's shoes. Pretend you are the character or person talking. Ask: "How would I feel if I were that person and how would my feeling contribute to the meaning I was trying to convey?" "What would I think about___?"

Step 2. *Use Details:* Read or listen for details, opinions, and values that suggest a person's specific point of view.

Step 3. *People Think Differently:* Try to understand your chosen character's point of view by recreating a mental image of the pictures on the Thinking Guide. Remember, to fully understand others, you may have to view from an opposite perspective items under discussion or events you read.

APPLYING THE THINKING GUIDE TO LITERATURE

Read to the students *The Three Little Pigs* by James Marshall (New York: Dial, 1989) and *The True Story of the Three Little Pigs* by John Scieszka (New York: Viking, 1989), any two versions of the same fairy tale listed on Blackline Master 8 in Lesson 2, or two books describing Christopher Columbus's voyage from different perspectives (*Encounter* by Jane Yolen, Boston: Houghton Mifflin, 1992, and *Follow the Dream: The Story of Christopher Columbus* by Peter Sis, New York:

Dell, 1992). Then ask students to apply the Thinking Guide by outlining on the Thinking Guide the main character's or author's point of view in each of the two stories. When they have finished, students' Thinking Guides should look similar to the one shown below. Last, assess students' work and discuss how the Thinking Guide assisted them in understanding different points of view in the same story.

© Addison-Wesley Publishing Company

ASSESSMENT OF PART 1

If you wish to end the lesson at this point or to assess how much students have learned, you can use one or more of the assessment options on pages 194–216, or allow students to select the option that enables them to best demonstrate what they have learned.

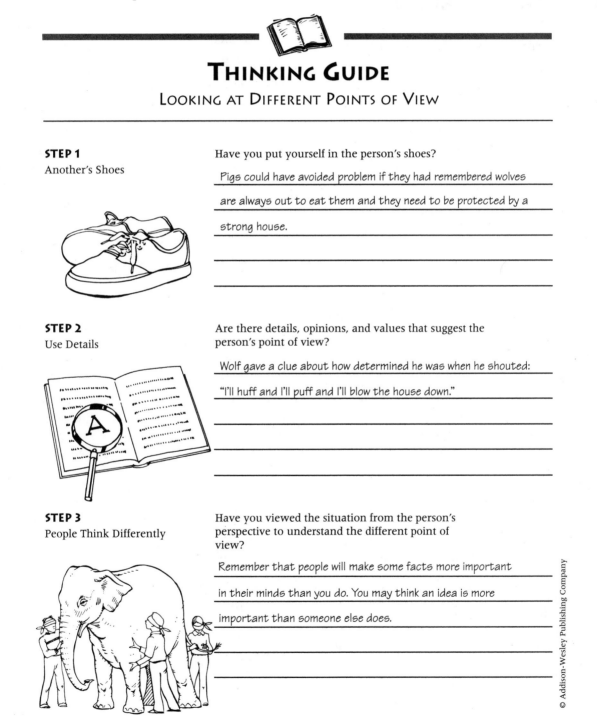

THINKING GUIDE
LOOKING AT DIFFERENT POINTS OF VIEW

STEP 1
Another's Shoes

Have you put yourself in the person's shoes?

Pigs could have avoided problem if they had remembered wolves

are always out to eat them and they need to be protected by a

strong house.

STEP 2
Use Details

Are there details, opinions, and values that suggest the person's point of view?

Wolf gave a clue about how determined he was when he shouted:

"I'll huff and I'll puff and I'll blow the house down."

STEP 3
People Think Differently

Have you viewed the situation from the person's perspective to understand the different point of view?

Remember that people will make some facts more important

in their minds than you do. You may think an idea is more

important than someone else does.

APPLYING THE STRATEGY

LOOKING AT DIFFERENT POINTS OF VIEW IN LITERATURE: FICTION

Review the Thinking Guide and introduce the following books in which authors write from different perspectives:

High Interest/Low Vocabulary

Cleary, Beverly. *Ramona Quimby; age 8*. New York: William Morrow, 1981.

Disney, Walt. *Cinderella*. New York: Gallery Books, 1986.

Galdone, Paul. *The Little Red Hen*. New York: Houghton Mifflin/Clarion Books, 1973.

Level 4–6

Babbitt, Natalie. *Tuck Everlasting*. New York: Farrar, Straus, & Giroux, 1975.

Burch, Robert. *Queenie Peavy*. New York: Viking Press, 1966.

Dahl, Roald. *The Witches*. New York: Farrar, Straus, & Giroux, 1983.

Grahame, Kenneth. *The Wind in the Willows*. New York: Adama Books, 1983.

Greene, Bette. *Philip Hall Like Me, I Reckon Maybe*. New York: Dell, 1974.

Howe, Deborah. *Bunnicula*. New York: Atheneum, 1979.

Lewis, C.S. *The Lion, the Witch, and the Wardrobe*. New York: Macmillan, 1983.

Lowry, Lois. *Anastasia Krupnik*. Boston: Houghton Mifflin, 1979.

MacLachlan, Patricia. *Sarah, Plain and Tall*. (video, film strip, record, and book) (Newbery Collection) New York: Harper & Row, 1985.

Taylor, Mildred D. *Let the Circle be Unbroken*. New York: Dial Press, 1981.

Taylor, Mildred D. *Roll of Thunder, Hear My Cry*. New York: Dial Press, 1976.

Taylor, Theodore. *The Cay*. Garden City, NY: Doubleday, 1969.

Level 7–8

O'Brien, Robert C. *Mrs. Frisby and the Rats of NIMH*. New York: Atheneum, 1971.

Paulsen, Gary. *Hatchet*. Puffin Books, 1988.

Introduce the books by reading a paragraph from two or three of them and asking students to determine the author's point of view and to share how they did so.

APPLYING THE STRATEGY TO EVERYDAY EVENTS

To help students practice using the Thinking Guide and to complete the objectives in this lesson, have students select an activity from those that follow or have them suggest an alternative through which they can practice looking at different points of view.

Students on Their Own   Take the students to the library, and have them check out one of the above books or another of interest. Referring to the Thinking Guide, instruct students to skim their book to locate information about two or three characters and write about these characters in their journals. Then have students read their library books for twenty minutes of the period and try to relate to a specific character's point of view as they read. Stipulate the character they select may not be the one that holds the main perspective through which the author is telling the story. Last, ask students to summarize their chosen character's point of view at the end of the first chapter and to write what steps on the Thinking Guide they used during reading.

Thinking with a Friend   Allow two students to read the same book, but ask them to assume the point of view of different characters in the book. At the end of each chapter, have students summarize their chosen character's point of view by writing which steps on the Thinking Guide they used during the reading to identify the point of view. Have both students: (a) create a compare-and-contrast diagram of their chosen characters' points of view, using the Thinking Guide "Comparing and Contrasting" (Blackline Master 4) or a Venn diagram, (b) write insights they had about the process of assuming a particular point of view, and (c) describe how the book would have ended differently had the author chosen to tell the story from both characters' points of view.

Role Play   Have students choose a partner with whom they would like to work and a book they would like to read. Ask students to skim their book and each choose a different character of interest. After students have chosen their characters, ask them to concentrate on the character's point of view as they read. Upon completion of the book, let students role play their character, making sure each portrays his or her character's point of view by using the steps in the Thinking Guide. Last, ask students as a class to describe differences among the points of view depicted in the play.

Group Reading   Have small groups of students take turns reading from multiple copies of the same book. At the end of the first section or chapter, have students discuss and outline the points of view of characters on the Thinking Guide. Have each small group make an overhead transparency of their Thinking Guide and present it to the class.

STUDENT SELF-ASSESSMENT

At the end of any activity in Part 2, students can elect to demonstrate their progress by peer conferencing. To do so, students choose a partner who read the same book and describe their chosen character's point of view to their partner by discussing how they used the Thinking Guide to understand the character's perspective. Then each partner reflects back strengths their classmate voiced about understanding another person's point of view as well as problems they had in doing so.

or

Students can elect to give a personal testimonial as to how they have incorporated understanding different points of view into their daily reading and how this strategy has helped them to understand different perspectives in experiences outside of school.

TEACHER ASSESSMENT

To assess student progress at the end of Part 2, ask students to read a new chapter from any book they select. Then have them write summaries for the main character's point of view on their Thinking Guide which they give to you to be graded.

or

Complete an informal assessment of how often students express a perspective different from their own in class discussions during the week following Part 2 of this lesson.

APPLYING THE STRATEGY ACROSS THE CURRICULUM

The following activities enable students to practice recognizing different points of view in several content areas.

Social Studies   Ask students to form pairs and choose a controversial current event. Ask each partner to choose either the pro or con side of the issue and research his or her position. Then have students choose a major public figure involved in their side of the issue and read and view news coverage of that person for two days. After developing their arguments, students take turns role playing the public figures' perspectives to each other. Last, have students discuss their ability to understand different points of view.

As an alternative or addition to this lesson, ask students to select one of the issues role played above and consider the issue from one of the points of view represented on Blackline Master 21. Students who have chosen the same point of view work together as a team. After each team meets to prepare their particular point of view, have them share their various points of view in a class discussion.

Science   Have small groups choose and assume the perspective of an endangered species. Ask students to use the Thinking Guide to write a letter in the voice of an animal of that species to convince people that their breed needs protection. Next ask students to explain their species' importance on earth and how it feels to be endangered. Last have students describe the research they did and what steps from the Thinking Guide they used in order to write their letters.

Music   Play several distinct selections of music, and ask students to describe their response to each selection in one word; e.g., relaxing, annoying, comforting, distracting. Afterwards, compare students' points of view concerning each selection. Point out that this activity demonstrates how different feelings and thoughts of different people can be. Finally, ask

students to pair with a classmate who recorded a description very different from their own, and have them take turns explaining how past experiences might have affected the way they felt about each selection. Have students refer to and comment upon steps on the Thinking Guide as they give their explanations.

Poetry   Ask the class to brainstorm different items that would be attractive from one perspective, and at the same time unattractive from another perspective. For example, a mouse might be scary to an elephant, but tasty to a cat. To help students better understand they are looking for two different perspectives about the same item, provide an idea that has two perspectives; for example, "I'm thinking of a mouse. Who or what would perceive a mouse as pleasing? (a cat); How would an elephant feel about a mouse? (scared). Continue until students have generated and you have listed ten combinations on the board. Then ask small groups to combine these ten thoughts on a chart to create a poem they will share with the class. Remind students words do not have to rhyme.

Art And Math   Have students choose one of the following books, read it, and describe how the book increased their ability to understand different points of view. Examples students may give appear in parenthesis after each title.

High Interest/Low Vocabulary

Ames, Lee J. *Draw 50 Cars, Trucks, and Motorcycles.* Garden City, NY: Doubleday, 1986. (confirms that understanding many points of view, prior to creating products, will increase the quality and applicability of the final product)

Garden, Beau. *The Look Again and Again Book.* New York: Lothrop, Lee, & Shepard Books, 1984. (illustrates optical illusions and how several objects can be viewed from many perspectives)

Heckman, Philip. *The Magic of Holography.* New York: Atheneum, 1986. (demonstrates how single incidents can produce infinite points of view)

White, Lawrence and Brockel, Ray. *Math-a-Magic: Number Trick for Magicians.* Niles, IL: Albert Whitman, 1990. (illustrates how points of view can distract people from viewing critical elements in an event or issue)

Wilson, April. *Look Again: The Second Ultimate Spot the Difference Book.* New York: Dial Books for Young Readers, 1992.

Levels 4–6

Escher, M.C. *The Graphic Works of M.C. Escher.* New York: Benedikt Taschen, 1992.

Hoban, Tana. *Look Again!* New York: Macmillan, 1971.

Jones, Ann. *Reflections.* New York: Greenwillow Books, 1987. (provides methods of mentally turning situations around)

Kenney, Margaret. *Tesselations Using Logs.* Palo Alto, CA: Dale Seymour Publications, 1987. (illustrates how points of view and frames of reference shift)

Levels 7–8

Escher, M.C. *Escher on Escher: Exploring the Infinite.* New York: H.N. Abrams, 1989.

MEETING INDIVIDUAL NEEDS

MULTICULTURAL CONNECTIONS

Introduce this activity by saying that the following are some countries that celebrate New Year's Day on January 1: United States, Australia, Belgium, Canada, France, Great Britain, Italy, Japan, Mexico, Netherlands, New Zealand, Spain, Switzerland, and Germany. Then ask students to divide into small groups, select a country other than the United States, and research how that country celebrates New Year's Day. After doing so, the students are to design a "sample" New Year's Day celebration from that country's perspective, and present it to the class. Assign each group a section of the room in which they will display their New Year's celebration. When all presentations are complete, students discuss differences and similarities between their country's and the United States perspective of New Year's Day.

STRATEGIES FOR LESS ABLE READERS

Review the Thinking Guide with students who wish to meet with you individually or in small groups. Then read or ask pairs of students to read reciprocally from one of the following books that illustrate different points of view in literature and life. In parentheses after each title is an activity or a topic of discussion in which less able readers can engage while reading that book.

High Interest/Low Vocabulary

Stolz, Mary S. *A Dog on Barkham Street*. New York: Harper & Row,1960.

Stolz, Mary S. *The Bully of Barkham Street*. New York: Harper & Row, 1963.

Levels 4–6

Blume, Judy. *The Pain And The Great One*. Scarsdale, NY: Bradbury Press,1974.

Merrill, Jean.*The Pushcart War*. New York: W.R. Scott, 1964.

Say, Allen. *The Bicycle Man*. Boston: Houghton Mifflin, 1982.

Levels 7–8

Gordon, James. *The Stone Boy* (a Junior Great Books Story). New York: Ace Books, 1984.

STRATEGIES FOR BETTER READERS

Explain the different points of view that authors use in their writing: (a) When a book is written in first person, authors use the words "I" and "we" and the person talking is telling the story from his or her point of view. (b) When a book is written from a second-person point of view, the author uses the word "you" frequently, and the story is what someone else did or what readers should do. (c) When writing in third person, authors use the words "he, she, and they," and readers do not always know how the person telling the story found out about the character or events. Once students understand these points of view, ask them to find stories or books written in first, second, and third person. Next, have them write how they knew each book was first, second, or third person. Have students list three advantages to each point of view and defend the point of view they prefer for their own writing. The following books, written from first and third points of view, can be used in this activity. Books written for youth in second-person point of view are rare.

BOOKS WRITTEN IN FIRST PERSON:

High Interest/Low Vocabulary

Howe, D. *Bunnicula*. New York: Atheneum, 1979.

Larson, Robert. *Mr. Revere and I*. Boston: Little, Brown, 1953.

Lawson, Robert. *Ben and Me*. Boston: Little, Brown, 1939.

Viorst, Judy. *Alexander and the Terrible, Horrible, No Good, Very Bad Day*. New York: Scholastic, 1989.

Levels 4–6

Blume, Judy. *The Pain and the Great One*. Scarsdale, NY: Bradbury Press, 1974.

Fritz, J. *Homesick: My Own Story*. New York: Putnam, 1982.

Kowgslung, E.L. *Throwing Shadows*. New York: Collier, 1988. (a collection of five first-person short stories in which pre-adolescent males learn more about their own personalities).

Levels 7–8

Danziger, P. *The Pistachio Prescription*. New York: Delacorte Press, 1978.

BOOKS WRITTEN IN THIRD PERSON:

High Interest/Low Vocabulary

Brown, M. *Cinderella*. Westminster, MD: Random House, 1974.

Lowry, L. *Antasia Krupnik*. Boston: Houghton Mifflin, 1979

Selden, G. *The Cricket in Times Square*. New York: Farrar, Strauss, & Giroux, 1960.

Levels 4–6

Babbitt, N. *Tuck Everlasting*. New York: Farrar, Straus, & Giroux, 1975.

George, J.C. *Julie of the Wolves*. New York: Harper & Row, 1972.

UNDERSTANDING OTHERS

Have students recall a conflict they have had with another family member and write about the conflict from that person's perspective. In this writing, students recreate the point of view of the family member who caused the conflict, what the nature of the conflict was, and how it might be best resolved from that person's point of view. At the end of the paper, ask students to write insights they had as they adopted the family member's point of view. You may use Blackline Master 22, "Putting Yourself in Someone Else's Shoes" for this activity.

ASSESSMENT OF PARTS 3 AND 4

After the last day of the lesson, ask students to write three ways that they are going to attempt to perceive situations from a different point of view, whether it is while reading or in conversations. Have students give insights, provide summaries, and ask questions to extend what they have learned in this lesson. Complete class and individual student assessment records. You may choose from:

- Class Monitoring Record, Blackline Master 62

- Journal Writing Assessment: Student Self-Evaluation, Blackline Master 64

- Journal Writing Assessment: Teacher Evaluation, Blackline Master 65

- Reading Wheel, Blackline Masters 69 and 70

- Assessing Thinking Abilities, Blackline Master 78

- Portfolio Assessment, Blackline Master 84

L E S S O N 5

ELIMINATING PROPAGANDA BEFORE MAKING A DECISION

STUDENT OBJECTIVES

In Part 1, students will learn to recognize propaganda in information they read and hear. They will interpret information in nonfiction literature. In Part 2, students will eliminate the persuasive effects of propaganda devices in editorials, advertisements, and other nonfiction writings as they interpret information about historical and current events.

READING AND LANGUAGE ARTS CONNECTIONS

- strengthening interpretive comprehension
- recognizing various persuasive devices
- reviewing and refining decoding strategies while reading personal and school-related materials
- interpreting editorials, advertisements, and nonfiction literature
- appreciating, recognizing, and responding to nonfiction literature for personal enjoyment
- varying word choice to accommodate the purpose and audience
- distinguishing facts from opinions
- recognizing persuasive writings and speeches

PART 1

EXPLORING THE STRATEGY

INTRODUCING THE LESSON

To introduce Lesson 5, explain to students that in this lesson they will discover how authors, speakers, and producers of commercials try to persuade them to do things. State that propaganda attempts to change people's ideas and behavior and that it uses deliberately slanted ideas and information to further a person's own cause or to damage an opposing cause. Add that such devices are usually subtle, such as a propagandist's choice of a word that has a positive or negative connotation. For example, share with students that "conversationalist" and "chatterbox" have the same dictionary meaning, but the first is more positively interpreted than the second. The first would likely persuade a reader to view the person to whom it refers in a more favorable light than the second. Emphasize that propaganda is also used when people voice opinions; seek support, money, or commitment from someone; or wish to gain an advantage for themselves. Discuss with students that as they learn to recognize propaganda they will not be as easily swayed to think or act in ways they don't necessarily agree with and that they will know they have learned to detect propaganda when they can describe incidents of its use in books and television.

Close the introduction by sharing a story from your life when recognizing a propaganda device saved you from taking an action that you may have later regretted. Ask students to add other examples from their experiences.

USING THE THINKING GUIDE

Distribute the Thinking Guide "Recognizing Propaganda" (Blackline Master 23). Explain that the Thinking Guide outlines the most commonly used propaganda devices. Read aloud the following definitions and ask students to share incidents from their reading, viewing, and listening in which a particular device has been used.

1. *Bandwagon:* Claiming that "everyone is doing it." Similar to this is the claim that something is "common knowledge," so everybody should believe it.

2. *Repetition:* Repeating the same word over and over again so you will remember it; for example, "excellence," "best," "first."

3. *Transfer:* Applying a set of symbols to a purpose for which they are not intended; for example, an anti-government group might display the United States flag and pictures of Washington and Lincoln at a meeting. These positive symbols help conceal the basic purpose of the group and help gain public support. A second example occurs when an incongruous image is coupled with an idea, such as a picture of a mother and child advertising a particular automobile so readers or viewers transfer the feelings of tenderness evoked by the picture to the concept of buying the car.

4. *Testimonials:* Getting some prominent person to endorse an idea or product, such as a television star endorsing a soft drink or a sports figure being pictured on a box of cereal.

5. *"Better Hurry":* Tells you "Offer will only last until__" or "Free with any purchase."

6. *Glittering Generalities:* Vague phrases that promise much; for example, "That act will benefit all Americans..." or "Everyone should..." or "Our way is the American way."

7. *Name Calling:* Using labels instead of discussing available information; for example, calling a politician a "crook" or a person whose ideas are unpopular a "fascist."

APPLYING THE THINKING GUIDE TO LITERATURE

Distribute Blackline Master 24, "The Costs to the Community." Tell students they will practice recognizing propaganda in nonfiction writing by checking whether the author uses any of the techniques described on the Thinking Guide. Ask students to write sentences from Blackline Master 24 in which propaganda appears. Then read Blackline Master 24 aloud as students underline sentences in which propaganda appears. Then have students go back to the Thinking Guide and add any items they missed the first time. Blackline Master 25 can be used as an answer key.

ASSESSMENT OF PART 1

If you wish to assess or have students self-assess how much they have learned at this point in the lesson, ask them to do one of the following:

■ Answer the question, "What have you learned from this lesson that you will use later in life?"

■ Generate new uses for the strategy.

■ Discuss and write with a partner about what you have learned.

■ Orally or in writing share insights with the class.

PART 2

APPLYING THE STRATEGY

RECOGNIZING PROPAGANDA IN LITERATURE: EDITORIALS

Review the Thinking Guide and explain to students that editorials are usually based on news and current issues but they report opinionated information. Ask students to bring to class several editorials and other reports of current events from sources such as newspapers, magazines, and *Zillions: Consumer Reports for Kids.* Then have students select two editorials before they choose an activity from Part 2 in which they will apply the strategy of eliminating propaganda before making decisions. Be sure all students select at least two pieces of writing about the same topic. If you prefer to not use editorials and current event literature, you may allow students to select another literature type in which propaganda devices appear and complete the Thinking Guide alone.

APPLYING THE STRATEGY TO EVERYDAY EVENTS

To help students practice eliminating the effects of propaganda devices, have them select one of the following activities or suggest an alternative in which they could do so.

Students on Their Own   Have students choose a topic and read two sources of information from periodicals about that topic, using a highlighter to mark incidents of propaganda and recording in their journals which of the two used the most persuasive techniques. Ask students to write in their journals about how they eliminated propaganda devices before forming opinions about the topic and whether this strategy improved the decision they made. You may want to allow students to work alone or with partners to complete each journal entry. After a twenty-minute working period, invite students to share with the class what they have learned about propaganda and decision making.

Collaborative Thinking   Have students divide into self-selected television-viewing groups and select a thirty-minute time period that evening during which they will all watch the same television channel. After you approve their selection, arrange for the group to meet on the following day to compare and summarize the following assignment and to report their results to the class. Instruct students to record on their Thinking Guides the types of propaganda they view in the commercials during their chosen time. Once you have given students instructions for the evening's television assignment, for the rest of the period have students read the two editorials they selected and record the propaganda devices on the Thinking Guide. On the following day, after the television-viewing groups have made their comparisons, using the "Comparing and Contrasting" Thinking Guide and their comparison strategies as they work, have students report their findings to the class.

Learning by Teaching   Suggest that students work in pairs or groups to design a role-play that uses as many of the propaganda devices on the Thinking Guide as possible. Have students spend the remainder of the class period practicing and presenting the role-play for your critique. On the next day, have two groups meet together and perform for each other, or have each group perform before the entire class. After each presentation, ask audience members to identify the propaganda devices used and have students self-assess their presentations in writing.

STUDENT SELF-ASSESSMENT

At the end of any activity in Part 2, suggest that students answer the following questions in their journals:

- What did you learn about the strategy of eliminating the effects of propaganda before you make decisions?

- How did the Thinking Guide help you think differently about commercials?

- How can you use this strategy in your daily life? Describe three specific events in your everyday activities in which eliminating propaganda before making a decision will be valuable to you.

or

Have students write a commercial about a product they value without using any propaganda devices.

TEACHER ASSESSMENT

Review students' written and oral presentations. As you evaluate students' abilities to eliminate propaganda devices, you may also look for:

- recognition of the use of individual propaganda devices as they read, listen, and view

- effectiveness in warning others about persuasive techniques

- incidents in which students point out to you propaganda devices in material they read

APPLYING THE STRATEGY ACROSS THE CURRICULUM

The following activities are designed to give students the opportunity to apply the strategy in several different areas of the curriculum. Review the Thinking Guide before students begin their activities.

Social Studies   Provide students with nonfiction accounts of Adolf Hitler and describe which persuasive devices he used most frequently. Before students begin their work, provide the following quotation as an example of Adolf Hitler's thinking:

> Through clever and constant application of propaganda, people can be made to see paradise as hell, and also the other way round, to consider the most wretched sort of life as paradise. — Adolf Hitler in *Mein Kampf*

Have students select one of the following books to read silently or choose from similar books from the library or that you make available. During their reading, have students write on the Thinking Guide examples of the types of propaganda Hitler used and include the page references in the book in which the examples appear. Once the twenty-minute period has elapsed, let students share their most vivid examples with classmates by reading from their books. Samples of the types of books from which students can read are:

High Interest/Low Vocabulary

Marrion, Albert. *Hitler*. New York: Viking Kestrel, 1987.

Levels 4–6

Bradley, Catherine. *Hitler and The Third Reich*. New York: Gloucester Press, 1990.

Elliott, B. J. *Hitler and Germany*. New York: McGraw Hill, 1968.

Wolfe, Burton H. *Hitler and the Nazis*. New York: G. P. Putnam, 1970.

Levels 7–8

Dolan, Jr. Edward F. *Adolf Hitler: A Portrait in Tyranny*. New York: Dodd, Mead, 1981.

Language Arts   Have students create and present to the class two one-minute speeches about a topic of choice. The first is to contain no propaganda devices, and the second is to contain three. The audience identifies the propaganda technique(s) used by each speaker and discusses the effects of hearing both speeches. After all speeches have been presented, students select which type of propaganda is most persuasive to them and what they can do to neutralize its effect on their own lives.

Art   Ask students to bring in magazine advertisements to analyze the types of propaganda conveyed through pictures.

PART 4

MEETING INDIVIDUAL NEEDS

STRATEGIES FOR LESS ABLE READERS

Review the Thinking Guide with students who wish to meet with you individually or in small groups. Read Blackline Master 25 and model how you identified the effects of each propaganda device represented and how you eliminated its effect as you interpreted the material. Then guide students to do the same as they read editorials that other students used in Part 2 of the lesson.

STRATEGIES FOR BETTER READERS

Ask better readers to expand their work with propaganda devices by having them form pairs and compete against other pairs to find as many examples of each propaganda device on the Thinking Guide as they can.

ASSESSMENT OF PARTS 3 AND 4

Ask students to recall, summarize, and give insights about what they have learned in this lesson. Then select and complete the class and individual student assessment records from pages 194–216. You may choose:

- Class Monitoring Record, Blackline Master 62

- Reading Wheel, Blackline Masters 69 and 70

- Student Self-Assessment of Thinking Abilities, Blackline Master 79

L E S S O N   6

MAKING DECISIONS BY RECOGNIZING FACTS, OPINIONS, AND REASONED JUDGMENTS

STUDENT OBJECTIVES

In Part l, students will learn strategies for distinguishing between fact and opinion and for combining facts and opinions with what they already know to make reasoned judgments as they read, listen, and think. In Parts 2 through 4, students will practice making reasoned judgments as they read a variety of literature and assess situations that occur in their own lives.

READING AND LANGUAGE ARTS CONNECTIONS

- strengthening inferential comprehension
- recognizing persuasive writing and speeches
- distinguishing facts from opinions
- making generalizations
- appreciating, recognizing, and responding to mysteries for personal enjoyment
- identifying important and less important details
- evaluating and making judgments
- identifying editorial writing
- understanding cause-and-effect relationships

EXPLORING THE STRATEGY

INTRODUCING THE LESSON

To begin the lesson, ask one student to tell something she or he knows is a fact and why it is a fact. Next have a second student tell something he or she thinks is an opinion. Ask a third student to think of a reasoned judgment. Write these statements on the chalkboard and create semantic webs by asking students to add new ideas to each of the three central concepts of facts, opinions, and reasoned judgments. Help students understand that making a reasoned judgment consists of assessing information that may be fact or opinion and determining what is most likely true. Stress that when making a reasoned judgment, students should be able to back up a point of view with some factual information.

Then ask students to think of something that was once thought of as a fact, but that has since been proven untrue, such as that the world is flat or the sun travels around the earth. Explain that the people who believed these things were making reasoned judgments based on information available at that time combined with what they already knew. Point out that people make reasoned judgments frequently, and discuss the importance of distinguishing between reasoned judgments, opinions, and facts. Remind students that this skill is necessary whether they are reading, listening, or speaking and that in this lesson they will have an opportunity to practice telling the difference between facts, opinions, and reasoned judgments.

Reveal to students that in this lesson they will improve their abilities to make decisions by learning to distinguish fact from opinion and by using facts and opinions to make reasoned judgments. Suggest that at the end of the lesson, students test their skills at distinguishing facts, opinions, and reasoned judgments in books that they choose to read. Tell them they will know they have increased their ability to make reasoned judgments when they can report their thinking processes when making a reasoned judgment.

USING THE THINKING GUIDE

Distribute the Thinking Guide "Making Reasoned Judgments" (Blackline Master 26) to students. Introduce the guide by showing that reasoned judgments are comprised of four parts: Boxes 1 and 2 represent facts and opinions and list common sources of each. Remind students that facts are information such as dates, places, and names and that opinions are what people think and believe. You may wish to use the example that it is a fact George Washington was the first president of the United States and it is an opinion he was the best president.

Now point out to students that reasoned judgments include information that they already know represented in Box 3 of the Thinking Guide. Finally, explain that reasoned judgments are made by combining facts, opinions, and prior knowledge and are represented in Box 4. Next caution students that opinions are often combined with facts in ways that are not immediately evident and it is important to question information they read and hear to be sure they know whether it is fact or opinion.

To illustrate, have students imagine they are reading the following advertisement for a diet product: "Doctors and scientists agree that you can eat all day and still lose weight with X Brand!" Next ask students to write this statement on the Thinking Guide in the box where they think it should go. Then lead a discussion about their responses, encouraging them to ask questions such as the following about the statement:

■ What facts support this statement?

■ Why do you think there is no information given to support the statement?

■ Who are the scientists and doctors who support this statement?

- If names of scientists were given who supported this statement, what would you want to know about them?

- Even if the statement were true, does it mean that it is automatically a good idea to eat all day or to take this product?

Finally, have students write the information they already know along with their questions and any ideas they have concerning this advertisement in Box 3 of the Thinking Guide. After they have done this, ask them to make a reasoned judgment about the claim "Doctors and scientists agree that you can eat all day and still lose weight with X Brand!" and write their judgment in Box 4.

APPLYING THE THINKING GUIDE TO LITERATURE

Read aloud or tell an excerpt from a mystery story without revealing the solution. (A list of mysteries students enjoy is on page 48). As you read, have students imagine they are detectives trying to understand what is occurring in the story. When you have finished reading, ask students to write the important points of the story on the Thinking Guide and to classify them as fact or opinion. As they do so, write their responses on the chalkboard using the structure of the Thinking Guide.

When students have filled in the guide, ask them to make a reasoned judgment about a particular character or the outcome of the story. Then have students write their judgment on a piece of paper. Finish reading the story and discuss how the actual solution to the mystery was similar to or different from students' own judgment. The following questions may help stimulate discussion:

- How was your solution similar to the one in the story?

- If your solution was different, was there any information you assumed was fact that was not?

- If your solution was different, can you give reasons why you think it could work just as well as the one in the story?

After the discussion, have students copy the new information they have gained through the discussion on their Thinking Guides, and write their solutions under Reasoned Judgment at the bottom of the guide.

🗒 ASSESSMENT OF PART 1

If you wish to assess or have students self-assess how much they have learned at this point in the lesson, ask them to do the following:

- Answer the question, "What have you learned from this lesson that you will use later in life?"

- Generate new uses for the strategy.

- Discuss and write with a partner about what you have learned.

- Orally or in writing share insights with the class.

PART 2

APPLYING THE STRATEGY

RECOGNIZING REASONED JUDGMENTS IN LITERATURE: MYSTERIES

Students may select from any type of literature to apply the strategy, but mysteries are especially appropriate because they contain many representations of facts, opinions, and reasoned judgments in their plots. You may want to make many of the following titles available for student selection. If you focus on mysteries as a genre study at this point in the lesson, help students understand that mysteries are fiction or nonfiction books that are fun to read because readers often don't know what is happening until the end of the story. Point out that many people like to try to figure out mysteries as they read and that this kind of detective work requires the ability to distinguish fact from opinion and to make reasoned judgments. Then have students choose a mystery from the classroom or school library such as one of the following:

High Interest/Low Vocabulary

Bunting, Eve. *Is Anybody There?* New York: HarperCollins, 1986.

Cooper, Susan. *Greenwitch.* New York: Atheneum, 1974.

Korman, Gordon. *Beware the Fish.* Apple Paperbacks/Scholastic, 1986.

Sobol, D. *Encyclopedia Brown* (Series). New York: Morrow, 1975–1985.

Wright, B.R. *Christina's Ghost.* New York: Holiday House, 1985.

Levels 4–6

Elmore, P. *Susannah and the Blue House Mystery.* New York: Dutton, 1980.

Fleischman, S. *The Bloodhound Gang's Secret Code Book.* New York: Random House, 1983.

Fitzhugh, Louise. *Harriet the Spy.* New York: Harper & Row, 1964.

Hahn, M.D. *Following the Mystery Man.* New York: Clarion Books, 1988.

Hildick, E. *The Case of the Bashful Bank Robber.* New York: Macmillan, 1981.

Hildick, E.W. *Deadline for McGurk.* New York: Macmillan, 1975.

Howe, James and Deborah. *Bunnicula.* New York: Atheneum, 1979.

Bride, E. *Tolliver's Secret.* New York: Crown Publishers, 1976.

Roberts, W.D. *What Could Go Wrong?* New York: Atheneum, 1989.

Rosenbloom, Joseph. *Maximilian You're the Greatest.* New York: Dutton, 1984.

Sadler, C. *The Adventures of Sherlock Holmes.* New York: Avon Books, 1988.

Wallace, Bill. *Danger in Quicksand Swamp.* New York: Holiday House, 1989.

Levels 7–8

Osborne, W. *Thirteen Ghosts: Strange But True Ghost Stories.* New York: Scholastic/Apple, 1988.

Slote, Alfred. *Omega Station.* New York: J.B. Lippincott, 1983.

APPLYING THE STRATEGY TO EVERYDAY EVENTS

To help students practice using the Thinking Guide to make reasoned judgments, have them choose from the following activities, or allow students to suggest an alternative. Review the Thinking Guide before students select their activities.

Students on Their Own or with a Partner
As they read a book of choice silently for a twenty-minute period, ask students to use the Thinking Guide to list facts, opinions, and rea-

soned judgments they find in their stories. At the end of the silent reading period, ask students to use the information they know and have integrated to make a reasoned judgment about some part of their stories they have not yet read. For example: Are the characters really who they seem to be? Who committed the crime? You may wish to collect Thinking Guides at this point and allow students to spend several additional days reading their books. When students have finished reading, return the Thinking Guides and have students write on the back of the guides how well they were able to make judgments about the characters or the outcomes of the story. Ask students to report how the thinking strategies from the Thinking Guide assisted them.

Working Collaboratively   Have students choose a topic about which there is disagreement; for example, a controversial political question in their hometown or city, an event they have recently studied, or a current event. Ask students to work in small groups to gather as much information as they can, using a variety of sources. Tell students that as they gather information they should classify it into the categories on the Thinking Guide. Allow students to work for two class periods researching and categorizing the ideas they find. Encourage them to seek the judgments and opinions of parents or other adults who know something about the topic. After two days have elapsed, have students make a reasoned judgment based on what they have learned, write it in Box 4 of the Thinking Guide, and present their judgments to the class.

Students on Their Own   Have students think of something they believe, such as that a particular piece of music is the best or that a specific product is superior to all others, and explain to students they will have the next class period to work in the library to gain more information about their belief. On the next day, have students list all new pieces of information on their

Thinking Guides as either facts, opinions, or reasoned judgments. Then ask students to evaluate all the information they have gathered and to make a reasoned judgment about the validity of their belief. Finally, ask students to discuss their findings in small groups, noting what effect using the Thinking Guide had on their beliefs. At the end of the class period have students write what they have learned about the differences between forming opinions and reasoned judgments on the back of their Thinking Guides.

STUDENT SELF-ASSESSMENT

At the end of any activity in Part 2, you can ask students to write in their journals how using the Thinking Guide has helped them make reasoned judgments, encouraging them to describe how their thinking or awareness may have changed.

or

Ask students to list the ways they might use this strategy in the future and subjects in which distinguishing fact from opinion could be important.

TEACHER ASSESSMENT

Review students' oral and written presentations. To evaluate whether students have improved their ability to make reasoned judgments, ask them to:

- select two newspaper reports about the same incident and record a factual statement, an opinion, and a reasoned statement that appears in each report; then have them complete the Thinking Guide to decide which account was most valid and reliable

- describe what they have learned in this lesson that will improve their decision-making abilities in the future

- design a lesson to teach younger classmates what they have learned. Be sure you approve the lesson before it is implemented.

APPLYING THE STRATEGY ACROSS THE CURRICULUM

The following activities provide students with the opportunity to apply the strategy in different areas of the curriculum. Review the Thinking Guide before students begin their activities.

Science   Have students work in small groups to research scientific "facts" that are no longer thought to be true or beliefs about natural phenomena they wish to confirm. You may wish to suggest one or more of the following topics and write additional student suggestions on the board to begin the lesson:

■ The sun revolves around the earth.

■ The earth is the center of the solar system.

■ The stars are tiny points of light appearing through holes in a huge dark screen.

■ The earth is flat.

Next ask students to collect information from encyclopedias regarding why people once believed these falsities to be true. For example, students can look at the sky to observe the apparent motion of the sun in relation to the Earth to understand why people thought the Earth did not move.

Allow students approximately twenty minutes to work in small groups on one topic. As students gather information, have them classify each piece in the appropriate boxes of the Thinking Guides as either opinion, fact, or reasoned judgment. Once the twenty-minute period has elapsed, ask students to make their Thinking Guides into overhead transparencies to be used as visual aids as they share their findings with the class. If time permits after all groups have shared, ask students to discuss beliefs we hold today that have not yet been proven true. For example, some people believe that ghosts exist, that UFOs have appeared in our atmosphere, and that establishing a gene bank can improve the human species. Have students use the Thinking Guide to list facts and opinions about such a contemporary belief and then to make a reasoned judgment about what students in the year 2200 who work on a similar activity will likely find to be true about that belief.

Social Studies   Divide the class into three groups. Ask each group to pick a current controversial topic. When they have chosen a topic, ask two of the groups to take opposing points of view and prepare to debate by thinking of all the reasons their point of view is the right one. Have the third group listen to the debate and classify on the Thinking Guide important points as either facts, opinions, or reasoned judgments. Based on the information each audience member records on the Thinking Guide, he or she votes for the side of the issue that is most reasonable. Votes are tallied at the end of the class.

Art   Have students create advertising posters expressing opinions in ways that make them seem like facts. First have students think of something they would like to advertise. Next have them list on the Thinking Guide all the facts and opinions they know about the item. Then tell students to write the copy for their advertisements, combining facts and opinions to make it difficult for readers to distinguish between the two. Encourage students to include pictures, drawings, or photographs that help make the point they are trying to communicate. At the end of the class period when all ads have been shared, have students write about their talents in the fields of communication and advertising and whether they might enjoy exploring such a career.

MEETING INDIVIDUAL NEEDS

STRATEGIES FOR LESS ABLE READERS

Review the Thinking Guide with students who wish to meet with you individually or in small groups and who may benefit by spending more time distinguishing fact from opinion. Have students read together with you photocopied pages from a mystery and ask them to use different-colored highlighter marking pens to highlight single sentences that are facts, opinions, or reasoned judgments. After each sentence is highlighted, ask volunteers to defend the choice they made as to why that statement is a fact, opinion, or reasoned judgment. After twenty minutes, ask students to explain what they have learned, why such distinctions are important, and times in their future reading and life experiences when they will need to pay special attention to making such distinctions.

STRATEGY EXTENSIONS FOR BETTER READERS

Have students expand their ability to distinguish factual, opinionated, and reasoned statements by having small groups select and read one editorial in the daily newspaper about a subject they agree on. Ask each student to work independently using the Thinking Guide to distinguish between facts and opinions in the editorial by listing them in Boxes 1 and 2. Then have them complete Box 3. When they have completed the first three boxes in the Guide, have them make a reasoned judgment and write it in Box 4. At the end of the class period, have students return to their small groups. Have students take turns reading their judgments to the other students in the group, and write on the back of their Thinking Guides which judgment they consider to be the best of the group and why.

MULTICULTURAL CONNECTIONS

On the day or evening preceding a classroom discussion have students look for advertisements or television commercials that use opinionated statements to influence people of certain cultural groups to buy their products. During the discussion ask students to tape to a bulletin board the ads they found. Then have students study the bulletin board and make generalized, reasoned statements about what types of appeals marketing teams are using for specific populations and why such appeals are used. After the class has completed these generalizations, ask them to make a reasoned judgment regarding whether such targeted ads are detrimental to creating a climate of inclusion in our society or whether such ads are beneficial in maintaining a healthy appreciation for the multicultural tapestry that distinguishes the United States. Ask students to choose whether to make these reasoned judgments in writing on their Thinking Guides or to share them orally.

Understanding Others   Share with students that throughout their lives they will be called upon to make a reasoned judgment when two experts or friends disagree. To do so they will benefit by visualizing their Thinking Guides, because they will need to assess the factual and opinionated dimensions of the disagreement before they offer their reasoned judgments. For example, they might need to determine whether the disagreement is based on misinterpretation of research findings or upon differing personal experiences. At this point in the activity, ask one student to describe a disagreement he or she was called upon to help solve in the past. Ask the rest of the class to list this problem at the top of the Thinking Guide and do a think-aloud (page 93) as you ask the first student to recall all the facts he or she knew and the opinionated statements made by both people involved in the dispute. Then ask students to report the reasoned judgments they would have made about that incident. Once all students have written their reasoned judgments in Box 4 of their Thinking Guides, ask the student who originally suggested the dispute under discussion to share the eventual outcome of that dispute. Ask students to compare the actual outcome to the reasoned judgment they would have rendered and to analyze the differences between them. If time permits at the end of class, you may want students to describe how they will use their Thinking Guides to make more reasoned judgments in the future and what this activity demonstrated to them about differences between factual statements, opinionated statements, and reasoned judgments.

ASSESSMENT OF PARTS 3 AND 4

Ask students to recall, summarize, and give insights about the steps on the Thinking Guide and other strategies they have learned to identify facts, opinions, and reasoned judgments. Then select and complete the class and individual student assessment records on pages 194–216. You may choose from:

- Class Monitoring Record, Blackline Master 62

- Reading Wheel, Blackline Masters 69 and 70

- Speech Critique, Blackline Master 72

- Informal Checklist for Usage, Blackline Master 73

- Portfolio Assessment, Blackline Master 84

L E S S O N   7

SOLVING PROBLEMS USING PSP

STUDENT OBJECTIVES

In Part l, students will learn PSP—the Problem-Solving Process—a step-by-step strategy they can apply to problems they encounter in life and the problems they read about in literature. In Parts 2 through 4, students will practice using the PSP strategy by applying it to the problems faced by characters in fiction, analyzing how fictional characters solve their problems, and by applying PSP to problems in their own lives.

READING AND LANGUAGE ARTS CONNECTIONS

- increasing awareness of how different cultures face similar problems

- recognizing problems and solutions in fiction

- appreciating, recognizing, and responding to fiction for personal enjoyment

- strengthening applied comprehension

- relating experiences using appropriate vocabulary in complete sentences

EXPLORING THE STRATEGY

INTRODUCING THE LESSON

To introduce Lesson 7, ask students to write about a problem they recently had, such a misunderstanding with another person, confusing schoolwork, or a broken piece of equipment. Then have students write the steps they took to solve that problem. Encourage them to list as many details as possible about their problem-solving processes. You may wish to help them enrich their writings or engage in a discussion after they complete their written reflections by posing the following questions:

- When you first noticed your problem, did it take some time before you were exactly sure what the problem was; that is, you were not really sure why you became upset until you had more time to think about the problem?

- When you were trying to find a solution, did you think about how it would feel if the problem were solved?

- How did you identify the best solution?

- Did you do anything to ensure that your solution would work?

- How did you decide the problem was solved?

Next, ask students to share their thoughts and ideas about solving problems, and explain that in this lesson they will learn an effective, step-by-step strategy they can use to solve many different problems. Add that they will know they have learned to solve problems when they can use the steps of this strategy to more effectively solve problems in their lives.

USING THE THINKING GUIDE

Distribute the Thinking Guide "Problem-Solving Process" (Blackline Master 27) and ask students to read silently while you read each section aloud. As you read, explain each section and

give examples from your life to illustrate each step of the strategy on the Thinking Guide.

Step 1: Sorting Out a Problem to Understand Clearly What Is Wrong   Tell students that the first step in solving their problem is to spend a lot of time describing in writing or orally what is wrong. Add that during this time it will be helpful to refer to Lesson 1 and the questions on the Thinking Guide "Asking Questions to Clarify" (Blackline Master 1) to clarify their thinking. Suggest that students continue asking themselves questions or discussing the problem until they have a strong positive feeling that they have found the true difficulty. Add that a sign the true problem has not been correctly identified is that students still have questions in their minds about what is wrong. Then, ask students to write the following questions that can also assist their thinking as they search for the true problem:

- When did it first happen?

- How long ago was it?

- What is wrong with how things are?

- Who is causing the problem?

- What is still "fuzzy" in my thinking?

- What do I need to explore before I can find the true problem?

Finally, tell students to name the exact problem.

Step 2: Brainstorming Ways to Change Explain to students that the second step in PSP is to look for ways to change what is wrong. Add that brainstorming (you may wish to have students reference the Thinking Guide in Lesson 12—Blackline Master 41) many different alternative solutions is the essence of Step 2. Help students understand that in such brainstorming it is valuable to list as many ideas as possible, regardless of how idealistic some may be.

Step 3: Describing What it Will Be Like When a Good Solution Is Found Explain to students that the third step is to list all the conditions that will exist when a good solution is found. Help students understand that Step 3 enables them to describe the goals they want in their solution. A detailed description will assist them in finding a better solution because the solution becomes more specific.

Step 4: Combining Information in Steps 2 and 3 to Select the Best Solution Explain that Step 4 of the PSP strategy is to decide what the best solution is by combining items from Steps 2 and 3. Suggest that students begin Step 4 by listing solutions from Steps 2 and 3 along with any new ideas and eliminating all solutions and ideas that would not work. Tell students they will stretch beyond their first ideas by combining as many items listed in Steps 2 and 3 as possible until as many goals as possible can be reached.

Step 5: Implementing a Plan of Action Explain to students that the last step of PSP is to implement a solution and stick with it to be sure the problem stays solved.

Now answer any questions students have, and tell them that you will use the PSP strategy together to see how a character in a story solves a problem. Choose a fictional book in which a character solves a problem; for example, *Grover Goes to School, Willie the Wimp, Benjamin Bunny, Martha Speaks, Sarah Plain and Tall*, or any serial book from the library, such as those listed on page 57.

APPLYING THE THINKING GUIDE TO LITERATURE

Read aloud the book *Grover Goes to School* (or another serial book or book from page 57), or if you prefer, tell students that in this story Grover was afraid that he wouldn't have any friends at school so he used the PSP strategy to overcome this problem. Then share the following events from the story in which steps in the problem-solving process are illustrated. Ask students to write a description of each step on their Thinking Guides after you discuss them:

Step 1 Grover was afraid he'd have no friends at his new school, so he should have spent time identifying why he was afraid. He did not ask himself questions (Lesson 1). He omitted the first step in problem solving. Because he did not use PSP, Grover increased his difficulties, as shown next.

Step 2 Instead of brainstorming solutions to his fear, Grover was not himself at his new school. Instead of listing ways he could overcome the fear of having no friends, he gave up his possessions to others, cleaned up other people's messes during classes, and played a game he disliked because he thought the people he did these things for would become his friends.

Step 3 Suddenly Grover realized he was unhappy, and he used Step 3 of PSP to identify all the goals that would make him happy.

Step 4 Grover also used Step 4, because he combined what he wanted to change (Step 2) with what he would like (Step 3) and selected the solution of becoming happy, showing his true self to others, not being a doormat, and becoming a helper/sharer as the best solution to his problem.

Step 5 Grover developed the plan of being friendly to people without doing anything against his will. He continued this plan of action throughout the remainder of the school year.

When you finish the reading or retelling of this story or another from a different book, ask students to describe what was difficult for Grover (or the main character) at the beginning of the problematic experience and to explain what the character was feeling. Write student responses on the chalkboard. Then read through the steps of the Thinking Guide, having students suggest other examples from the story for each step on the guide.

When you have completed the Thinking Guide with the students, lead a discussion about how well the character in the story solved his or her problem. Ask students how the problem might have been solved differently if all the steps of PSP had been used.

ASSESSMENT OF PART 1

If you wish to assess or have students self-assess
how much they have learned at this point in the
lesson, ask them to do one of the following:

- Answer the question, "What have you
  learned from this lesson that you will use
  later in life?"

- Generate new uses for the strategy.

- Discuss and write about what they have
  learned in pairs.

- Share insights as a class orally or in writing.

APPLYING THE STRATEGY

RECOGNIZING PSP IN LITERATURE: FICTION

Review the Thinking Guide and explain that students will now have the opportunity to practice using PSP as they read fiction. You may want students to review the definition of fiction before they begin. Point out that works of fiction include short stories, novels, and plays and that they usually portray imaginary characters and events. Once students understand the definition, have them select a fiction book. Serial books are excellent for this lesson. They enable students to use familiar settings and character traits from past readings in the series to predict the steps of PSP that their main characters are likely to take. Some serial fiction books in which main characters must solve problems are:

High Interest/Low Vocabulary

Brown, Marc. *Arthur*. Boston: Little, Brown, 1983–1993.

Cleary, Beverly. *Ramona*. New York: Morrow, 1977.

Delton, Judy. *Pee Wee Scouts*. New York: Dell and Jubilee Publishers, 1989–1993.

Parish, Peggy. *Amelia Bedelia*. New York: Harper & Row, 1963.

Potter, Beatrix. *Tales of Benjamin Bunny*. New York: F. Warner and Company, 1989.

Ross, Pat. *M & M Twins*. New York: Pantheon and Viking, 1950–1987.

Sharmat, Marjorie Weinman. *Nate the Great*. New York: Coward, McCann and Geoghegan, 1972.

Sobel, Donald. *Encyclopedia Brown*. New York: Morrow, 1975–1985.

Levels 4–6

Adler, David. *Cam Jansen Adventures*. New York: Viking, 1980–1992.

Dixon, C. *Hardy Boy Mysteries*. 1950–1979.

Keene, Carolyn. *Nancy Drew Mysteries*. 1950–1981.

Simon, Seymour. *Einstein Anderson*. New York: Viking, 1980–1983.

Wilder, Laura Ingalls. *Little House on the Prairie*. New York: Harper & Row, 1935.

Levels 7–8

Lewis, C.S. *Chronicles of Narnia*. New York: Macmillan, 1954.

Before students read, explain that their main characters will face some kind of problem in the first chapter and that they are to read the chapter in order to help the character solve a problem, understand how characters deal with their problems, or learn more about how to solve problems for themselves. Ask students to select one of the objectives or to record a personal objective for reading Chapter l of their book at the top of their Thinking Guides. At this point, reread the above objective choices and allow students to record their preferences. After twenty minutes of silent reading, ask students to share examples of the steps of PSP that their characters used.

APPLYING THE THINKING GUIDE TO EVERYDAY EVENTS

To help students practice using the Thinking Guide and to experience the concepts in this lesson, ask them to choose from the activities that follow, or allow students to create their own activity.

Students on Their Own Have students read the second chapter of their book (or read silently for twenty minutes) and complete the objective that they selected. Then, ask students to use the Thinking Guide to analyze how well their character applied the steps in PSP to their problem and to write incidents of individual steps on their Thinking Guides. After twenty minutes, have students write a description of the problem, what the character did to solve it, and what they would suggest the character do differently if ever faced with a similar problem in the future.

Working Collaboratively   Have students who wish to work in pairs or small groups select the same book to read. Tell them that they are to read for twenty minutes and to use the Thinking Guide to identify how their characters solve a problem. Encourage them to look for places in the story in which a character did not follow the problem-solving steps in PSP and to analyze the results. Give the following example before students begin: Two of the three little pigs did not arrive at good solutions for their home needs and were almost eaten by the wolf because they neglected to brainstorm alternative solutions to their initial problem. (Step 2) After twenty minutes, ask students to share what they have learned about the effects of eliminating PSP steps in reaching a solution and how it can increase the difficulty of the problem.

APPLYING THE THINKING GUIDE TO STUDENTS' OWN LIVES

Have students work with you as a class or in a small group to apply the Thinking Guide to a problem they face in school. Begin the activity by listing possible problems that students suggest on the board. Students may select the problem, but ask them to choose one that most or all of them have experienced. Then have them in groups or as a whole class go through the steps, writing down their ideas for each step. When students have finished this process, ask each student to write down independently his or her idea for a clear solution to the problem. Have the class discuss these ideas and decide whether they feel they have arrived at a realistic solution to the problem. If they wish to implement one of their solutions, have them list the steps they want to use in implementing it.

STUDENT SELF-ASSESSMENT

At the end of any activity in Part 2, have students write how PSP has helped them understand ways that other people solve problems and to discover new methods to solve their own problems.

or

Ask students to list questions they still have about PSP and aspects of problem solving that still are difficult for them.

TEACHER ASSESSMENT

Review students' written and oral presentations by evaluating their understanding of each step and the plausibility of the solutions they derived. You may also give students a problem they are likely to experience in their lives outside of school and ask them to suggest the best solution. As you evaluate students' problem-solving abilities, look for evidence that students:

- initiate PSP without prompting

- volunteer insights as to steps literary characters omit in their problem-solving processes

- recognize why past personal problems were not resolved as successfully as desired

APPLYING THE STRATEGY ACROSS THE CURRICULUM

The following activities are designed to give students the opportunity to use PSP in several different curriculum areas. Review the Thinking Guide before students begin their activities.

Mathematics   Divide the class into small groups and ask students to use the Thinking Guide to solve a word problem in mathematics. Assign each group two different problems. Before you begin, give the following example and ask the entire class to think aloud with you as you write each step of PSP on the board. Ask students to describe the thoughts they have as they use the information in the following word problem to reach the solution:

> One night Linda is picking out clothes to wear for the next day. The electricity is out and her room is dark. Linda only wears red or yellow socks and wants to find a matching pair. She knows that there are 18 pairs of loose socks in her drawer. How many socks should she take out to be sure she has a pair that matches? (Answer: 3 socks)

Model for students how they can sort out important and unimportant information (Step l), brainstorm ideas (Step 2), think of goals or conditions the solution must meet (Step 3), select an answer (Step 4), and mentally check to see if the answer makes sense by visualizing the drawer (Step 5). Tell students that when they solve the problem they are to write the solution without saying it aloud so that other students will have a chance to work on it. Ask each group to write on their Thinking Guides the steps they follow in solving their problem and to share answers with the class when all have finished. After all answers have been shared, discuss how PSP can be used in other mathematical problems and why it will be helpful for students to use it.

Social Studies   Have small groups of students select a current problem that interests them, such as environmental pollution, people not having enough food, or the protection of ocean resources. Explain that these are complex problems without simple answers and that PSP can help students arrive at possible solutions. Encourage students to think of what they can do to solve the problems they selected, pointing out that even small solutions can help solve big problems. Ask students to think about the problem at home that night and to bring any resources they have and information from discussion with their parents to school the next day. Then ask students to spend one full day researching the problem. On the third day, let the small groups apply PSP to the problem and share their solutions with the entire class.

From Reading to Writing   Have students write a story in which a character solves a problem. Stipulate that students use the Thinking Guide to help plan their stories, using the steps as a rough outline for the plot and suggest serial books as good models to follow in developing their stories. Point out that because they know their characters so well they can predict a sequel more easily. Suggest that students also draw upon their own experiences and imaginations for story ideas, settings, or characters. Encourage them to include details that will assist readers to better understand the problem the character has and to sympathize with the experience. After students have finished their stories, have them share them in small groups.

This lesson lends itself well to the introduction of instruction on how to write vivid and effective settings. You may wish to use one or more of the following books to demonstrate how their authors created effective settings before students begin to write:

High Interest/Low Vocabulary

White, E.B. *Charlotte's Web*. New York: Harper, 1980.

Levels 4–6

Babbitt, Natalie. *Tuck Everlasting*. New York: Farrar, Straus, & Giroux, 1975.

Fritz, Jean. *Homesick: My Own Story*. New York: Putnam, 1982.

Lasky, Kathryn. *Beyond the Divide*. New York: Macmillan, 1983.

L'Engle, Madeleine. *A Wrinkle in Time*. New York: Farrar, Straus, & Giroux, 1962.

Paterson, Katherine. *Bridge to Terabithia*. New York: Thomas Y. Crowell, 1977.

Speare, Elizabeth George. *The Witch of Blackbird Pond*. New York: Dell, 1978.

Van Allsburg, Chris. *Jumanji*. Boston, MA: Houghton Mifflin, 1981.

Wilder, Laura Ingalls. *The Long Winter*. New York: Harper, 1953.

Science   Give students the following problem:

> Several students went on a camping trip with their families. Everyone spotted a cave. All the adults except one went inside the cave to see if it was safe for children to enter. Just as the adults entered, a large boulder rolled in front of the doorway to the cave, and the adults could not get out.

Ask students to think what they would do, and divide the class into small groups to solve the problem. Specify a time limit. After the specified time, have each group share its solution with the class. Have students diagram and write their solution on the Thinking Guide. Share solutions and have each student vote and defend her or his preferred solution in writing on the back of the Thinking Guide. Tabulate the preferred solutions (lst, 2nd, 3rd, and so on) and announce them on the following day. List the reasons students gave as to why these applications of PSP were judged best. Ask students what they learned that will help them become more successful users of PSP, and to predict times in their lives, like the cave incident, when they will use it.

MEETING INDIVIDUAL NEEDS

STRATEGIES FOR LESS ABLE READERS

Review the PSP strategy with students who wish to meet with you individually or in small groups. Review the steps of the Thinking Guide and then read aloud a simple story in which a character solves a problem. As you read, point out examples of each step of the problem-solving process and explain how it helps the character solve his or her problem. An excellent story for this activity is *The Tales of Benjamin Bunny* by Beatrix Potter. The story is easy to read and adheres to PSP in plot development: Peter and Benjamin establish certain criteria before entering the garden to retrieve Peter's clothes, and they assess their plan of action as they implement it. You could also stop the story at Step 2 and ask students to brainstorm their own solution to Peter's problem. When the story is over, ask students to discuss how they feel about the character's solution and to apply PSP to a problem they face in their own lives by writing the steps from memory.

STRATEGIES FOR BETTER READERS

Ask students to expand their application of PSP by suggesting different ways it could be used at school and in their lives outside of school. Then give this group the option of solving a problem you describe, making up a real-life situation in which PSP would be helpful, and solving it or describing and solving with PSP a current problem in their lives. If students choose the first option, describe in detail the behavior of a hypothetical bully in the classroom.

MULTICULTURAL CONNECTIONS

Ask students to consider the problem of racial tension as it exists in their nation, hometown, or school. Have students apply PSP as a class or in small groups by writing each step in detail on their Thinking Guides. When groups have completed their work, have students share their solutions by making their Thinking Guides into overhead transparencies. When all solutions have been shared, discuss how the class can implement one of the plans.

ASSESSMENT OF PARTS 3 AND 4

Ask students to recall, summarize, and give insights about the problem-solving process they have learned in this lesson. Then select and complete the class and individual student assessments records on pages 194–216. You may select:

- Class Monitoring Record, Blackline Master 62

- Conference Log, Blackline Master 66

- Reading Wheel, Blackline Masters 69 and 70

- Student Self-Assessment of Thinking Abilities, Blackline Master 79

L E S S O N   8

SOLVING SMALL PROBLEMS INDEPENDENTLY

STUDENT OBJECTIVES

In Part l, students will learn to identify strategies literary figures use to solve their problems and to select their own strategies to solve small problems they will encounter in life. In Parts 2 through 4, students will practice identifying strategies used by characters in fiction, analyze how fictional characters solve problems, and build their own problem-solving skills by selecting the strategies they prefer to use in their own lives.

READING AND LANGUAGE ARTS CONNECTIONS

- recognizing problems and solutions in fiction
- increasing literal comprehension
- appreciating, recognizing, and responding to fiction for personal enjoyment

EXPLORING THE STRATEGY

INTRODUCING THE LESSON

To introduce Lesson 8, ask students to think about a bad habit they want to change and assure them that all people have qualities about themselves they wish to change. Give an example of a habit you would like to change for yourself. List students' habits on the board as they share them. Have students describe in their journals this habit or a problem they recently had related to this habit, such as not putting things back in their proper place or being late to school. Then have them write what strategy they used to solve the problem. Encourage students to elaborate by listing as much as they can remember about their problem-solving process. You may wish to use the following questions as prompts for students to recall details.

■ When you were trying to find a solution, did you have a sense of what it would mean to solve the problem?

■ How did you find the most appropriate solution?

■ How did you decide on a way to solve the problem?

■ How could you tell the problem had been solved?

When students have finished writing, explain to them that when they want to solve a problem—e.g., the bad habits listed on the board, losing possessions, or losing their temper—they can use the new strategies they learn in this lesson. Tell students they will know they have learned these strategies when they find it easier to overcome a bad habit and when little annoyances are solved more rapidly.

USING THE THINKING GUIDE

Distribute the Thinking Guide "Selecting My Own Problem-Solving Strategy" (Blackline Master 28), and ask students to read silently

while you read each section of the Guide aloud. Go through the sections, explaining the steps and giving examples. You may wish to paraphrase the following descriptions of strategies in the Thinking Guide.

Strategy 1: Give Myself A Hint   Explain to students that giving themselves hints can be a good way to solve minor problems. Help students understand that hints are mental clues or prompts. For example, ask students to think of the last time they were stumped on a mathematical problem. Explain that if the next time they say to themselves, "What do I need to do?" or "What now?" they may be able to solve the problem more rapidly. Instruct students that giving themselves hints can help their problem-solving process because hints remind the brain to recall what they learned previously, help them refocus on the task at hand, and stimulate new thoughts. Ask how many students have used hints in the past and how these hints have helped in problem solving. Also explain that the "hint strategy" is one reason people often discuss their problems with other people; such discussions produce hints for their next course of action. Ask students to write an example from the discussion or from their own lives in which they could use hints. Have them write these examples on their Thinking Guides as a reminder of the meaning of Strategy l.

Strategy 2: Make Repeated Minor Changes
Students learn that their first step in problem solving is not necessarily to aim for a total solution. By using Strategy 2, they discover that even small solutions can help to solve big problems. For example, when a person is writing and a sentence does not sound exactly correct, demonstrate that a good problem-solving strategy is to use a specific word even though it does not say exactly what the person wants, rather than crossing out an entire sentence and starting all over. Often, making minor changes is all that is necessary. Reiterate that when students see a

new problem develop, they should avoid thinking that everything they have done to that point is wrong or that everything about the situation is wrong. Instead, tell students to try to find one small change that could improve their work, and, if the problem still exists, to alter a second small part, continuing in such a manner until their work satisfies them. Ask students to give other examples of times when they made minor changes. Ask what the resulting effects were. Then ask students to select one of the examples from the discussion or from their own lives and to write it on their Thinking Guides as a reminder of Strategy 2.

Strategy 3: Think of a story as if I'm reading

State that throughout history, people have recalled stories from books and their own lives in which problems similar to the one faced now were solved effectively. Explain that if students can learn to recall situations similar to the one at hand, they can use the lessons from that situation to solve current minor problems. Add that when others consult them for suggestions or advice, they can assist by sharing a story from their own lives in which they solved a similar difficulty. Next, share that even skilled technicians use stories as a method of repairing engines and other complicated machines. Such experts analyze problems by remembering stories their mentors told them or ones in which they observed their mentors solving similar difficulties. Conclude your remarks by challenging students to think of a similar situation whenever they face a difficulty. They can use this recollection to help them decide what to do. To aid their thinking, they can also remember how a problem was solved in a favorite book as well as the advice given in the book. Ask students to select one of the habits on the board listed in the initial class discussion. Ask students to write on the Thinking Guides an event in their lives when they could have succumbed to the bad habit but didn't, and to write that story as a reminder of the meaning of Strategy 3. For example, students could write about a time they were nervous but did not bite their fingernails and instead talked to a friend to overcome their nervousness.

Strategy 4: "What if _____ were _____?"

Define this strategy to students as reminding themselves to think "What if _____ were _____?" each time they can't figure out how to make minor changes to solve a problem. Add that this strategy can help students see that situations can usually be changed and improved, but that without this strategy even the best problem solvers can have difficulty identifying more than a limited variety of options, because most people's initial approaches to problem solving are limited by their own cultures, experiences, and individual needs. Most people tend to think in the same way over and over again and this questioning strategy can be an effective way to open thinking to new ideas and possibilities.

Ask students to explore the strategy by writing their own "What if _____ were _____?" statements about the habit in their own lives they identified earlier. Before students begin, demonstrate the activity by writing about a habit of your own as students watch and listen to you read what you write. For example, you could share that once you could not solve the problem of making time to exercise as much as you desired. You remembered to ask yourself, "What if I asked my best friend to walk with me every day after school?" By using this strategy, you solved your problem. Conclude by reiterating that when students get stuck in their thinking, they should trigger their minds to think "What if ___ were ___?" and to just change one part of the situation to something they already know how to do. For example, have students pretend their parents asked them to figure out how much of a tip to leave at a restaurant and they are unsure how to figure it out. They could use the "What if _____ were _____?" to solve their difficulty. They could think, "I know I am supposed to leave 15% of the total bill, so I think to myself, 'What if I only had to tip 10%?' I know how to do this, because 10% of $26.40 is $2.64. I also know that 5% is 1/2 of 10% so I can add 1/2 of $2.64 to $2.64 to get the total tip I need to leave, which is _____." (Ask students to compute the answer: $3.96.) Pause and let students write their own "What if _____ were _____?" example.

Review the strategies by asking students to tell you what they have learned. Answer students' questions about these four strategies, and tell them you will use the guide together to notice how a character in a story solves a problem. Then choose any short story in which a character solves a problem. *The Great Rat Island Adventure, Swimmy, Lon Po Po,* or *The Pushcart War* are good books you could also choose to use. Read aloud one of the stories listed above or have students read it on their own. When they are finished, ask them to describe what was difficult for the main character at the beginning of the story and to explain what the character was feeling. Write student responses on the chalkboard. Then read through the steps of the Thinking Guide, having students suggest examples in the story where each strategy could have been used. For example, Swimmy used the

"What if _____ were _____?" strategy to convince another school of fish there is safety in numbers. You may want to read aloud pages from *Swimmy* to illustrate where this strategy appears in the story. You can find these on the tenth and twelfth pages of the book, counting the title page as page 1. Discuss how well the character in the story solves his or her problem.

ASSESSMENT OF PART 1

If you wish to end the lesson at this point, to assess how much students have learned, or to ask students to self-assess their learning, you can use one or more of the assessment options on pages 194–216, or allow students to select the option that enables them to demonstrate what they have learned.

APPLYING THE STRATEGY

RECOGNIZING PROBLEM-SOLVING STRATEGIES IN LITERATURE: FICTION

Tell students they will now have the opportunity to practice using the Thinking Guide as they read a work of fiction. You may wish to point out that works of fiction include short stories, novels, and plays, and usually portray imaginary characters and events.

Have students select a story from the list below or provide alternative appropriate stories in which main characters solve difficulties. Before students begin to read, tell them they will be reading about a character or characters who face a problem and that they should read in order to help the character solve a problem, understand how characters deal with their problems, or learn more about how to solve problems for themselves. Encourage students to record a personal objective they may have before they begin, insights they receive as they read, and a description of why they chose the problem-solving strategy they did. Review the Thinking Guide before students begin. The following are some appropriate books for this activity:

High Interest/Low Vocabulary

Brittain, Bill. *Dr. Dridd's Wagon of Wonders.* New York: Harper & Row, 1987.

Freedman, Russell. *The Wright Brothers: How They Invented The Airplane.* New York: Holiday House, 1991.

Gretz, Susanna. *Frog, Duck, And Rabbit.* New York: Four Winds Press, 1992.

Lionni, Leo. *Swimmy.* New York: Pantheon, 1963.

Shannon, George. *Stories to Solve: Folktales From Around the World.* New York: Greenwillow Books, 1985.

Wood, Don and Audrey. *The Little Mouse, The Red Ripe Strawberry, and The Big Hungry Bear.* Child's Play International, 1984.

Woodruff, Elvira. *Dear Napoleon, I know you're dead, but...* New York: Holiday House, 1992.

Young, Ed, translator. *Lon PoPo.* New York: Philomel Books, 1989.

Levels 4–6

Beattie, Owen and Geiger, John. *Buried in Ice: The Mystery of A Lost Arctic Expedition.* New York: Scholastic/Madison Press Book, 1992.

Bunting, Eve. *Wednesday Surprise.* New York: Houghton Mifflin, 1991.

Dahl, Roald. *James and the Giant Peach.* New York: Puffin Books, 1961.

Dahl, Roald. *Matilda.* New York: Viking Kestrel, 1988.

Haas, Dorothy. *The Secret Life of Dilly McBean.* New York: Bradbury Press, 1986.

Hutchins, Pat. *The Doorbell Rang.* New York: Greenwillow Books, 1986.

Lion, George Ella. *Together.* New York: Orchard Books, 1989.

Merrill, Jean. *The Pushcart War.* New York: W.R. Scott, 1964.

Mosel, Arlene. *The Funny Little Woman.* New York: E. P. Dutton, 1972.

Slavin, Bill. *The Cat Came Back.* Mortongrove, IL: Whitman, 1992.

Speare, Elizabeth George. *The Witch of Blackbird Pond.* Boston: Houghton Mifflin, 1958.

Talbota, Charlene.*The Great Rat Island Adventure.* New York: Atheneum, 1977.

Levels 7–8

Ratz de Taggos, Paul. *A Coney Tale.* New York: Clarion Books, 1992.

Serial Books That Students Select Based on Personal Interests:

High Interest/Low Vocabulary

Cleary, Beverly. *Ramona Series*. New York: Dell, 1990.

Parish, Peggy. *Amelia Bedelia Series*. New York: Harper & Row, 1963–1988.

Rey, H.A. *Curious George Series*. Boston: Houghton Mifflin, 1941.

Levels 4–6

Adler, David A. *Cam Jansen Adventures Series*. New York: Viking, 1980–1993.

Fitzgerald, John D. *The Great Brain Series*. New York: Dial Press, 1967–1985.

Sharmat, Marjorie Weinman. *Nate the Great Series*. New York: Coward, McCann and Geoghegan, 1972–1990.

Levels 7–8

Sibley, Brian. *Land of Narnia: Brian Sibley Explores the World of C. S. Lewis*. New York: Harper & Row, 1990.

APPLYING THE STRATEGY TO EVERYDAY EVENTS

Collaborative Thinking   Have students work in pairs or small groups and choose works of fiction to read. Tell them they can use the Thinking Guide to identify which strategy a character in their story uses to solve a problem. After twenty minutes of silent reading, ask students to record their answers and the title of the book on the Thinking Guide. Post the Thinking Guides on the bulletin board to review orally as a class. The posted Thinking Guides can help students identify new books about characters who face problems similar to their own.

Students on Their Own   Have students silently read the book they selected for twenty minutes. As they read, ask them to incorporate the Thinking Guide into an analysis of how the character in the story solved a problem. After completing this task, have students respond in their journals to the following questions about the problem:

- What was the problem?

- What did the character do?

- What could you have done differently?

- What about this story could you recall at a later date to help you solve problems for yourself?

Dramatic Thinking   Have students create a humorous or dramatic role-play of a scene including acts of problem solving from one of the books they read. Let them perform their role-plays for the class.

APPLYING THE STRATEGY TO STUDENTS' OWN LIVES

Have students work together as a class to apply the Thinking Guide to a problem they face at home or at school. Ask them to choose a problem they have in common. Then have students choose which strategy they would like to implement. After they have finished this process, have each student write down his or her idea for a clear solution to the problem. Have the class as a whole discuss these ideas and decide whether they feel they have arrived at a realistic solution to the problem.

STUDENT SELF-ASSESSMENT

At the end of any activity in Part 2, students can elect to monitor their own progress by a series of peer conferences.

or

Have students write problem-solving entries in their journals to share with you.

TEACHER ASSESSMENT

To assess students' progress at the end of Part 2, you may wish to do one of the following:

- Observe the students in various settings (cafeteria, playground, classroom) as they go about their daily routine. Are the problem-solving strategies on the Thinking Guide being exercised?

- Create a written quiz of fictional problems and evaluate students' choice and implementation of the strategies previously discussed.

APPLYING THE STRATEGY ACROSS THE CURRICULUM

The following activities are designed to give students the opportunity to apply the strategy in several different areas of the curriculum. Review the Thinking Guide before students engage in their activities.

Language Arts Have students write a story about a character who has a problem. Tell them to include a detailed description of the problem. Encourage students to use their experiences as a basis for the story. Then ask them to use their Thinking Guides to determine which strategy the character in the story will use to solve the problem. Students may choose to share their stories with the class.

Mathematics Encourage students to refer to their Thinking Guides while solving numerical equations in mathematics. For example, when given the equation 11 + 5 = __, students can implement the "What if _____were _____?" by saying, "I'm not sure what 11 + 5 is, but I know that 10 + 5 = 15, so, 'what if 11 were 10, and 5 were 6?' The answer would be 16."

Science/Social Studies Have students choose a prominent world problem, such as starvation, the deterioration of the ozone layer, or the national deficit. Explain to students that these are complex problems without simple answers and that they should use the Thinking Guide to arrive at some possible solutions.

Encourage students to think of what other people can do to solve these problems and to think of things they might do themselves. Point out that even small solutions can help solve big problems. EXTENSION: Let students write a letter to the principal listing actions they want to take to contribute to the solution of the problem they analyzed.

Physical Education Have students arrange themselves in a circle. Explain that they will be having a relay race and will need to divide themselves into six equal lines. Time students to see how long is required to form six equal lines. (A class of twenty-four students will need four students in each line to make six equal lines.) Encourage students to make a mental picture of their Thinking Guide to assist them. When the task is completed, ask students which strategy they used to solve the problem. If students have difficulty, discuss the problem and time them a second time. When students return to the classroom, discuss how the strategies on the Thinking Guide can improve their performances in the games and sports they play. For instance, when they play baseball, they can use Strategy 4 and ask themselves when they step up to bat, "If I were a member of the opposing team, what would I expect the batter to do now that two people are on base? How can I hit the ball in an unexpected way to score a run for our team?"

MEETING INDIVIDUAL NEEDS

Students who are having difficulty may benefit from more extensive work with the Thinking Guide. Review the strategies of the Guide and then read aloud or retell a simple story from one of the books in this lesson in which a character solves a problem. As you read, point out examples of the problem-solving strategies depicted on the Thinking Guide, and explain how the character used or could have used each of the strategies to solve his or her problem. When the story is over, ask students to discuss how they feel about the character's solution and to write about or draw a future time in their lives when they might use one or more of the strategies.

STRATEGIES FOR BETTER READERS

Ask students to divide into pairs, pretend they are teachers, and design a lesson with which they can teach one of the problem-solving strategies of their choice to other students. Suggest they begin with a problem younger students can easily understand and work collaboratively to write clear information for each step that will enable them to teach it to others. After you review and evaluate students' written work, allow them to teach the strategies to another group.

UNDERSTANDING SELF

Establish that students can learn more about how they solve problems when they think about how they arrived at a solution. Ask students to recall a problem they have recently encountered at home or school. Have them look up a book from pages 67–68 in which characters overcome problems similar to their own. Following this introduction, ask students to use the Thinking Guide to test a problem's solution in their own minds. Explain that this is how Einstein discovered relativity. He visualized concrete objects, such as trains and whistles, for years, until he finally created a story in his mind in which he stood on a beam of light, traveled through space, and left earth behind him.

ASSESSMENT OF PARTS 3 AND 4

Ask students to recall, summarize, and give insights about what they have learned. Then select and complete the class and individual assessment records on pages 194–216. You may select one or more of the following:

- Class Monitoring Record, Blackline Master 62

- Reading Wheel, Blackline Masters 69 and 70

- Story Map, Blackline Master 74

- Assessing Thinking Abilities, Blackline Master 78

- Students Self-Assessment of Thinking Abilities, Blackline Master 79

- Portfolio Assessment, Blackline Master 84

RECOGNIZING STRENGTHS AND WEAKNESSES

STUDENT OBJECTIVES

In Part 1, students will learn to identify strengths and weaknesses they have in reading, speaking, listening, writing, and thinking. In Parts 2 through 4, students will have opportunities to (a) identify the strengths and weaknesses of characters in fiction, myths, legends, and fairy tales; (b) compare literary characters' strengths and weaknesses with their own; and (c) determine how characters' and their own strengths affect outcomes in life and literature.

READING AND LANGUAGE ARTS CONNECTIONS

- identifying important and less important details
- strengthening literal comprehension in order to make generalizations
- discovering that fiction can be an information-gaining resource
- developing facility in oral reading for an audience
- relating experiences using appropriate vocabulary in complete sentences
- appreciating, recognizing, and responding to fiction, myths, legends, and fairy tales for personal enjoyment

EXPLORING THE STRATEGY

INTRODUCING THE LESSON

To introduce Lesson 9, ask students to divide a sheet of paper into two vertical columns. In the left-hand column, ask students to list their personal strengths in reading, writing, speaking, listening, and thinking. Next, ask them to list their weaknesses in the right-hand column. When students have completed their lists, ask them to evaluate how they know they do these things well and whether they would like to learn how to recognize more of their personal strengths and weaknesses. Explain that by identifying their strengths and weaknesses they can learn more, foresee problems more easily, and use more of their strengths to overcome difficulties. Add that students will have an opportunity to practice this strategy, called *thinking metacognitively,* by reading about and identifying with characters in fairy tales and myths.

Define metacognitive thinking as being aware of how their thought processes work. For example, students can realize when their minds wander away from the subject in a class discussion and consciously refocus on the topic. Add that students will know they are increasing their awareness of their strengths and weaknesses if they can add at least two additional strengths or weaknesses to their lists by using some of the strategy's steps. Identifying their strengths will help students face real difficulties.

Conclude the introduction by asking students if they understand why it is important to identify their strengths and weaknesses, and whether or not they were able to do so easily in the past.

USING THE THINKING GUIDE

Distribute the Thinking Guide "Recognizing What I Do Well" (Blackline Master 39) and ask students to read the steps as you explain them. As students use the Thinking Guide, they will concentrate on the strengths they listed in the previous activity. Instruct them to fill in at least two examples under each step on the guide. Then present the following steps from the Thinking Guide, and allow time for students to discuss and write personal examples of their reading, writing, speaking, thinking, and listening abilities before proceeding to the next step.

Step 1: What Do I Do Well?   Explain to students that whenever they want to learn more about their strengths, they can ask themselves: "What have my parents, teachers, or other adults told me I do well? What have adults noticed I do well? What have my friends noticed I do well?" Remind students to pay attention to compliments others give them. Then, in the right- and left-hand columns of their lists, ask students to write examples from their lives that this step helped them to recognize.

Step 2: Seeing Myself in Other People
Share with students that each time they finish a book, movie, or television show they can come to understand themselves better by asking, "Which characters in books and movies do I identify with easily? Which of their good qualities am I developing, and how can their actions assist me to develop these qualities more completely?" Have students give an example of a main character in a book that has qualities they possess and explain how identifying with that character made their own strengths easier to recognize. Ask a few students to name their favorite characters from books that possess strengths of theirs. In the left-hand column of the Thinking Guide have students write a few new strengths they have in common with these favorite characters. Some students may even notice a few weaknesses both they and their favorite characters want to overcome.

Step 3: My Strengths Show in Activities I Enjoy Doing   Explain to students the third step will help them identify their strengths through reflecting on activities they enjoy. Ask students to list on Step 3 of the Thinking Guide several activities in the language arts they enjoy. Ask students to examine their lists and consider whether the activities they chose have anything in common. Explain that by identifying common parts to activities they enjoy, students can see how their strengths make those activities more enjoyable. For example, suggest that if students enjoy debating, writing about their opinions, and reading about people who had strong opinions, they may discover that a thinking strength they have is analyzing opinions and making reasoned judgments as they learned in Lesson 6.

Step 4: Use a Strength to Improve a Weakness. Explain that when students are attempting something difficult, they should ask themselves, "What part of this activity can I change so that it uses more of my strengths or is more enjoyable?" For example, depending on the length of a person's attention span, taking a small break from working on a difficult task might improve its quality. Students also can consider whether they prefer working in groups or alone and how an activity can be altered so they can work with the number of people they prefer. Do students want quiet surroundings when they are reading? Do students want to be able to look outside while they work or have all distractions blocked from view? Allow students to raise their hands as you read each of the above examples so they can see how many of their classmates have the same preferences as themselves.

Then ask students for suggestions of other parts of activities they could change so they would be able to use more of their strengths, e.g., "How can you use your ability to write well to increase your spelling ability?" List the ideas on the board. After students have shared, ask them to write new strengths they have recognized in their learning styles and personalities that they can add to the left-hand column of their lists.

Ask students to reflect on a weakness they had in the past, such as not being as patient with their brothers and sisters as they are now, not paying attention in school, having trouble in writing, and so on. After students have identified a weakness they overcame, ask them to identify a strength in their personality that

assisted in their success. Ask them to add these elements to the left-hand column of their list.

Conclude this introduction by asking students for examples of when thinking metacognitively will be valuable in their lives. You may also want to cite the following examples of the strategy's use, or use examples from your own life:

"Recognizing a strength in my life helped me decide to become a teacher. My parents had commented on how well I related to children. Then, as I spent more time with children, I realized that I enjoyed it a lot. Characters in my favorite books and movies also helped me choose teaching as a vocation. For example, I remember watching The *Sound of Music* when I was a little girl. I really identified with Maria, the main character, because she was someone who loved children and wanted to help them. Thinking metacognitively helped me realize that working with children is one of my strengths."

"I have been able to overcome one of my weaknesses by analyzing my thinking. I am sometimes a poor listener. Others tell me that I often do not listen attentively because I anticipate what people are going to say and interrupt them. I realized that this was a weakness because people told me (Step 1); because I enjoy talking more than listening (Step 2); and because I enjoy being with groups of two to four people (Step 3). Because I did this analysis I can now consciously think about listening better, remember to listen until the end of people's statements, and to ask questions to further clarify what people have told me to ensure that I don't misunderstand."

You may also want to ask students to share examples. Have students assess whether this lesson increased their knowledge of themselves and whether they added at least two strengths or weaknesses to the list they began at the beginning of the lesson. Share with them that if they did, they are increasing their abilities to think metacognitively and to recognize their strengths and weaknesses.

APPLYING THE THINKING GUIDE TO LITERATURE

Explain to students that they can use this strategy continuously throughout their lives with each new experience they have and new book they read. Add that if they keep the Thinking Guides in mind as they read each day, they will increase their self-knowledge and grow to understand their personal strengths and weaknesses. To demonstrate, ask students to think about a book they read in class recently. Have them write on the Thinking Guide specific ideas they gained about themselves through reading about ways the characters in that book used their strengths.

Confirm for students that each time they reuse the steps of the strategy, they will enhance their metacognitive thinking abilities.

If you wish to assess or have students self-assess how much they have learned at this point in the lesson, ask them to

- Answer the question, "What have you learned from this lesson that you will use later in life?"

- Generate new uses for the strategy.

- Discuss and write with a partner about what they have learned.

- Orally or in writing share insights with the class.

PART 2

APPLYING THE STRATEGY

RECOGNIZING STRENGTHS AND WEAKNESSES IN LITERARY CHARACTERS: MYTHS AND LEGENDS

Review the steps of metacognitive thinking on the Thinking Guide and define myths and legends as forms of folktales that appear in all societies of the world. Continue the explanation by sharing that ancient Greek myths are widely known because their stories affect many contemporary civilizations; for example, the planets in the solar system are named after the gods in Greek mythology. Ask if students are familiar with American legends or myths such as Paul Bunyan and Johnny Appleseed. Add to the discussion that characters in myths and legends have obvious strengths and weaknesses that influence and add interest to the stories about them. Examining mythical figures is a good way to practice identifying strengths and weaknesses.

Provide all or some of the following books that contain myths and legends or, if you prefer, students can also use any selection of literature, fiction, or short stories from basal readers or anthologies in which they can easily identify character traits. If you provide some of the following books for students' selection, state that some are complete novels and some contain shorter stories.

High Interest/Low Vocabulary

Low, Alice. *The Macmillan Book of Greek Gods and Heroes.* New York: Macmillan, 1985.

Levels 4–6

Brooks. *Elfstones of Shannara.* New York: Ballantine, 1982.

Brooks. *Sword of Shannara.* New York: Ballantine, 1991.

Brooks. *Wishsong of Shannara.* New York: Ballantine, 1985.

Hickman and Weis. *Dragon Lance Legends.* New York: Random House, 1988.

Tolkien, J.R.R. *Farmer Giles of Ham.* Boston: Houghton Mifflin, 1991.

Stebbins, R.A. *Magician.* New York: Krieger, 1993.

Levels 7–8

Burn, Lucilla. *Greek Myths.* Austin: University of Texas Press, 1991.

Eddings, D. *The Belgariad.* (five-book series) Garden City, New York: Nelson Doubleday, 1983-1984.

Tolkien, J.R.R. *The Hobbit.* Boston: Houghton Mifflin, 1984.

Tolkien, J.R.R. *Lord of The Rings.* (trilogy) New York: Ballantine Books, 1965.

APPLYING THE STRATEGY TO EVERYDAY EVENTS

To help students practice metacognitive thinking, allow them to choose from the activities below or to suggest an alternative in which they can identify their strengths and weaknesses.

Students on Their Own   Have students select a book or story from the above list and read it for a period of twenty minutes. As they read they are to use as many of the steps in the strategy as possible and to choose their favorite character. At the end of the twenty-minute reading students will analyze their writing or speaking abilities alone or with a partner. Give them a minute to choose their desired format. If they choose to improve their writing abilities, have them answer the following questions by composing an essay. If they want to analyze their speaking abilities, they can record on cassette their answers to the following questions:

■   Why is this character your favorite?

- What are his or her strengths?

- What are his or her weaknesses?

- Do you have any strengths or weaknesses in common with this character? How do you know?

- Could you use one of your strengths to help you overcome one of your weaknesses? Can you identify a way that your favorite characters could use one of their strengths to overcome one of their weaknesses?

If students have taped their responses, have them listen to their tapes and analyze their use of crutch words, grammar, tone, rate of speech, and other areas of possible weakness. If students have responded in writing, have them analyze their grammar and style. Finally, ask all students to describe how they will use one of their strengths to eliminate one of their weaknesses during this grading period and to turn this analysis in to you. Use this paper during an end-of-the-grading-period conference with the student.

Collaborative Thinking Have small groups of students read the same story. After students have read silently for about twenty minutes, ask them to discuss how a character in the story identified his or her own strengths or weaknesses, or how the author made that character's strengths and weaknesses clear to the reader. Next, have each group member write a summary of the discussion and use steps on the Thinking Guide to report the insights they gained about their personal strengths and weaknesses.

Students on Their Own Have students work alone as they write on the Thinking Guide and complete Blackline Master 32 to explore their strengths and weaknesses.

STUDENT SELF-ASSESSMENT

At the end of any activity in Part 2, have students report in their journals what they learned about their strengths and weaknesses.

or

Have students meet with you in a conference to assess their mastery of the strategy taught in the Thinking Guide.

TEACHER ASSESSMENT

To assess students' progress at the end of Part 2, you may wish to note the following qualities in students' work:

- increased use of learning strengths

- less frustration when placed in areas where they have fewer strengths

- self-initiated plans to improve in areas of need

You can also ask students to write a short essay giving advice to a hypothetical person about how to identify personal strengths and weaknesses.

PART 3

APPLYING THE STRATEGY ACROSS THE CURRICULUM

The following activities are designed so students can learn to identify their strengths and weaknesses in several different areas of the curriculum. Review the Thinking Guide before students begin their activities.

Writing   Have students select their favorite piece of personal writing. Have them analyze it by completing the Thinking Guide and by asking themselves the following questions concerning that writing.

- What three qualities of this writing do I like most? Are these qualities what made this writing my favorite?

- What parts of the writing were hardest for me? What personal weaknesses contributed to my difficulty? What strengths can I use to overcome this difficulty in the future?

- What qualities about myself did I discover as I wrote this piece? What qualities did I just discover as I analyzed this selection?

- How is this writing like other activities I have completed with high levels of success?

Physical Education   Have students complete the Thinking Guide as it relates to a sports activity or favorite recess game. After they have finished, ask a few students to share what they wrote. Discuss how the Thinking Guide and analyzing this thinking (metacognitively) helped them.

Mathematics   Arrange a group discussion about a topic students are studying in mathematics class. Ask students what they find easy or challenging about the topic and why. Point out to students that they can learn from each other and build upon one another's strengths.

Recognizing Strengths and Weaknesses

MEETING INDIVIDUAL NEEDS

STRATEGIES FOR LESS ABLE READERS

Review the Thinking Guide with students who wish to meet with you individually or in small groups. Have students select a book that appeals to them, read alone or with a partner, and then share what they have learned about recognizing strengths and weaknesses in a discussion at the end of the period or in writing after they have finished the book.

UNDERSTANDING OTHERS

Have students who wish to work on overcoming personal weaknesses meet in small groups. Ask students to discuss their weaknesses with other group members and invite classmates to give advice on how to overcome these weaknesses.

MULTICULTURAL CONNECTIONS

Ask the school librarian to assist you in locating as many folktales as possible from different regions of the world. List the cultures and their folktales on the board. Have students divide into small groups and select folktales from at least three different cultures. Ask each group to analyze the strengths and weaknesses depicted in each tale's main characters. Have students discuss ways in which the strengths of each character are similar and ways they differ. Ask students to write and share with the class their analyses and how the cultural values as depicted in their characters differ. Recently published folk literature that could be obtained for this activity include:

Africa:

High Interest/Low Vocabulary

Aardema, V. *Anansi Finds a Fool.* New York: Dial Books for Young Readers, 1992.

Gleeson, B. *Koi and the Kola Nuts.* Saxonville, MA: Picture Book Studio, 1992.

Kimmel, E.A. *Anansi Goes Fishing.* New York: Holiday House, 1992.

Levels 4–6

Gerson, Mary-Juan. *Why the Sky Is Far Away.* Boston: Little, Brown, 1992.

McDermott, G. *Zomo the Rabbit.* San Diego: Harcourt Brace, 1992.

Brazil:

Levels 4–6

Stiles, M.B. *James the Vine Puller.* Minneapolis, MN: Carolrhoda Books, 1992.

England:

High Interest/Low Vocabulary

Garner, Alan. *Jack and the Beanstalk.* New York: Doubleday Book for Young Readers, 1992.

Kimmel, E.A. *Old Woman and Her Pig.* New York: Holiday House, 1992.

Germany:

High Interest/Low Vocabulary

Grimm, Jacob. *Bremen Town Musicians.* New York: Philomel, 1992.

Grimm, Jacob. *Rapunzel.* New York: Philomel, 1992.

Grimm, Jacob. *Snow White and Rose Red.* New York: Philomel, 1992.

Grimm, Jacob. *The Fisherman and His Wife.* New York: Philomel, 1992.

Mexico:

Levels 4–6

Brenner, Anita. *The Boy Who Could Do Anything and Other Mexican Folk Tales.* New York: W.R. Scott, 1942.

Native American:

High Interest/Low Vocabulary

Lacapa, Michael. *Antelope Woman*. Flagstaff, AZ: Northland Publishing Co., 1992.

Troughton, Joanna. *How the Seasons Came*. New York: Blackie, 1992.

Levels 4–6

Begay, S. *Ma'ii and Cousin Horned Toad*. New York: Scholastic Books, 1992.

Hinton, J. *Ishi's Tale of Lizard*. New York: Farrar, Straus, Giroux, 1992.

Levels 7–8

Wood, M. *Spirits, Heroes and Hunters from North American Indian Mythology*. New York: Scholastic, 1982.

Russia:

Levels 4–6

Cech, J. *First Snow, Magic Snow*. New York: Four Winds Press, 1992.

Souci, San R.D. *Tsar's Promise*. New York: Philomel, 1992.

Switzerland:

High Interest/Low Vocabulary

Stone, M. *Singing Fir Tree*. New York: Putnam, 1992.

Central and Southern Asia

China:

High Interest/Low Vocabulary

Bang, Molly. *Tye May and the Magic Brush*. New York: William Morrow, 1993.

Leaf, Margaret. *Eyes of the Dragon*. New York: William Morrow, 1981.

Lobel, Arnold. *Ming Lo Moves The Mountain*. New York: William Morrow, 1981.

McClung, Robert. *Lili: a Giant Panda of Sichaun*. New York: William Morrow, 1993.

Singer, Marilyn. *The Painted Fan*. New York: William Morrow, 1993.

Levels 4–6

Pattison, Darcy. *The River Dragon*. New York: William Morrow, 1993.

Japan:

High Interest/Low Vocabulary

Havill, Juanita. *Sato and the Elephants*. New York: William Morrow, 1993.

Melmed, Laura Krauss. *The First Song Ever Sung*. New York: William Morrow, 1993

Sato, Satoru. *I Wish I Had a Big, Big Tree*. New York: William Morrow, 1993.

Wisniewski, David. *The Warrior and The Wise Man*. New York: William Morrow, 1993.

Levels 4–6

Blumberg, Rhonda. *Commodore Perry in the Land of the Shogun*. New York: William Morrow, 1984.

Hughes, M. *Little Fingerling*. Nashville: Ideals, 1992.

Merrill, J. *The Girl Who Loved Caterpillars*. New York: Philomel, 1992.

Shute, Linda. *Momotaro The Peach Boy: A Traditional Japanese Tale*. New York: William Morrow, 1993.

Souci, San. *Samurai's Daughter*. New York: Dial Books for Young Readers, 1992.

Levels 7–8

Godden, Rumer. *Great Grandfather's House*. New York: William Morrow, 1993.

Maruki, Toshi. *Hiroshima No Pika*. New York: William Morrow, 1991.

Korea:

Levels 7–8

Watkins, Yoko Kawashima. *So Far From the Bamboo Grove*. New York: William Morrow, 1985.

Taiwan:

High Interest/Low Vocabulary

Reddix, Valerie. *Dragon Kite of the Autumn Moon.* New York: William Morrow, 1993.

Indonesia:

High Interest/Low Vocabulary

Sis, Peter. *Komodo!* New York: William Morrow, 1992.

Philippine Islands:

Levels 4–6

Aruego, Jose and Dewey, Ariane. *Rockabye, Crocodile.* New York: William Morrow, 1993.

Thailand:

Levels 7–8

Ho, Minfong. *Rice Without Rain.* New York: William Morrow, 1989.

Vietnam:

Levels 4–6

Keller, Holly. *Grandfather's Dream.* New York: William Morrow, 1993.

Kid, Diana. *Onion Tears.* New York: William Morrow, 1993.

Vuong, Lynette. *The Golden Carp and Other Tales of Vietnam.* New York: William Morrow, 1993.

India:

High Interest/Low Vocabulary

Rodanas, Kristina. *The Story of Wali Dad.* New York: William Morrow, 1993.

Levels 4–6

Napal: Mantinband, Gerda. *Three Clever Mice.* New York: William Morrow, 1993.

ASSESSMENT OF PARTS 3 AND 4

Students give insights, provide summaries, and ask questions to extend what they have learned in this lesson. Select and complete class and individual student assessment records from pages 194–216. You may select from:

- Class Monitoring Record, Blackline Master 62
- Reading Wheel, Blackline Masters 69 and 70
- Oral-Language Needs Monitor, Blackline Master 71
- Editing Checklist, Blackline Master 75
- Clues to Improving Handwriting, Blackline Master 77
- Student Self-Assessment of Thinking Abililties, Blackline Master 79
- Problem-Solving Assessment, Blackline Master 82

LESSON 10

MONITORING UNDERSTANDING AND INCREASING COMPREHENSION

STUDENT OBJECTIVES

In Part l, students will learn how to pay attention to their thinking and monitor whether words and ideas make sense when reading. In Parts 2 through 4, students will practice thinking metacognitively as they learn about the genre of mysteries and as they read other types of literature.

READING AND LANGUAGE ARTS CONNECTIONS

- appreciating, recognizing, and responding to mysteries for personal enjoyment
- strengthening interpretive comprehension
- strengthening literal comprehension
- increasing metacognitive thinking
- identifying main idea statements

PART 1

EXPLORING THE STRATEGY

INTRODUCING THE LESSON

To introduce Lesson 10, explain to students that there are certain ways people think when they misunderstand something they are reading. They may know what is happening in the text, they may think they know, or they may be unsure whether they know what the author meant. Tell students that in this lesson they will learn a new way to think while reading that will help them to more fully comprehend what they read. Explain that there are three steps in this thinking process and that they will know they have increased their ability to learn when they employ these steps easily and independently each time they read.

USING THE THINKING GUIDE

Distribute the Thinking Guide "Do I Understand?" (Blackline Master 31). Tell students that the Thinking Guide outlines the three steps they will use to build their comprehension. Each step will be represented by a symbol: I don't know if I know—(?); I know I don't know—(*) ; I know I know—(☺). As you read each section of the Thinking Guide aloud, ask students to share examples of times when they were confused and what they did to clarify their thoughts. Have students discuss what it means to have enough information when reading. Ask them to consider how sufficient information helps them to ask themselves "who," "what," "where," "when," "why," and "how" as they read and what it means to have the confidence to put new pieces of information together.

Applying the Thinking Guide to Literature
Model for students how to use the Thinking Guide by reading "The Case of the Hitchhiker" (Blackline Master 32) from the *Two-Minute Mysteries* series. Display the master on an overhead projector and use the think-aloud below as you read the story aloud. Stop after each section

to share with students the thoughts in parentheses as an example of what a reader might be thinking.

"Boy, thanks for the lift," exclaimed the young man as he slid off his knapsack and climbed into the front seat of the air-conditioned patrol car beside Sheriff Monahan.

(In my mind, I'm thinking, "I don't know if I know what the author is saying. It seems strange that a sheriff would pick up a hitchhiker. But I know I'm not confused; I just don't have enough information, so I'll read on.")

"Say aren't you going to arrest me for bumming a ride?"

"Not today," replied the sheriff. "Too busy."

(I'm confused now—since when is a sheriff too busy to make an arrest? Well, I will just keep reading to find out more.)

The young man grinned in relief. He took a chocolate bar from his knapsack, broke off a piece, and offered the rest to the sheriff.

(I know I understand this. The man seems to be pretty friendly to the sheriff. I know I would be scared, then again, I don't think I would be hitchhiking. This doesn't have much to do with the story.)

"No, thanks," said the police officer, accelerating the car.

"You chasing someone?" asked the hitchhiker.

"Four men just held up the First National Bank. They escaped in a big black sedan."

(I understand everything that is going on, I just don't know why this sheriff is so open with a hitchhiker.)

82   Lesson 10

"Hey," gasped the hitchhiker. "I saw a black sedan about ten minutes ago. It had four men in it. They nearly ran me off the road. First car I saw in an hour. But they took a left turn. They're headed west, not north."

(I know I don't know why this hitchhiker has so much information for the sheriff.)

Sheriff Monahan braked the patrol car and swung it around. The young man began peeling an orange, putting the rinds tidily into a paper bag.

(I know I don't know why he is so neat for being an illegal passenger, and also the sheriff just turned the car around. Why? I wonder.)

"Look at the heat shine off the road ahead," said the sheriff. "Must be eighty-five in the shade today."

(Now I'm confused. How could this hitchhiker have stayed an hour in the sun if it was eighty-five in the shade?)

"Must be," agreed the hitchhiker. "Wait—you passed the turn-off—where're you going?" "To the police station," snapped the sheriff—a decision to which Haledijian heartily agreed upon hearing the hitchhiker's story.

How come?

(I don't know if I know "how come?" so I will go to Step 1. Is it a word I don't understand that confused me? No, it's not a word. Is it my lack of background? No, I understand what a hitchhiker does. Was it too long a sentence? No, I understood all of the sentences. Was my concentration broken? Yes, my concentration was broken because I got caught up with why a hitchhiker would be standing out in the hot sun for so long. Now I will concentrate on putting the other details together to answer "how come?" Step 3 says I should trust my ability to put together new information to comprehend. I have the information and I put all the words correctly together. I now understand that the hitchhiker was too helpful and knew too much. It was almost as if he was trying to throw the sheriff off. Also, if he had been standing in the hot sun for an hour, the candy bar would have no longer been brittle. I think the sheriff suspects the hitchhiker is a part of the hold-up gang. I'm going to check my comprehension by turning to the end of the mystery now.) [See Blackline Master 38 for the answer.]

Stories on Blackline Masters 32–35 are taken from *Two-Minute Mysteries* and *More Two Mysteries* by Donald J. Sobel, Scholastic Book Services.

PART 2

APPLYING THE STRATEGY

Have available five two-minute mysteries for students' use (see Blackline Masters 32–35). Then ask students to select a mystery and use the Thinking Guide independently. After all students have finished, discuss how the steps on the Thinking Guide can be used to face misunderstandings in everyday life.

APPLYING THE STRATEGY TO EVERYDAY EVENTS

To help students practice using the Thinking Guide and to illustrate the concepts in this lesson, have them choose from the activities below or design their own in which they demonstrate their use of metacognitive thinking.

Students on Their Own   Have students select a different mystery to read from Part 1. Then ask students to read that mystery and use the Thinking Guide to help them reflect upon their own metacognitive thinking as they read. Direct them to write next to the appropriate paragraph the symbols that reflect the strategies they are using as they read. (See sample for "The Case of The Hitchhiker" on pages 82 and 83).

Collaborative Thinking   Have students who have read the same mystery form small reading response groups. After a period of silent reading during which they write page numbers on the Thinking Guide when they reference it, ask students to write about the benefits of using metacognitive thinking during reading. Students could also record and compare the number of times each step on the Thinking Guide was used in their group.

Dramatic Thinking   Have students create a humorous or dramatic role-play of the mystery they read, including the questions from Steps 1–3. In this role-play characters tell the audience the thoughts they are having as each character says something to them. Have students present role-plays to the class. Some students may wish to open the play by asking the class to be prepared to say what they think happened at the end before the actual ending is dramatized.

Working with the Teacher   Have students meet with you to explain parts of the Thinking Guide that are confusing to them. You can also discuss ways to build confidence as you talk about reasons Step 3 is difficult for individual students.

STUDENT SELF-ASSESSMENT

At the end of Part 2, students can report what they have learned about the value of building their metacognitive abilities.

or

Students can keep a diary or tally of the questions they asked from Steps 1–3 over a two-week period.

TEACHER ASSESSMENT

To evaluate how much students have learned, tally the number and quality of the results and the learning taking place over a two-week period. Also evaluate metacognitive strengths and weaknesses. Present your findings to the students in individual conferences and design ways to help improve their comprehension.

APPLYING THE STRATEGY ACROSS THE CURRICULUM

The following activities are designed to give students the opportunity to apply metacognitive thinking to several areas of the curriculum. Review the Thinking Guide before students engage in their activities.

History   Have students read *The Case of The Stolen Bible* (Blackline Master 35) and *The Case of The Lincoln Letter* (Blackline Master 33) to be motivated to learn more about the historical events referred to in the stories. They are to find answers to one of their questions through library research and report their "investigative work" to the class before the endings to these cases are read. As students read, ask them to record their metacognitive thinking by using the symbols on the Thinking Guide. After adequate time has elapsed for students to complete their research, ask them to share what they learned about their metacognition and how they worked independently to improve their reading abilities.

Language Arts   Direct students to apply the Thinking Guide by asking themselves questions before reading and by completing the Reading Log, Blackline Master 37. After twenty minutes of silent reading time, have pairs of students assist each other in answering the questions that were not found in their readings. Then ask small groups of students to read and complete their reading logs, with each group member reading the same selection of literature. After the group constructs the questions they want to answer, have them read silently for twenty minutes and then share their answers. Each member should also share one way he or she wants to improve his or her reading ability while other group members suggest strategies that appear on the Thinking Guide or that they have used successfully in the past. For the last ten minutes of the period, have students write or diagram what they learned about metacognition and their own reading ability as a result of this lesson.

Mathematics And Science   When students are doing an experiment or a mathematics problem, they can decide whether they know all the information or what they still need to find out by following the three steps of the Thinking Guide and using the symbols as they work each word problem.

Social Studies   Have students apply the Thinking Guide as they hold a group meeting during a social studies class to discuss a new concept. During the discussion have students write in the margins of the Thinking Guide what they did or could have done to better understand statements made by their peers during the meeting. Stop the activity a few minutes before the end of the class period and hold a class discussion, asking students to share what they learned.

PART 4

MEETING INDIVIDUAL NEEDS

STRATEGIES FOR LESS ABLE READERS

Review the Thinking Guide with students who wish to meet with you individually or in groups. After the review, have students work with you to write a news broadcast in which all questions on Steps 1–3 of the Thinking Guide are presented. Have students present their work to classmates. After the broadcasts are finished, have students discuss how the information on the Thinking Guide aided their comprehension.

Understanding Self   Have students keep a journal of events that happen in their lives. Direct students to include information about "who," " what," "where," "when," "why," and "how" in relation to each event.

or

Have students complete a chart to tally the number of times when they don't have enough information (on the "Not Enough Information" form, Blackline Master 38). After two weeks, ask students to bring the form to a conference with you.

or

Have students make a chart of why they were confused or complete the form, "It's OK Not to Know" (Blackline Master 39). After two weeks, have students devise a plan to overcome the major comprehension problem they face.

STRATEGIES FOR BETTER READERS

Have students use the Thinking Guide to analyze an event or incident that occurred in their life or a topic in another content area. Ask students to write about how the Thinking Guide helped them understand that event or topic better.

ASSESSMENT OF PARTS 3 AND 4

Ask the students to recall, summarize, and give insights about what they have learned in this lesson. Then, select and complete the class and individual student assessment records from pages 194–216. You may select from:

- Class Monitoring Record, Blackline Master 62

- Reading Wheel, Blackline Masters 69 and 70

- Assessing Thinking Abilities, Blackline Master 78

- Problem-Solving Assessment, Blackline Master 82

- Portfolio Assessment, Blackline Master 84

CREATING MENTAL IMAGES TO STAY FOCUSED

STUDENT OBJECTIVES

In Part 1, students will learn to form mental pictures while they read, listen, and think so they increase their comprehension. In Parts 2 through 4, students will practice creating mental pictures as they hear a book read to them and while they read silently and/or listen.

READING AND LANGUAGE ARTS CONNECTIONS

- strengthening interpretive comprehension
- developing creative thinking abilities
- strengthening reading and listening retention
- describing the time and setting of the story
- relating unknown to known information by constructing a mental image
- producing, coordinating, and subordinating sentence elements to construe meaning
- recognizing and using personification as a literary device
- activating prior knowledge

PART 1

EXPLORING THE STRATEGY

INTRODUCING THE LESSON

To introduce Lesson 11, ask students to recall if they have ever pictured in their minds what they were reading. Explain that mental imaging is the ability to form a picture in their minds so they can remember what they are thinking, reading, hearing, or saying. Explain that mental images enable readers to organize information into categories (schemas) which strengthen their ability to remember those concepts in the future. Share that students will have an opportunity to practice this thinking strategy as you read to them and as they read silently. Then they will either draw or describe what they pictured in their minds during the reading. Finally, tell students they will know they have learned the strategy when they begin to create pictures in their minds automatically as they comprehend and remember what authors and speakers are saying.

To promote students' interest in this lesson, share a story that describes the benefits students can receive by learning to image. The story you share can be from your life or from a former student's testimonial, such as, "After last year's class finished this lesson, Michael said he understood the lesson because he had created mental images while reading a book about a big red dog. He explained that when the dog got his leg stuck in some pipes, he imagined how he would have saved the dog if he were there, and because he created this mental picture he could remember everything that happened in the book." Tell students you want them to experience such success in comprehending and that you think imaging will help them do so.

USING THE THINKING GUIDE

Distribute the Thinking Guide "Creating Mental Images" (Blackline Master 40), and ask students to read each section as you discuss it. Point out there are four steps to create mental images.

After reading each step, give examples of times you have observed students doing these steps in class, and ask them to share examples of when they have imaged in that way.

APPLYING THE THINKING GUIDE TO LITERATURE

Read one of the following stories or another book containing events that are easy to image.

A. Sheehan. *The Butterfly.* New York: Warwick Press, 1976. (Levels 4–6).

Christine Howes. *Life in the Desert.* New York: Macmillan, 1993. (High Interest/Low Vocabulary).

Jane Cutler. *No Dogs Allowed.* New York: Farrar, Straus & Giroux, 1992. (Levels 4–6).

As you read, ask students to create a picture in their minds as if they were one of the characters in the story. As soon as you have finished reading, have students draw one image they created and invite them to share it with the class. As students share their descriptions and drawings, point out that it doesn't matter that images vary. Discuss with students why learning to create mental pictures will improve their comprehension and retention.

ASSESSMENT OF PART 1

If you wish to end the lesson at this point or to assess how much students have learned, you can use one or more of the assessment options on pages 194–216 or allow students to select the option that enables them to demonstrate what they have learned.

PART 2

APPLYING THE STRATEGY

CREATING MENTAL IMAGES WHEN READING LITERATURE: FICTION

If the books listed below are not available, select other literature in which events are easy for students to visualize. Review the Thinking Guide. Then ask students to define and review fiction, ensuring they understand that fictional works describe events that are imagined and not factual. Add that reading and writing fiction stories can expand a person's creativity and imagination. Introduce a collection of fiction books in which the main characters are women, represent particular cultural groups, or overcome obstacles to achieve their goals. Ask pairs of students to read the same selection as they reference the Thinking Guide. After twenty minutes, have students discuss the book and draw their most vivid mental image from that book. Share each pair's images with the class and discuss the value of creating mental images. The following books work well for this activity:

High Interest/Low Vocabulary

- Aliki. *A Weed is a Flower: The Life of George Washington Carver.* Englewood Cliffs, NJ: Prentice-Hall, 1965.

- Park, Barbara. *Skinnybones.* New York: Knopf, 1982.

Levels 4–6

- Dalglish, Alice. *The Courage of Sarah Noble.* New York: Charles Scribner, 1986.

- DeClements, Barthe. *Nothing's Fair in Fifth Grade.* New York: Puffin Books, 1990.

- Gilson, Jamie. *Itchy Richard.* New York: Clarion Books, 1991.

Levels 7–8

- Mathers, Petra. *Maria Teresa.* New York: Harper & Row, 1985.

APPLYING THE STRATEGY TO EVERYDAY EVENTS

To help students practice using the Thinking Guide and to increase their ability to image, have them select one or more of the following activities, or suggest an alternative through which they can practice creating mental images to improve comprehension.

Students on Their Own   Have available multiple copies of a fiction book and ask students to read the book silently to themselves. When they have finished, ask students to draw an event they imagined and write a short explanation of how they created mental pictures. Last, have students list the number of steps on the Thinking Guide they used and describe how they will continue to improve their ability to image.

Collaborative Thinking   Divide students into groups of five, and designate one reader for each group. When the groups finish reading, have each student draw him- or herself in a scene and post the drawing beneath a banner that has the title and author of the group's book printed on it. On the next day, ask students to retell in writing what they remember from the book. Post these retellings beneath each drawing, and ask students if the imaging assisted their recall.

Group Reading   Read half of a book to the entire class and have students imagine what the ending of the book will be. Ask students to either write or draw the ending they imagine. Then ask selected students to read aloud their imaged conclusions or show their drawings that depict their endings. Read the author's ending and discuss how students' images differed.

STUDENT SELF-ASSESSMENT

Students can elect to monitor their own progress in imaging through self-reports in journal entries for a week.

or

Students can choose a content area in which they want to improve their learning and consciously image during that class period every day for a week. At the end of the week, have students record in their journals what they learned and how imaging assisted that learning.

TEACHER ASSESSMENT

Review oral, written, and drawn presentations to evaluate students' progress at the end of Part 2. Also use teacher conferencing and journal entry reviews to assess students' increase in comprehension.

APPLYING THE STRATEGY ACROSS THE CURRICULUM

The following activities are designed to give students the opportunity to apply the imaging strategy in several different areas of the curriculum. Review the Thinking Guide before students engage in their activities.

Art Hold up an object in full view of all students for one minute. After you remove the object from view, have students draw the object in as much detail as possible. Following this experience, ask students to recall similar objects, situations in which they were used, and past experiences with that object. Next, read a story with high imagery potential, but do not show any illustrations or the cover of the book. After you finish reading, ask students to depict the last scene or an appropriate cover in a drawing they share with classmates. Through this sharing activity, students can understand that each image can be different and that it is based on what is important to the person who creates it.

Creative Dramatics Remind students they can refer to mental images whenever they are asked questions or challenged to retell events they have read or heard. Add that they can strengthen their recall by focusing on a black spot on a wall or looking away from people and objects as they remember their images. Engage students in the following activity to practice recalling images:

Let's imagine there is a boy standing in the corner of this room. Let's give him a hat. What does the hat look like? What color is the hat? Let's give him a jacket and a pair of pants. What color jacket shall we give him? Describe the jacket you see. Is he wearing jeans, slacks, or something else? Let's put some shoes on him. What kind of shoes are they?

Now change the color of his hat. What color did you change it to? Change it again. What color is it this time? Change it again. What color? Look at his jacket. What color is it? Change it to another color. Change the color of his pants. Change them

both again. What is he holding in his hand? Change it. What is he holding now? Make him jump in the air. Make him jump higher. Have him stand on one foot and hold the other leg straight out in from of him. Have him walk to another corner of the room. Which corner is he in now?

If you wish, after students have completed the activity, invite them to act out the images they have created.

Language Arts Divide the class into small groups to complete the following science experiment. Have students fill a glass beaker with a colored liquid ($\frac{1}{2}$ cup vinegar and 5 drops food coloring), but do not tell them what the liquid is. Next, ask students to sprinkle a small amount of powder (one tablespoon baking soda) into the beaker, but do not tell them what the powder is or the purpose of the experiment. Once the powder enters the beaker, the liquid will begin to bubble, foam, and expand until it erupts from the beaker. Ask students to use their imaginations to create mental-image responses to the following questions:

- Who created the formula for such a potion and what does this person look like?

- Why did he or she create it?

- What does this potion do?

- To whom does the creator give the potion?

- What consequences might result?

As each group brainstorms, ask them to place their answers in storymaps, citing the setting, characters, conflict, solution, resolution, and author's message. Then ask each group to write their story using the storymap and end the story with a question another group can explore. Have students exchange stories, research and prepare their responses to the question, and list the steps in imagery they followed during this lesson.

Spelling   Students can improve their spelling by learning how to image words. To make imaging easier, show students how to animate words so that the visual image becomes more distinct: see the examples of animated words below. Share some with students and point out how each step has been animated in a way that conveys its meaning. Ask students to practice making images by identifying ten words they have spelled incorrectly in their journals and personifying each word in a similar manner.

Any Subject Area   Ask students to listen and image as you read a segment of the textbook chapter the class is studying. After ten minutes of reading, stop and ask students to draw and/or write about their most vivid memories from the segment. Then ask students to read silently from the point in the chapter where you left off. Discuss how visualizing helped them remember more. Ask students if they remembered more from their listening or their reading and to consider whether they imaged more during either experience.

MEETING INDIVIDUAL NEEDS

STRATEGIES FOR LESS ABLE READERS

Review the Thinking Guide with students who wish to meet with you individually or in small groups. Share with students that they can more easily relate unknown to known information when they begin a new content area chapter by constructing a mental image sequence of chapter headings, maps, graphs, and review questions. Demonstrate how to do so through a "think-aloud" of a chapter you want students to read: Tell them your thoughts as you picture each subheading one after the other and place the maps and graphs below each heading in your mind. Next read the first page of that chapter orally while students read silently. Draw and describe what you imaged on the board, modeling a set of images you created from that page. Clarify for students how and why you created the mental pictures that you did. Guide students to draw or describe in writing what they imaged on subsequent pages of the chapter. Discuss each page after they have finished.

UNDERSTANDING OTHERS

Read *Rembrandt's Beret* by Johnny Alcon, New York: Tambourine, 1991. In this book, Tiberius is accidentally locked in a museum on a rainy afternoon. While he is the only person in the museum, he soon discovers that he is not alone as the portraits of Rembrandt and other old masters spring to life. Before Rembrandt climbs back into his frame, he paints one last portrait that will change Tiberius' life forever. Have students read in encyclopedias and trade books about the cultural conditions that existed at the time Rembrandt lived. Then have them draw and share their mental image of what that portrait will be. After students have shared their visual pictures, read the ending and discuss it.

STRATEGIES FOR BETTER READERS

Have better readers extend their ability to use mental images by challenging them to read books with surprising conclusions. First ask students to select a book from one of the following that contain surprise endings. Alert students to the fact that into each book the author has purposely built a plausible but startling ending. Then ask all readers to create mental images as they read and to note these images in their journals. Ask students to pause before the last chapter and draw or describe in writing an episode they can imagine that might occur in the last chapter. Tell students they can create more than one image if they desire. After students have created that image and read the ending, have them write why their ending was the same or as plausible as the author's. Books to use for this activity include:

High Interest/Low Vocabulary

DeWeese, Gene. *Whatever Became of Aunt Margaret?* New York: Putnam, 1990.

Samuel, Paul. *Born Into Light*. New York: Scholastic, 1988.

Yolen, Jane, illustrated by Bruce Degen. *Commander Toad and the Planet of the Grapes*. New York: Cowan, McCann, 1982.

Yolen, Jane, illustrated by Bruce Degen. *Commander Toad and the Dis-Asteroid*. New York: Cowan, McCann, 1985.

Yolen, Jane. *Heart's Blood*. New York: Delacorte Press, 1984.

Levels 4–6

Etra, Jonathan and Stephanie Spinner. *Aliens for Lunch* (A Stepping Stone book). New York: Random House, 1991.

Buller, Jon and Susan Schade. *Space Rock*. New York: Random House, 1988.

L'Engle, Madeleine. *A Wrinkle in Time*. New York: Farrar, Straus, & Giroux, 1991.

Pinkwater, Daniel Manns. *Fat Men from Space*. New York: Dodd, Mead, 1977.

Service, Pamela F. *Stinker from Space*. New York: Scribner, 1988.

Zelazny, Roger. *A Dark Traveling*. New York: Walker, 1987.

Levels 7–8

Asimov, Janet & Isaac. *Norby Down to Earth*. New York: Walker, 1989.

UNDERSTANDING SELF

Explain to students that many people visualize themselves successfully engaged in an upcoming event in which they want to be successful. Unfortunately, some who are fearful of an upcoming event are inclined to visualize all the things that could go wrong that might undermine their future performance. Ask students to think about what they do and to practice making mental images that portray their success in an upcoming event. Have students write about how they can change their mental preperformance images to be more positive in the future.

Once students have completed the first section of the activity, ask them to list three simple tasks they complete outside of school in which mental images could be helpful. For example, making a list of items to buy at the grocery store as they visualize the grocery store's physical lay-out will enable them to list items in the approximate order in which they appear in the store. When students have completed this list, share that they can use mental imagery in another way whenever they need to outside of school. When students face a difficulty, if they visualize what it would be like "if they lived in a perfect world" and then draw or write the details of that solution, their abilities to reach a resolution to their difficulty will be enhanced. Ask students to practice doing so by discussing with their partners their difficulty, an ideal world, and the effect creating these mental images had upon their feelings and creation of probable solutions.

ASSESSMENT OF PARTS 3 AND 4

Ask students to recall, summarize, and give insights about what they have learned in this lesson. Then select and complete the class and individual student assessment record from pages 194–216. You may select from:

- Class Monitoring Record, Blackline Master 62

- Running Record of Language Arts and Thinking Strategies, Blackline Master 63

- Reading Wheel, Blackline Masters 69 and 70

- Writing Overview, Blackline Master 76

- Student Self-Assessment of Thinking Abilities, Blackline Master 79

- Associative Word Test of Creative Thinking, Blackline Master 83

LESSON 12

BRAINSTORMING TO BECOME MORE CREATIVE

STUDENT OBJECTIVES

In Part 1, students will learn the brainstorming strategy to increase their creativity, broaden their thinking, and expand their abilities to apply what they read and hear to novel situations. In Parts 2 through 4, students will apply the brainstorming strategy as they compose and read essays, editorials, and content-area materials.

READING AND LANGUAGE ARTS CONNECTIONS

- strengthening applied comprehension
- predicting probable outcomes or actions
- selecting and narrowing a topic for a specific purpose
- distinguishing facts from opinions
- relating supporting sentences to main topic sentences
- recognizing persuasive writing and speeches
- developing facility in oral reading for audience
- explaining and relating to feelings and emotions of characters
- developing creative-thinking abilities

EXPLORING THE STRATEGY

INTRODUCING THE LESSON

To introduce Lesson 12, ask students to share what they know about the brainstorming process and ways it can be used successfully in and outside of school. List students' ideas in a semantic map or outline on the board. Discuss with students the difficulties involved in creating new ideas and workable plans, and tell them certain strategies can help generate new ideas and plans. Specify brainstorming as one of these strategies and define brainstorming as the process by which a person or group of people writes as many ideas as come to mind about a topic, idea, or plan they are developing. In essence, brainstorming is making a list of as many ideas as possible, regardless of how crazy they may seem. Once all ideas are listed, they can more easily be combined and refined into a practical plan of action. Add that researchers have discovered that in general the greater the number of ideas produced, the greater the probability the quality of ideas will be higher, because ideas produced in the latter stages of brainstorming sessions tend to be of higher quality than those created in the early stages.

Explain that students will practice brainstorming as they read and write essays, book reviews, and editorials and that they will know they have learned to brainstorm when they can initiate the strategy for themselves or suggest that others use it when ideas are not coming easily. Clarify that brainstorming can be used at times when students' thinking is "stuck" or when they face a problem and don't know what to do.

USING THE THINKING GUIDE

Distribute the Thinking Guide "Brainstorming" (Blackline Master 41) and ask students to read as you describe each step. Ask students to begin with Step 1: "All ideas are welcome." Tell students this means that in a brainstorming session no one should be afraid their ideas are strange or not good, because all ideas are acceptable. For this reason, the first rule of brainstorming is that no one comments on the quality of an idea given. State that the second step in brainstorming is to give as many ideas as you can. The longer the list, the more likely it will contain a number of workable ideas.

The third step in successful brainstorming is to add to other people's ideas. Tell students this step will remind them to build better ideas by adding the best parts of other people's previous ideas together. The fourth step in brainstorming is to think of crazy and new ideas and to not hinder the free flow of thoughts by telling themselves that an idea is silly or impossible. When they hear someone else's idea, it may trigger a new thought for them. The last step is to record and combine all the ideas.

Next show an example of a brainstorming session that began with the topic "animals" and grew as each student added their ideas about the topic (see Blackline Master 42). The brainstorming session enabled students to identify areas of interest to them.

Finally, ask students to ask specific questions about the process or to share incidents when they were not sure they used the strategy successfully.

APPLYING THE THINKING GUIDE TO LITERATURE

Divide the class into groups of four or five. Have them read silently the selected portion of "Letter from a Birmingham Jail" by Martin Luther King, Jr., printed in Blackline Masters 43 and 44. Then ask students to read aloud the passage in their small groups, with students taking turns reading while the rest of the group follows. Direct them to use the ideas in the letter to brainstorm ideas for a group letter they would write to someone concerning civil rights or another topic.

Have students write their ideas during their brainstorming session on the Thinking Guide and examine the brainstorming activity they just completed. Discuss difficulties they encountered or successes they had in finding a topic and sub-topics to develop their letters.

ASSESSMENT OF PART 1

If you wish to end the lesson at this point or to assess how much students have learned, you can use one or more of the assessment options on pages 194–216 or allow students to select the option that best enables them to demonstrate what they have learned.

PART 2

APPLYING THE STRATEGY

BRAINSTORMING TO CREATE LITERATURE: EDITORIALS, BOOK REVIEWS, AND ESSAYS

Review the Thinking Guide and allow students to select any type of literature or essays, book reviews, or editorials for this section of the lesson. Define essays as brief, nonfiction compositions about a specific topic. Add that essays give writers an opportunity to express their opinions or personal thoughts. Essays can persuade, inform, argue, or compare and contrast. Define editorials as opinions expressed by a staff or individuals. They are usually brief and unsigned, and found in newspapers, magazines, or journals. Book reviews differ from editorials in that they always state opinions about books and they are often signed with a byline. Show the editorial, movie review, and essay on transparencies made from Blackline Masters 45, 46, 47, and 48, or provide other editorials from your local newspaper.

APPLYING THE STRATEGY IN EVERYDAY EVENTS

To help students practice brainstorming using the Thinking Guide, choose from the activities below or allow students to choose or design their own.

Group Reading   Have students choose to read any type of literature or one of the editorials, book reviews, or essays included here or that you have provided. Ask students to group themselves based on the selections they made. Ask each group to engage in two brainstorming sessions. In the first they should select the most innovative topic for their group to explore related to improving the classroom in a realistic and effective way. Once they have completed this first brainstorming session, students can brainstorm what to include in an editorial about improving the classroom. After all editorials are

completed and read to the class, an improvement is selected and implemented.

On the next day, instruct students to write individual editorials, book reviews, or essays and share them aloud with the group. Allow students to work until the end of the class period, complete their work at home, and rejoin the group on the following day to combine writings and finalize the group product. Ask groups to share their work with the class.

Group or Individual Writing   Have students choose to work in groups or alone to complete the letters they began in Part 1 or to write an editorial for the school or city newspaper. Ask students to brainstorm and compose their ideas. Stop the discussion after fifteen minutes and have students switch from brainstorming ideas to writing their editorials. If students have not finished by the end of the period, ask them to complete the editorials after class, dividing tasks among members if they are working in groups. On the next day, make editorials into overhead transparencies and ask each group to share their final work.

Students on Their Own   Have students prepare to compose a personal compare-and-contrast essay by brainstorming a list of their likes and dislikes. Ask students to write personal essays based on their lists. The finished essays can be placed in a book in the classroom library so students can learn more about their classmates. In addition, you may wish to challenge students to brainstorm creative openings and conclusions to their essays before they write.

Thinking with a Friend   Ask pairs of students to locate essays or editorials and facts about a topic that interests them. Have students spend one full class period locating sources in the library. On the second day have them brainstorm to compose two editorials, one arguing for a position and the second arguing against the same position. Each editorial should contain at least two facts students located through library research. On the third day, ask pairs to share their editorials with the class.

STUDENT SELF-ASSESSMENT

At the end of any activity in Part 2, students can elect to monitor their progress in using brainstorming by recording self-selected evidences of their growth in journal entries that you evaluate.

or

Students can turn in the first drafts they write for a two-week period and assess how often they used brainstorming to improve their writing.

TEACHER ASSESSMENT

To evaluate how much students have learned, tally the number and quality of ideas students express over a two-week period in class discussions, and assess whether they are following the steps on the Thinking Guide in generating responses to others and creating better ideas in group work. Then ask students to suggest ways that brainstorming has improved their creative thinking and to explain which step was the most difficult for them to learn and why.

APPLYING THE STRATEGY ACROSS THE CURRICULUM

The following activities are designed so students can use brainstorming in several different areas of the curriculum. Review the Thinking Guide with students before they engage in the activities.

Science   Ask students to form small groups and use a ten-minute brainstorming session to brainstorm new uses for a recent scientific discovery. After the brainstorming is complete, have students explain the benefits of brainstorming ideas and why scientists use this strategy. For example, it expands traditional patterns of thinking.

History   Have students use brainstorming to project possible future events they hope will occur in the United States. Instruct each pair to complete two brainstorming sessions. In the first they should identify a specific and far-reaching change they could study, limit the topic to an issue they are presently studying in social studies lessons, and list their ideas on the board. Once all students' ideas are on the board, ask the class to agree on a few topics and have individuals select the small interest group in which they want to work. Instruct students to spend one class period researching their topic, but to brainstorm before they begin to select the method through which the group can find the most facts about their topic. Ask students to prepare a report of their work for the class. To conclude, ask students how the skills they learned in this lesson can be used in future careers so students can think about the relevance of brainstorming to content area disciplines.

Physical Education   Ask students to use brainstorming to improve a contemporary sport of their choice. Have students select their favorite sport and divide into groups based on the sport selected. Instruct students to brainstorm to find an aspect of the game that could be improved. To stimulate their thinking, cite examples such as the 25-second clock rule being created in football and basketball so quarterbacks and basketball players cannot delay the game unnecessarily or the designated hitter becoming a part of one of our baseball leagues to increase the excitement of the game. After fifteen minutes of brainstorming, ask groups to share their four best ideas with the class.

Then ask each group to prepare a demonstration of one change to present the next day during physical education class or a special class trip to the gymnasium. Finally, when students return to class, ask them to express in writing the benefits and drawbacks of each plan they observed. Summarize the comments to stimulate a class discussion on the following day.

Just For Fun/Any Subject Area   Have students use brainstorming to plan a party or special surprise for someone at home. Have students work alone, in pairs, or small groups, and specify that they are to include three different brainstorming topics in their work. For example, they can prepare a brainstorming list or semantic map of ideas concerning the music, food, and theme for a party. Have students brainstorm about the three topics of their choosing for ten minutes for each topic. During the last segment of the class have students write about, graphically depict, or draw the designs they have for their party, as well as describe how brainstorming assisted in the quality of the ideas produced. Conclude the activity by asking students to write about how they can use brainstorming in the future at home.

MEETING INDIVIDUAL NEEDS

STRATEGIES FOR BETTER READERS

Ask students to brainstorm a new Thinking Guide format that communicates the theme of brainstorming in a more innovative fashion and highlights the information in each step.

or

Before students begin this activity, obtain information from *Who's Who* and almanacs concerning the author of a nationally syndicated editorial or column or an author from your local newspaper. Have students review the Thinking Guide. Then ask students to read copies of the editorial, underline facts, and circle opinions. Next instruct students to brainstorm about the extent of the experience the author has had regarding the topic and the likely position this person holds on the newspaper staff. Have students share the results of their brainstorming with each other. Then share with students the true information about the writer, or ask that person to come to class to discuss the topic and hear students' comments, if a local newspaper columnist's work is used as the content for this lesson.

UNDERSTANDING OTHERS

Ask students to brainstorm to identify new methods to keep the noise level from rising during certain activities. After students have completed their individual lists, have them form small groups, brainstorm together, and combine their lists to present three ideas they suggest the class implement in such situations. After twenty minutes, ask each group to share their ideas with the class. Then have the class vote on the best ideas. Finally, have students compare their list to the following generated by another class during this lesson.

Ideas for a Quiet Classroom:

- Have a "noise checker" in each small group.
- All people pledge to whisper.
- One person speaks at a time in each small group.
- When noise gets too loud, all groups have to stop for the day.
- The class elects a "roving noise monitor."
- Tape loud mouths shut.
- Ban loud mouths from the groups.
- Give a prize for the quietest voice each day.
- Use a chip system; each person starts with two chips. Each time someone talks too loud, that person has a chip taken away. If both chips are taken away, that person cannot talk any more during the group work.
- Take away points from the grade of noisy groups.
- Put quiet signs on each desk.

This class selected three options:

- One person speaks at a time in each group.
- Assign a noise checker to each group.
- Give points for the quietest voice each day.

STRATEGIES FOR LESS ABLE READERS

Ask students to divide into small groups and brainstorm different types of stereotypical information presented on television and in books about preteens that they find annoying. For example, they are portrayed as scatterbrained and not responsible enough to handle money or be on their own sometimes. Then instruct students to brainstorm and select three ways that television and books can more accurately depict preteens. After groups have made their selections, invite the class to send some of their ideas to publishers or broadcast networks.

ASSESSMENT OF PARTS 3 AND 4

Ask students to recall, summarize, and give insights to extend what they have learned in this lesson. Then select and complete the class and individual student assessment records from pages 194–216. You may select from:

- Class Monitoring Record, Blackline Master 62

- Running Record of Language Arts and Thinking Strategies, Blackline Master 63
- Reading Wheel, Blackline Masters 69 and 70
- Story Map, Blackline Master 74
- Editing Checklist, Blackline Master 75
- Writing Overview, Blackline Master 76
- Assessing Thinking Abilities, Blackline Master 78
- Student Self-Assessment of Thinking Abilities, Blackline Master 79
- Associative Word Test of Creative Thinking, Blackline Master 83

L E S S O N 13

WORKING COOPERATIVELY IN GROUPS

STUDENT OBJECTIVES

In Part 1, students will learn how to work cooperatively and effectively in groups. In Parts 2–4, students will demonstrate their cooperative group strategies as they study poetry and different content areas.

READING AND LANGUAGE ARTS CONNECTIONS

- responding to and appreciating poetry, biographies, autobiographies, and proverbs for personal enjoyment
- developing creative-thinking abilities
- strengthening applied comprehension
- relating supporting sentences to main topic sentences
- developing facility in oral reading for an audience
- relating experiences using appropriate vocabulary in complete sentences
- arranging events in sequential order, including time and degree of importance
- recognizing various persuasive devices

EXPLORING THE STRATEGY

INTRODUCING THE LESSON

To introduce Lesson 13, ask students to think of the best groups in which they have worked in the past. List the characteristics they remember about these groups on the board. When students have completed their sharing, help them understand that learning to attain group goals and to work cooperatively with others will be important in their professional and personal lives. Add that in this lesson they will (1) learn four strategies to use in cooperative settings the rest of their lives, (2) divide into groups to establish a goal and practice using these strategies, (3) evaluate their group's success, and (4) identify weaknesses in their prior group work experiences. Also specify that they will know they have learned these strategies if they reach group goals with less difficulty in the future.

To increase students' motivation, you may share the following testimonials from former students describing what they gained from this lesson: "I liked this lesson because it taught us to work in a group. It also helped us to handle group situations better…. I thought it was really fun and I would like to do it again." "I liked getting into groups and hearing their point of view as well as mine. I learned to list negative and positive solutions." "I learned to team up with someone who likes to write a lot, and if someone is in trouble to think about what I would do if I were them." "I will try to do better in my group and try to help out and do more than what I have been doing."

USING THE THINKING GUIDE

Distribute the Thinking Guide "Working Cooperatively in Groups" (Blackline Master 49). Ask students to read along as you provide the following descriptions from the Thinking Guide of keys to cooperative group work. After you share each description, pause to ask students to suggest methods to accomplish each step. Have students write these methods in the blank boxes on the Thinking Guide. Sample methods that might stimulate students' thinking follow.

Key 1: Set goals together. Participation is key because, as successful businessman Bill Bethel stated, "a successful team is a group of many hands but one mind." Help students understand they can include everyone in their group and assist all in contributing equally by using one or more of the following methods.

■ All group members express their ideas, but before they present a new thought they first state something positive about the previous person's idea.

■ All group members assist in establishing specific groups and refrain from complaining.

■ Before every group goal is finalized and before each group discussion ends, each person volunteers a talent or resource to contribute to that goal.

Before you present the next key to successful group work, ask students to give examples of incidents when their groups have used Key 1 and to suggest other methods that encourage everyone to contribute to goal-setting discussions. Have students list their responses on their individual Thinking Guides as you add them to an overhead transparency of the Thinking Guide. Students should write these suggestions and several of the above methods to the right of Key 1.

Key 2: Everyone shares equally while developing a plan of action. Methods of sharing equally include the following:

■ Use the "wraparound strategy." In "wraparounds" everyone has the opportunity to make a first comment or to pass before anyone makes a second comment. People who decide not to contribute during the first round of ideas are called upon to summarize or extend the group's thoughts at the end of the first wraparound session. After all group members have contributed, the second wraparound begins.

- Listen carefully to each other. Emphasize this point by sharing words from former President George Bush's 1988 Inaugural address in which he gave three suggestions to improve listening during group discussions. He said, ". . . in crucial things, seek unity; in important things, seek diversity; and in all things be led by generosity." Pause to ask students what these words mean to them, assisting them to understand that when a point is made that will be essential to the group's goal, listeners should make follow-up comments to modify that idea so all group members can support it; when an idea is important, but not a priority, listeners should provide alternatives based on this idea; and when a complex or unfocused idea is expressed, listeners should identify possible relevance or potential in the remark.

- Before a final plan of action is decided upon, develop three alternatives. By seeking a first, second, and third alternative, the "we's" and "they's" in a group can more often rally around the final plan, and more people can find a way to contribute.

Before proceeding in the discussion of the Thinking Guide, ask students to suggest other methods through which all people can contribute to developing a plan of action. Have students write some of these suggestions and the above methods in the block below Key 2.

Key 3: Identify the good ideas of others in the group by doing the following:

- Help others overcome areas of weakness.

- Identify the knowledge required for a plan and the people outside the group who can help.

- Identify each group member's strengths and help them to contribute these strengths to the group's project.

Before moving to Key 4, ask students to suggest methods of ensuring all people do the work needed in a group. Have students write some of these suggestions and the above methods in the block in the box to the left of Key 3.

Key 4: Eliminate stumbling blocks that are unjust to people or the goal by doing the following:

- Try to anticipate objections before the plan is presented to others and to develop ways to overcome these objections as the group works.

- Discuss ideas and do not criticize people. When different points of view are expressed in a discussion, ensure that comments focus on improving ideas, and not on attacking the people who voice them. To improve ideas, search for alternatives that address all people's needs and concerns rather than focusing comments on reasons why single ideas are inferior.

Before continuing any further, ask students to suggest other methods of eliminating stumbling blocks. Have students write some of these suggestions and the above methods in the blank blocks to the left of Key 4.

Key 5: Evaluate how well you worked together by doing the following:

- Evaluate what went well and what can be improved at the end of each group session, even if assessments are single evaluative statements made by each member.

APPLYING THE THINKING GUIDE TO LITERATURE

Distribute Blackline Masters 50 and 51. Ask students to read "If I Were in Charge of the World." Tell students this poem came from an assignment to write a poem after reading *If I Were in Charge of the World* by Judith Viorst. Then ask five student volunteers to join you in a small group to demonstrate the strategies on the Thinking Guide. Instruct the five volunteers to bring their chairs and the Thinking Guide for this lesson (Blackline Master 49) with them as they form a circle with you. The remainder of the class will watch you and these students interact as you attempt to use these strategies on the Thinking Guide. Explain to students that they should use the strategies on the Thinking Guide whenever a group works together to solve a problem or develop a plan.

Instruct the class to watch as you and these five students work to implement the strategies on the Thinking Guide. Ask the class to write specific incidents in which people implemented individual strategies.

Now turn your attention to the five students who have become members of the small group. Explain to them that in many professions problems are solved in groups. What they are to do today is to use strategies from the Thinking Guide as you and they work together to establish a goal, develop a plan, discuss how to implement it, and evaluate the successes and weaknesses of the group's work. Explain that throughout the fifteen-minute session, you will work as one of the group members.

Pause for moment and ask students to review the keys to successful group work from the Thinking Guides. Throughout the fifteen-minute group meeting, allow students to take the lead in implementing the steps on the Thinking Guide, but if they neglect a strategy, initiate it yourself, since the purpose of this session is to model strategies for the class.

If students omit specific cooperative work strategies, use the following prompts to remind them:

To prompt the use of Key 1, you might say: "What is the most important goal we could reach in studying poetry?" "What could we do so everyone in the class could contribute something special?"

To prompt the use of Key 2, you might say: "Let's use the wraparound strategy to gather ideas for activities we should do." "Let's look for a third alternative." "I think that is a critical idea. How can everyone in the class accomplish it?" "I think that idea is an important one. Can we provide different ways people can do it?" "How can we include people in our class who already know a lot about poetry and also those who do not know very much?"

To prompt the use of Key 3, you might say: "That's a great idea!" "What knowledge do we need?" "Who can help us?"

To prompt the use of Key 4, you might say: "What are some of the objections people might have to our plan and how can we demonstrate they should not be fearful?" "If someone gets 'writer's block' and believes they cannot write a poem, what can we plan to help them?"

To prompt student evaluation at the end of the session, you can ask them to discuss the strengths and weaknesses of the discussion, such as: "What did we want to accomplish? What needed to be done? Who did it? What materials could we have used that we didn't think about using? Were the dates we set as deadlines realistic? Did we assign people to check that certain tasks were done on time?"

For the discussion itself, pose the following problem to the small group of students and ask them to use the strategies as a group to solve the problem for the class: "We are about to begin a study of poetry. What do you want to learn about poetry, how do you want to learn it, and how do you think we can measure how much we have learned?"

After fifteen minutes, have students return to their original places in the class. Ask classmates to share specific strategies they witnessed during the small group session. Then ask students if they have any questions concerning the Thinking Guide or the keys for working effectively in groups.

ASSESSMENT OF PART 1

If you wish to end the lesson at this point or to assess how much students have learned in Part 1, you can use one or more of the evaluation strategies on pages 194–216 or allow students to select an option that best enables them to demonstrate what they have learned.

PART 2

APPLYING THE STRATEGY

RECOGNIZING COOPERATIVE GROUP STRATEGIES IN LITERATURE: POETRY

Review the strategies of cooperative group work on the Thinking Guide. Tell students they can work cooperatively as they study poetry. Then define poetry as an arrangement of words in verse, especially a rhythmical composition, sometimes rhymed, expressing facts, ideas, or emotions in a style more concentrated, imaginative, and powerful than ordinary speech.

APPLYING THE STRATEGY TO EVERYDAY EVENTS

To provide practice using the Thinking Guide and to complete the objectives in this lesson, let students select an activity from those that follow, or suggest an alternative in which they can practice working effectively in groups.

Collaborative Writing In this activity, students experience the joy of writing in a group. Have groups of students construct a group poem and use the Thinking Guide in the process. Encourage students to study the poems on Blackline Masters 50 and 51 before they begin and to write about an event that members of the class have experienced. At the end of the twenty minutes, have the group reference the Thinking Guide and assess how well they worked together.

Building Team Spirit Have students complete each of the following actions and then evaluate how well they worked together in doing so:

- Use one piece of paper and one marker per group.

- Write a group poem.

- Set group goals to learn about poetry.

- Decide on a name for the poem.

- Decide on a name for the group.

- Brainstorm similarities among group members and what each can contribute to a study of poetry.

Working Cooperatively for a Week
Students can establish their own goals concerning the poetry they will read and write. Have them begin by reading and discussing the poems on Blackline Masters 50 and 51. Each day students work, ask them to complete Blackline Masters 52 and 53 to assess their use of effective group work skills and their knowledge of poetry.

STUDENT SELF-ASSESSMENT

At the end of any activity in Part 2, have students self-assess their cooperative group strategy use by completing one of the group assessment forms on Blackline Masters 80 and 81.

or

Ask students to analyze specific ways they can improve their individual implementation of each strategy on the Thinking Guide in future group work settings.

TEACHER ASSESSMENT

Review students' written and oral presentations to evaluate whether their cooperative group work abilities have increased. You may also "debrief" students by referring to group working situations that occurred in class prior to students learning the strategies in this lesson, and ask them to write about ways they would overcome individual problems in the future.

APPLYING THE STRATEGY ACROSS THE CURRICULUM

The following activities enable students to use group work skills in various content areas. Review the Thinking Guide before students begin their activities.

Language Arts   Divide the class into small groups. Have students select from the following goals:

- Create a puppet show to demonstrate how people use cooperative working strategies (see Blackline Master 56 for ideas of materials to use for puppets).

- Write a poem that could be presented as a choral reading. After each group finishes their project, have them present it before the class, and ask audience members to tell group members aspects of the project and ways the group worked together that they judged to be particularly effective. Last have each group member write an individual evaluative statement on his or her Thinking Guide to assess how well the group implemented each strategy.

Any Subject Area/Social Studies   Allow students to select a responsibility they wish to assume in their groups that utilizes their talents. Among the responsibilities students can assume are: Checker of Work, Helper of Others, Organizer, Finalizer/Summarizer, Recorder, Filer, Resource Gatherer, Leader, or Creator of Ideas. After students assume these responsibilities to complete a unit or chapter of study, ask them to discuss their feelings about group investigations and group work projects. Have students discuss why it is important for each person to take some responsibility in group tasks. What are some of the pros and cons of group investigations? What should be done when work is being divided unequally?

MEETING INDIVIDUAL NEEDS

STRATEGIES FOR LESS ABLE READERS

Review the Thinking Guide for students who wish to meet with you individually or in small groups. Then share with students the following event that occurred with another group of students their age who learned the cooperative working strategies in this lesson. The teacher of those students said: "Once a student in my class named Jim thought he could do things better by himself. He did not want to try to help other people, and he did not want any help from them. Jim was very good at math, but he had a hard time reading big words. So one day I asked him if he would please help David with his math. At first he did not want to help, but he remembered what he had learned in this lesson, and as a special favor to me he agreed. He helped David see math in a whole new way so that he could understand it. Jim found out that he liked helping others. As a result he also decided to let David help him with his reading. After that Jim liked working in groups." Distribute Blackline Master 53 and ask students to write strategies for each key to effective group work that Jim could use.

Read aloud or have students read excerpts from the book *Doing Things Together* by Carl and Elizabeth James or another book in which students work well together. Discuss the incidents from this book, and ask students to identify aspects of working together that are difficult for them. Have the group set a goal to overcome a difficulty they experienced. Reconvene the group at the end of the week to assess their progress.

STRATEGIES FOR BETTER READERS

Ask better readers to expand their abilities to work cooperatively by working in groups of five. Have each group select a current school, community, national, or global issue about which two strong opinions exist. Have each member select a different stance on the issue from one of these five:

- entirely neutral
- wanting to convince others that your positive stance on the issue is correct
- wanting to convince others that your negative stance on the issue is correct
- mildly agreeing with the negative position on the issue
- mildly agreeing with the positive position on the issue

Once students select their positions, have them maintain the same positions throughout the discussion as they use the strategies on the Thinking Guide to work effectively together to reach a group plan of action concerning their position. After the plan is finished, students should share it with the class and state which strategies on the Thinking Guide were most effective to them in reaching an understanding of others' points of view.

UNDERSTANDING SELF

Ask students to identify what they were likely to do in a group situation whenever disagreements arose before they studied this lesson. To stimulate their thinking, you may wish to distribute a list similiar to the following and ask them to check the ones they used:

___ Discuss or stand firm.

___ Persuade by justifying or reasoning.

___ Ask for a vote and let majority rule.

___ Compromise by combining and modifying.

___ Try to mediate between others.

___ Ask people not to decide now but wait until tomorrow.

___ Give in or play the martyr.

___ Use humor to move away from confrontation.

___ Ignore a difficult item or try to postpone it indefinitely.

Instruct students to identify a new strategy they will use in the future whenever they are tempted to take any of actions above, particularly the ones they checked.

ASSESSMENT OF PARTS 3 AND 4

Ask students to recall, summarize, and give insights about the steps on the Thinking Guide and other group-work skills. Then select and complete the class and individual student assessment records from pages 194–216. You may select from the following:

■ Class Monitoring Record, Blackline Master 62

■ Reading Wheel, Blackline Masters 69 and 70

■ Speech Critique, Blackline Master 72

■ Informal Checklist for Usage, Blackline Master 73

■ Student Self-Assessment of Cooperative Groups, Blackline Master 80

■ Student Self-Assessment for Group Work During Consensus Building, Blackline Master 81

■ Portfolio Assessment, Blackline Master 84

LESSON 14

GAINING CONFIDENCE AND BECOMING MORE RESPONSIBLE

STUDENT OBJECTIVES

In Part 1, students will learn strategies to gain confidence and to become more responsible in setting their own language-arts goals as well as goals in other areas of their lives. In Parts 2 through 4, they will use the strategies by creating their own fables in which a character takes responsibility for his or her actions and by engaging in a variety of other activities and readings.

READING AND LANGUAGE ARTS CONNECTIONS

- appreciating, recognizing, and responding to fables for personal enjoyment
- developing facility in oral reading for audience
- assuming responsibilities effectively
- strengthening interpretive comprehension
- recognizing one of the components of literal comprehension
- relating experiences using appropriate vocabulary in complete sentences

EXPLORING THE STRATEGY

INTRODUCING THE LESSON

To Introduce Lesson 14, explain to students that there are strategies people use to gain confidence and assume responsibilities more effectively. Share with students they will have an opportunity to practice gaining confidence and assuming responsibilities in their reading and writing abilities by participating in role-plays and by creating their own fables. Tell students they will know they have learned to increase their confidence and accept more responsibilities when they use these strategies without being reminded. Conclude this introduction with a story from your own life in which you learned to take responsibility and increase your confidence, or tell the following story by another teacher:

"When I was in school my mother worked, and I arrived home each day before my mother. I always had a great deal of homework to do, but on one was home to make me do it. I would sit in front of the television until I heard my mother drive up. Then after supper, I would have to spend the entire evening finishing my assignments, so I could not be with my mother. Finally I realized I was not taking responsibility for my learning. I knew I had no business watching television after school. I decided I would not allow myself to watch television until I had completed my homework. From then on, I walked in the door, grabbed a snack, and went to the table to do my homework. I wrote down all my assignments on my assignment sheet at school, and when I got home I went down the list and did my homework. I made sure there were no distractions so I could concentrate and finish my homework. By taking responsibility for my actions, I enjoyed my homework and time with my mother more."

Ask students to share other examples from their lives.

USING THE THINKING GUIDE

Distribute the Thinking Guide "Taking Responsibility" (Blackline Master 55) and explain the steps as students read them. First focus students' attention on the left section as you describe the elements and suggest students set a deadline when they have tasks that need to be done. Add that it is a good idea to set this deadline before the work is due to allow for any problems or unnecessary stress. Second, explain to students that breaking difficult tasks into parts will make them seem easier. It will also help to list similar items that can be accomplished at the same time. Third, suggest students can list an easy task first so they feel a sense of reward when the task is completed, or offer the alternative that they can take a brief pause before beginning difficult tasks. Fourth, point out that students could get up early to allow more time to get organized. Fifth, suggest that when given a choice, students should volunteer to be first. Sixth and finally, stress that it is important for students to remove themselves from distractions and to situate themselves in a comfortable environment where they can work and learn. Conclude the left section of the Thinking Guide by stating that all of these suggestions can help students take responsibility for their work and keep them from postponing difficult jobs.

Now ask students to read the right section of the Thinking Guide as you describe the steps of taking responsibility when something goes wrong or a mistake is made. First suggest students admit when they make a mistake. Next encourage them to apologize for what they did as soon as possible. Emphasize the possible difficulty, but ultimate value, in these actions. Explain the importance of recognizing mistakes and realizing how it helps to take responsibility for one's own actions as soon as possible.

Finally, emphasize that students can build on these three steps and plan their future behavior so mistakes are corrected as soon as possible and further damage is avoided.

After reviewing the Thinking Guide, ask students to give examples of times when they might use the suggestions in the future or to share benefits they have experienced in using one or more of these ways of taking responsibility in the past. Have students share examples of mistakes they have made in the past and describe how what they have learned in this lesson might be applied to similar situations in the future. Last, have students set a goal to use the Thinking Guide in some subject this week.

APPLYING THE THINKING GUIDE TO LITERATURE

Have students divide into groups of four and read together, or listen to you read, any selection of literature or one of the following books in which the main characters gain confidence and become more responsible:

High Interest/Low Vocabulary

Fox, Paula. *One-Eyed Cat*. New York: Bradbury, 1984.

Galdone, Paul. *The Little Red Hen*. New York: Houghton Mifflin, 1987.

Levels 4–6

Christopher, Matt. *Undercover Tailback*. New York: Houghton Mifflin, 1992.

King-Smith, Dick. *Pretty Polly*. New York: Houghton Mifflin, 1992.

Le Roy, Gen. *Emma's Dilemma*. New York: Morrow, 1990.

Shreve, Susan. *Wait For Me*. New York: Tambourine Books, 1992.

Sutton, Elizabeth. *The Pony Champions*. New York: Houghton Mifflin, 1992.

Then using each step on the Thinking Guide, have students compile a list of what the characters could have done to take responsibility for themselves.

ASSESSMENT OF PART 1

If you wish to end the lesson at this point, to assess how much students learned in Part 1 or for students to self-assess how much they have learned you can use one or more of the evaluation strategies on pages 194–216 or allow students to select an option that enables them to demonstrate how much they have learned.

APPLYING THE STRATEGY

RECOGNIZING STRATEGIES FOR GAINING CONFIDENCE AND BECOMING MORE RESPONSIBLE IN LITERATURE: FABLES

You may use any type of literature with this lesson, or you may wish to use the lesson as an opportunity to instruct students in the genre of fables. If you choose the latter option, ask students to define fables. Help them understand fables are short, fictitious stories that teach morals. Add that fables often have characters that are personified plants, animals, or objects that act and talk like humans. Tell students many fables give morals in the form of a proverb at the end. Many fables have been told for over two thousand years and people enjoy fables because they portray truths to which most people can relate. Explain that most of the fables popular in the United States can be traced back to ancient Greece and India, with most Greek fables credited to Aesop, a Greek slave known for telling wise, witty tales about animals. Refer students to the fables in Blackline Masters 56, 57, and 58 or ones from the following list you make available to them.

High Interest/Low Vocabulary

Allison, Christine. *I'll Tell You A Story, I'll Sing You A Song.* New York: Delta, 1991.

"The Boy Who Cried Wolf"

"The Crow and The Pitcher"

"The Farmer and His Sons"

"The Fox and The Goat"

Aesop. Galdone, Paul (illustrator). *The Hare and The Tortoise.* New York: McGraw-Hill, 1962.

Aesop. Galdone, Paul (illustrator). *The Monkey and The Crocodile.* New York: Houghton Mifflin/Clarion Books, 1969.

Levels 4–6

Aesop. *Aesop's Fables.* New York: Grosset and Dunlop, 1947 (and many other editions published until 1992).

"The City Mouse and The Country Mouse"

"The Fox and The Crow"

"The Fox and The Grapes"

"The Lion and The Mouse"

USING THE THINKING GUIDE IN PART 2

Review the Thinking Guide with students. To help students practice using the Thinking Guide and to complete the objectives of this lesson, have students select an activity from those that follow, or have them suggest an alternative through which they can practice taking responsibility for their actions.

Role-Play   Have students choose a fable from the above list and prepare to act out the fable in front of the class. Instruct students to emphasize in their dramatizations the steps from the Thinking Guide that their character used to take responsibility for their actions. If the characters in the fable they select did not take responsibility for their actions, ask students to enact what the characters could have done.

Collaborative Thinking   Have students form small groups and read two or three fables from the recommended list to gain an understanding of fables. Each group should choose a recorder who receives a copy of the Thinking Guide and lists all the characteristics group members want to include in their fables. After they finish their reading, have each group create their own fable to teach the steps on the Thinking Guide. Suggest the recorder write the fable on large chart paper and ask a group narrator to share the fable with the class. Invite the entire group to recite in unison the moral at the end of the fable. You may wish to share the examples on Blackline Master 59 of fables other students wrote during this lesson.

Thinking with A Friend   Have pairs of students choose two fables from the list on page 114 or from Blackline Masters 56–58 if not used previously. One person reads the first fable to the other partner. Then the reader asks the partner whether the main character took responsibility for his or her actions. If so, how? If not, how could the character have done so? Have students compose a summary of what they learned and list new items they would like to add to the Thinking Guide.

Students on Their Own   Have students read about how famous people take responsibility for their actions. Encourage them to read a book about a person they admire and as they read to identify specifically what that person did to accomplish difficult tasks and overcome mistakes. Next have students describe to the class methods this person used that could be added to the Thinking Guide. Students can select from books such as:

High Interest/Low Vocabulary

Adler, David. *Martin Luther King, Jr.: Free At Last.* New York: Holiday House, 1986.

Adler, David. *Thomas Jefferson: Father of Our Democracy.* New York: Holiday House, 1987.

Gutman, Bill. *Magic Johnson: Hero On and Off The Court.* Brookfield, CT: Millbrook Press, 1992.

Levels 4–6

Fowler, Carol. *Daisy Hooee Nampeya.* Minneapolis, MN: Dillon Press, 1977.

Hamilton, Virginia. *The People Could Fly.* New York: Knopf, 1987.

O'Dell, Scott. *The Road to Damietta.* Boston: Houghton Mifflin, 1985.

Levels 7–8

Wade, Mary Dodson. *Amelia Earhart: Flying for Adventure.* Brookfield, CT: Millbrook Press, 1992.

STUDENT SELF-ASSESSMENT

At the end of any activity in Part 2, students can complete the charts on Blackline Master 60 following the directions appearing on that page.

or

Students can write insights gained from this lesson that they will use in one situation at school and one situation outside of school.

TEACHER ASSESSMENT

To assess students' progress at the end of Part 2, you may wish to ask students to answer the following questions either in writing or orally:

- Did you accomplish the goal you set in Part 1 of this lesson?

- What actions did you take during this lesson to accomplish that goal?

- What did you do to obtain these results?

- How were you responsible for your results?

- How did you follow the steps in the Thinking Guide to accomplish this?

- How were you responsible for your learning of the lesson?

- Was there something else you could have done that would have made the results more to your liking?

- How will you use the steps in the Thinking Guide to better take responsibility for your actions in the future?

- What did you learn about taking responsibility for your own success and failure?

PART 3

APPLYING THE STRATEGY ACROSS THE CURRICULUM

The following activities are designed to give students an opportunity to take responsibility in several different areas of the curriculum. Review the Thinking Guide before students engage in their activities.

Science and Social Studies Divide students into small groups. Read or have students read one or more of the following books concerning ecology:

High Interest/Low Vocabulary

Cross, James. *George Washington: A Picture Book Biography.* New York: Scholastic, 1992.

Gretz, Susana. *Frog, Duck, And Rabbit.* New York: Four Winds Press, 1992.

Mayer, Mercer. *Just A Mess.* Western Publishing Company/Golden Book, 1990.

Ross, Tony. (retelling) *The Boy Who Cried Wolf.* New York: Dial Books for Young Readers, 1985.

Van Allsburg, Chris. *Two Bad Ants.* Boston: Houghton Mifflin, 1987.

Levels 4–6

Levine, Evan. *Not The Piano, Mrs. Medley.* New York: Orchard Books, 1991.

Nabb, Magdalen. *Josie Smith and Eileen.* New York: M.K. McElderry Books, 1992.

Williams, Barbara. *Donna Jean's Disaster.* Niles, IL: Albert Whitman, 1986.

Next have groups of four students pick a topic in their science or social studies curriculum for which they would like to take responsibility for teaching classmates. Have them use the Thinking Guide as they complete the project. Have students write the actions they took on the back of the Thinking Guide. Then ask students to teach their topic and use Blackline Master 80 to assess their group's ability to take responsibility.

Homework Is My Responsibility Ask students to devise a plan for taking responsibility for their homework (or chores at home if they do not have homework). Suggest they use the steps presented in the Thinking Guide to write their plans. Ask students to follow this plan for one week. At the end of the week, discuss as a class the effects this plan had on students' homework performance.

Language Arts Using the Thinking Guide, ask students to choose a book by their favorite author and describe responsibilities the main character accepted. Then have students meet in pairs and describe how their character took responsibilities and the challenges of accepting them. Conclude the activity by reconvening the class and making a master list of all strategies main characters used to assume their responsibilities.

PART 4

MEETING INDIVIDUAL NEEDS

STRATEGIES FOR LESS ABLE READERS

Review the Thinking Guide with students who wish to meet with you individually or in small groups. Ask each student to identify an aspect of language arts or social skills they find difficult; e.g., speaking before the class, organizing materials, or responding to peer pressure. Ask students to discuss as a group how each student could use one of these strategies from the Thinking Guide to take more responsibility for improving in their area of difficulty. For students who cannot think of an area they wish to explore, you may wish to recommend they read one of the books listed on page 115 prior to meeting with you and to identify what the main character did to overcome his or her problems.

MULTICULTURAL CONNECTIONS

Ask students to select several of the following fables or folktales from different cultures and compare them. Have students compare how each book suggests that people take responsibility for their actions. Fables and folktales include:

High Interest/Low Vocabulary

Courlander, Harold. *The Crest and the Hide and Other African Stories of Heroes, Chiefs, Bards, Hunters, Sorcerers, and Common People.* New York: Coward, McCann, and Geoghegan, 1982.

Isele, Elizabeth (retold by). *The Frog Princess.* New York: Thomas Y. Crowell, 1984.

Lee, Jeanne M (retold by). *Toad is the Uncle of Heaven: A Vietnamese Folk Tale.* New York: Holt, Rinehart, and Winston, 1985.

Young, Ed. *Lon PoPo: A Red Riding Hood Story From China.* New York: Philomel Books, 1989.

Levels 4–6

Aardema, Verna. *Tales for the Third Ear* (from Equatorial Africa). New York: Dutton, 1969.

Baker, Olaf. *Where the Buffaloes Begin.* New York: Frederick Warne, 1981.

Carpenter, Frances. *People From the Sky: Ainu Tales From Northern Japan.* Garden City, New York: Doubleday, 1972.

Ginsburg, Mirra (translated by). *Fox Stories From Russia: One Trick Too Many.* New York: Dial Press, 1973.

Gold, Sharlya and Caspi, Mishael Maswari. *The Answered Prayer and Other Yemenite Folktales.* New York: the Jewish Publication Society, 1990.

Jones, Hettie (retold by). *Coyote Tales.* New York: Holt, Rinehart, and Winston, 1974.

Singh, Rani. *The Indian Story Book.* London: Heinemann, 1984.

Levels 7–8

Greaves, Margaret. *A Chinese Legend: Once There Were No Pandas.* New York: Dutton, 1985.

Hague, Kathleen and Michael. *East of the Sun and West of the Moon* (classic Scandinavian fairy tale). New York: Harcourt Brace Jovanovich, 1980.

UNDERSTANDING SELF

Ask students to pretend someone challenged them to create a way they could demonstrate more of the things they have learned on their next class project than they did on their last one. Then suggest students review the Thinking Guide to identify the strategies that could assist them in creating a better project. Finally, ask students to write in their journals ideas they have gained from this lesson that they will use to learn as much as possible from future class assignments. Encourage students to be as specific as possible and to state rewards they would like to receive from increasing the amount they know.

ASSESSMENT OF PARTS 3 AND 4

Ask students to recall, summarize, give insights, and ask questions to extend what they have learned in this lesson. Then select and complete the class and individual student records from pages 194–216. You may choose from:

- Class Monitoring Record, Blackline Master 62
- Running Record of Language Arts and Thinking Strategies, Blackline Master 63
- Journal Writing Assessment: Student Self-Evaluation, Blackline Master 64
- Journal Writing Assessment: Teacher Evaluation, Blackline Master 65
- Reading Wheel, Blackline Masters 69 and 70
- Assessing Thinking Abilities, Blackline Master 78
- Student Self-Assessment of Thinking Abilities, Blackline Master 79
- Portfolio Assessment, Blackline Master 84

LESSON 15

SETTING ACHIEVABLE GOALS

STUDENT OBJECTIVES

In Part 1, students will learn to establish achievable goals for their reading and writing. In Parts 2 through 4, students will practice setting goals for themselves as they read nonfiction and fiction literature in which main characters overcome obstacles through goal-setting.

READING AND LANGUAGE ARTS CONNECTIONS

- increasing literal, interpretive, and applied comprehension by establishing goals to overcome weaknesses

- appreciating, recognizing, and responding to autobiographies and biographies, as well as fictional stories in which literary figures reach their goals

- developing an appreciation for literature as a resource for improving one's competencies

- self-selecting, reviewing, and refining specific weaknesses in decoding, comprehending, spelling, composing, speaking, or listening

EXPLORING THE STRATEGY

INTRODUCING THE LESSON

To introduce Lesson 15, ask pairs of students to tell one another how they establish goals. State that each student should also give an example of an important goal he or she achieved.

After students have shared with their partners, ask the pairs to describe to the class problems they have had in setting and reaching goals. During the discussion, write students' ideas in two columns on the chalkboard. One column contains problems students have experienced; the second identifies suggestions peers offer for solving these problems.

Read the following quote by Aristotle: "We are what we repeatedly do. Excellence, then, is not an act, but a habit." Ask students how some of the suggestions they have given for solving problems when they set goals could become habits of excellence. Tell students that this lesson will give them the steps of establishing achievable goals. They will read about famous people who set such goals and evaluate their own success in goal-setting by comparing their achievement at the end of the lesson to the goal they set at the beginning.

You may add that students who have studied this lesson in previous years valued what they learned. Share the following examples: "I have noticed being much more patient in doing my homework and not being so frustrated since I learned to set better goals." "When I get home, the first thing I do is plan or sketch out the next day so that I will be prepared."

USING THE THINKING GUIDE

Distribute the Thinking Guide "Setting Goals" (Blackline Master 61). Ask students to read along as you describe each section. Begin by explaining that a research group called the "Power of Positive Students Program" conducted a study and concluded that (a) only three people in every one hundred write their goals;

and (b) those who write goals achieve at least fifty percent more than those who do not. Tell students it is for this reason that you will ask them to develop the habit of writing their goals. Then ask students to write on the top of the Thinking Guide a specific goal they would like to achieve. It should be one they feel capable of achieving by the end of this week.

After students have written their goals, tell them they will return to this goal later in the lesson. Ask students to look at the section of the Thinking Guide entitled "Plan of Action." Share that at times all people have difficulty working on projects and reaching their goals. Because attaining larger goals often requires patience, persistence, and time, developing a "Plan of Action" for smaller steps makes larger goals achievable.

Tell students that one way a plan of action helps is to keep people from ignoring inconvenient and annoying details or omitting smaller, important responsibilities and loose ends. You may want to give an example of an action plan by describing the one that Coach Jimmy Johnson of the Dallas Cowboys used from the beginning of his NFL coaching career: He stated that his goal was to win one game at a time, and he prepared his players for all the details in the game that week before looking ahead to the next game. Four years later the Cowboys won the Superbowl.

Assist students in learning to break their larger goals into smaller actions by giving them the following example. Ask students to assume that their goal is to achieve a higher grade than last time on the next test in a specific subject. The first step in their action plan could be to study for fifteen minutes every day after school; the second step could be to end each class period by summarizing what they learned; and the third step could be that at the end of each class period they could ask a friend any questions they still have about the information presented in class on that day. Now ask students to develop an action plan for the goal they wrote at the top of the Thinking Guide and to specify the time of day or week when they will perform each action.

Next direct students' attention to the circle at the middle of the Thinking Guide. Explain that visualizing how they will feel when their goal has been reached is the next step in goal setting. Tell students that when they take the time to picture what will happen in their lives and how they will feel when their goal is reached, their goals become more specific. Moreover, when a goal is as specific as possible, it is easier to believe it can be achieved. Next, tell students that when they visualize desired outcomes, they will be less easily distracted by superficial products and deceiving short cuts. Confirm that while distractions may seem more attractive, they cannot deliver what is possible through a more thorough and thoughtful plan of action. You may elect to close your description of Step 2 by sharing this poem delivered in a speech by Roger Mager at the 1991 IRA Convention:

> To rise from a zero
>
> To a big campus hero,
>
> The answers to three questions
>
> I must surmise:
>
> Where am I going?
>
> How will I get there? and,
>
> How will I know I have arrived?

Now ask students to draw a picture or write in the rectangle at the center of the Thinking Guide how they will feel when they have reached their goal and what will be happening in their lives when that goal is achieved.

Next direct students' attention to the calendar pages and clock at the bottom of the Thinking Guide. State that the last step in goal-setting is to establish a realistic date (or time of day) when the plan should be accomplished. Share with students that when a goal is completely under their control, it becomes more challenging and fun to achieve when they set a deadline. Even when goals are not completely within students' control, deadlines increase the likelihood of success because they tie goals to very specific points in time. Pause now as you allow students to write a deadline for the goal they wrote at the top of the Thinking Guide.

APPLYING THE STRATEGY TO LITERATURE

Have students read a story about any famous person or a selection from one of the books listed below. Tell students that they will read silently for twenty minutes about a famous person or story character and ask students to write that person's goal, plan of action, and how and when this person knew she or he had reached the goal. Have students use the back of the Thinking Guide on which they wrote their own goal and plan of action.

Also ask students to notice specific strategies the famous person used to reach goals, since the class will discuss these at a later time. For instance, Oral Hershiser, a famous Los Angeles Dodgers' baseball player, kept a diary to record conditions that contributed to his success in games; and jazz musician Sonny Rollins set his goals by going outside to be alone and think of his goal while he played his trumpet. He continued to play until a plan of action came to mind.

You may select from the following autobioghraphies/biographies or fictional books:

High Interest/Low Vocabulary

Haskins, Jim. *One More River to Cross: The Stories of Twelve Black Americans*. New York: Scholastic, 1992.

Kraus, Robert. *Noel The Coward*. New York: Simon & Schuster, 1988.

Lindgren, Astrid. *Pippi Longstocking*. New York: Puffin, 1973.

Miles, Betty. *The Real Me*. New York: Knopf, 1974.

Levels 4–6

Corbett, Scott. *The Hockey Girls*. New York: Dutton, 1976.

Crayder, Dorothy. *She, The Adventuress*. New York: Atheneum, 1973.

Cummings, Pat. *Talking with Artists*. New York: Bradbury, 1992.

de la Mare, Walter. *Mollie Whuppie*. New York: Farrar, Straus, & Giroux, 1983.

Gaines, Ernest. *The Autobiography of Miss Jane Pittman*. New York: Dial, 1971.

George, Jean. *Julie of the Wolves*. Boston: G.K. Hall, 1973.

Gutman, Bill. *Jim Abbott: Star Pitcher*. Brookfield, CT: Millbrook Press, 1992.

Lindgren, Astrid. *Ronia, the Robber's Daughter*. New York: Viking, 1983.

Lofts, Norah. *The Maude Reed Tale*. New York: T. Nelson, 1972.

Lurie, Alison. *Clever Gretchen and Other Forgotten Folktales*. New York: Crowell, 1980.

Lyons, Mary. *Letters from a Slave Girl: The Story of Harriett Jacobs*. New York: Scribner, 1992.

McKissack, Patricia. *Sojourner Truth: Ain't I a Woman?* New York: Scholastic, 1992.

Levels 7–8

de Paola, Tomie. *Helga's Dowry: A Love Story*. New York: Harcourt Brace Jovanovich, 1977.

ASSESSMENT OF PART 1

If you wish to end the lesson at this point or to assess how much students have learned in Part 1, you can use one or more of the evaluation strategies on pages 194–216 or allow students to select an option that enables them to demonstrate how much they have learned.

APPLYING THE STRATEGY

GOAL-SETTING AS IT APPEARS IN LITERATURE: FICTION AND NONFICTION

Review the Thinking Guide and the characteristics of fiction and nonfiction literature. Share that many books describe people who attain goals. Suggest that whenever they read in the future students should notice strategies that literary figures use to achieve their goals, as some of these devices could become valuable to them as well.

APPLYING THE STRATEGY TO EVERYDAY EVENTS

To help students practice using the Thinking Guide and to complete the objectives in this lesson, have students select an activity from those that follow, or suggest an alternative in which they can practice establishing achievable goals for themselves.

Students on Their Own   Have students work for one week to implement the action plan they wrote during Part 1 of this lesson. At the end of the week, invite students to describe what they learned, their progress toward their goal, modifications they wish to make in future plans of action, and a new goal they wish to reach.

Thinking with a Partner   Have students work in pairs to establish a goal together. Ask each pair to write their goal and plan of action on a Thinking Guide and give them one week to achieve the goal. At the end of that time, have the pairs report their results to you and the class orally or in writing.

Working with the Teacher   Ask students to establish a class goal for one class period a day for one full week. Help them fill out a Thinking Guide that describes their plan of action. At the end of the week, have students refer to the Thinking Guide and assess the class's success in meeting their daily goals. Also ask students to suggest new strategies to add to future plans of action so the class can achieve more. If you desire, you can complete this cycle on the following week so students can see their growth in goal-setting abilities.

STUDENT SELF-ASSESSMENT

At the end of any activity in Part 2, students can report to you what they learned and discuss goals they did and did not attain.

or

Students can keep a diary of the insights they had about goal-setting and share these during a class discussion.

TEACHER ASSESSMENT

Review students' oral and written work and evaluate how much they have learned by asking them to write a story with themselves or a fictional character as the main character. In the story, the main character should reach his or her goal by enacting the steps on the Thinking Guide. The story ends by describing the next goal this character establishes and how much he or she learned about goal-setting.

APPLYING THE STRATEGY ACROSS THE CURRICULUM

The following activities enable students to establish goals in different content areas. Review the Thinking Guide before students engage in their activities.

All Content Areas   Pair students and allow them to apply goal-setting strategies to become "content experts." On a Monday, in one content area, announce that during the following Thursday's class period, students will complete the steps on the Thinking Guide so as to develop a plan for how to teach one section of the content area which they select. On Tuesday of that same week have students spend a few minutes completing the Thinking Guide to establish the goal they wish to achieve on the following Thursday. After you have approved students' goals, for a few moments during Wednesday's class period discuss resources that will be needed on the next day. On Thursday have students pursue their goals. Finally, on Friday, ask as many students as possible to present their goals and results to the class in as creative and effective a manner as possible, since the purpose is to assist their classmates in learning what they have mastered. During the last five minutes of that period, ask students to describe how much they have improved their goal-setting abilities and what they will do in coming weeks to expand their own self-initiated goal-setting competencies.

Language Arts   Ask students to use goal-setting to overcome a weakness in an area of their speaking, listening, reading, or writing. Then have them select one of the books listed below about additional goal-setting strategies. Students can read in a small group or you can read aloud the one they select.

High Interest/Low Vocabulary

Zadra, Dan. *Arthur's Pet Shop, The Secrets of Goal Setting*. Mankato, MN: Creative Education, Inc., 1986.

Levels 4–6

Hinton, S. E. *The Outsiders*. Boston: Little, Brown, 1990.

Levels 7–8

Zadra, Dan. *The Secret of the Slight Edge*. Mankato, MN: Creative Education, 1987.

After reading or listening to the story have students write on the Thinking Guide an insight they gained from the book and use it for one week. Invite students to report its value at the end of that week through a class discussion or journal entry.

Social Studies   You may want to use this activity during social studies on the same day as the activity in Part 1. After students have read the books in Part 1 of this lesson, have them discuss the strategies the characters they studied used to reach their goals. Then have students select their favorite strategy and use it to attain goals they establish for the present social studies unit.

Fine Arts/Drama/Language Arts   Have students read the items on the assessment forms of your choice (pages 194–216) and use the Thinking Guide to develop a plan of action to overcome a problem in their own creative, speaking, writing, handwriting, grammar, or reading abilities.

MEETING INDIVIDUAL NEEDS

UNDERSTANDING SELF

Ask students to analyze the goals they set during this lesson. Share with them that through analyzing their strengths and weaknesses in goal-setting, they can better understand themselves and increase the number of goals they attain. For example, by determining why they reached some goals and not others, students can recognize new strategies to develop. For instance, if a student sets a goal to learn a series of content area facts within one week and doesn't reach that goal, he or she may wish to include smaller steps or allow longer periods of time to complete future plans of action.

STRATEGIES FOR LESS ABLE READERS

Review the Thinking Guide with students who wish to meet with you individually or in small groups. Have students choose one of the following books that describe main characters who used goal-setting to eliminate problems they face. These problems are the same as or very similar to those faced by some fourth graders. Ask students to select a book and write a goal and plan of action to address a similar problem they face. Students may use the following list or the one that appears on pages 121–122.

High Interest/Low Vocabulary

Carlson, Nancy. *I Like Me*. New York: Viking Kestrel, 1988.

Hines, Anna Grossnickle. *Tell Me Your Best Thing*. New York: Dutton Children's Books, 1991.

Sharmat, Marjorie W. *I'm Terrific*. New York: Holiday House, 1976.

William, Barbara. *Donna Jean's Disaster*. Niles, IL: Albert Whitman, 1986.

Levels 4–6

Danziger, Paula. *The Cat Ate My Gymsuit*. New York: Delacorte Press, 1974.

Fowler, Carol. *Daisy Hooee Nampeyo*. Minneapolis: Dillon Press, 1977.

Levinson, Marilyn. *The Fourth-Grade Four*. New York: Henry Holt, 1989.

Whelan, Gloria. *Hanna*. New York: Random House, 1991.

Levels 7–8

O'Dell, Scott. *The Road To Damietta*. Boston: Houghton Mifflin, 1985.

UNDERSTANDING OTHERS

After students complete the goal-setting activities in Parts 1 and 2, ask them to discuss their successes and difficulties. Through examining these goals, students can come to understand their classmates' strengths. Also peers can suggest strategies they used to reach their goals.

ASSESSMENT OF PARTS 3 AND 4

Ask students to recall, summarize, and give insights about the steps on the Thinking Guide and other goal-setting strategies they have learned. Then select and complete the class and individual student assessment records from pages 194–216. You may select from the following:

- Class Monitoring Record, Blackline Master 62

- Reading Wheel, Blackline Masters 69 and 70

- Oral-Language Needs Monitor, Blackline Master 71

- Speech Critique, Blackline Master 72

- Informal Checklist for Usage, Blackline Master 73

- Story Map, Blackline Master 74

- Clues to Improving Handwriting, Blackline Master 77

- Student Self-Assessment of Thinking Abilities, Blackline Master 79

LESSON 16

REVIEW

You may assign or have students select as many of the following review activities as appropriate. Each assists students in integrating and retaining the strategies they learned in Volume One of *Reason to Read*.

1. On Blackline Masters 85–88 are reduced copies of each Thinking Guide in Volume One. The titles have been removed. Students can use these guides in many ways to review what they have learned. They can label each with the strategic process it demonstrates, order the guides by their own preferences of use and describe their reasons for these preferences, and/or write about incidents in which they used one or more guides.

2. Have students work in groups and demonstrate to the class selected aspects of what they learned from Lessons 1–15.

3. Have students describe how they will remember to use each strategy in Volume One in the future.

4. Ask students to teach their favorite strategy to another class in the school.

5. Have students modify one or more strategies using their own creativity, prepare a new Thinking Guide, and teach it to the class.

6. Invite students to perform a dramatic, musical, or artistic reenactment that demonstrates as many strategic processes in action as possible.

7. Have students share with a peer a case study of themselves that includes a description of how many strategies they initiated within a set period of time and a description of additional strategies they want to learn.

8. Have students form groups and create their own strategy lesson about one of the strategies to teach to the rest of the class.

9. Invite a group of volunteers to form a panel that fields questions from students in a different class concerning difficulties these schoolmates face. In answering the questions, instruct panelists to refer to as many strategies and Thinking Guides on Blackline Masters 85–88 as appropriate.

10. Ask students to report backup strategies they want to rely on in reading and thinking relative to each strategy learned in Volume One.

11. Invite students to report successful experiences outside of reading class in which they opted to use particular strategies.

12. Have students complete exercises in applied citizenship in which they interview community leaders about problems they face. Then have students use the strategies they have learned to provide suggestions to address one or more of the problems. Invite the community leaders to respond to the feasibility of the suggestions and to suggest additional strategies they may need to consider.

13. Students can create their own student-made test about the strategies in Volume One that they can administer to classmates.

14. Have students create diagrams that integrate the strategies from Volume One in innovative ways.

15. Present to the class a list of the strategies contained in Volumes Two and Three of *Reason to Read*. Allow students to select one or more strategies they want to learn, based on the amount of time available until the end of the school year.

ASSESSMENT OF LESSON 16

Ask students to recall, summarize, and give insights about the strategies they have learned in this program. Then select and complete the class and individual student assessment records from pages 194–216. You may prefer to use one or more of the following:

- Running Record of Language Arts and Thinking Strategies, Blackline Master 63

- Genres Introduced in *Reason to Read*, Blackline Master 67

- Attitude/Interest Inventory (a posttest given after Lesson 1), Blackline Master 68

- Oral-Language Needs Monitor (a posttest and compare to pretest given after Lesson 1), Blackline Master 71

- Clues to Improving Handwriting, Blackline Master 77

- Assessing Thinking Abilities, Blackline Master 78

- Student Self-Assessment of Thinking Abilities, Blackline Master 79

- Problem-Solving Assessment (as a transfer test and compare to the one administered after Lesson 9), Blackline Master 82

- Portfolio Assessment, Blackline Master 84

THINKING GUIDE

ASKING QUESTIONS TO CLARIFY

? ? ? ? ? ? ? ? ? ? ? ? ? ? ? ? ?

1. Why?

2. Is the most important point _____ or _____?

3. What do you mean by "_____"?

4. If I understand, you mean _____. Is that right?

5. Where will the point you are making not apply? How does ___ relate to _____?

6. If your idea is accepted, what is the greatest change that will occur?

7. Would you say more about _____?

8. What is the difference between _____ and _____?

9. Would this be an example?

10. Is it possible that _____? What else could we do?

11. If _____ happened, what would be the result?

LEARNING TO ASK QUESTIONS

PART 1

President Roosevelt was campaigning to be reelected for his second term. During the campaign, he gave speeches from a train that traveled from the east to the west coast. Then, as now, newspaper reporters traveled with the President. They reported news from the trip and wrote stories about the President's speeches for their newspapers.

By the time the President had finished his third speech, he knew who you were. You were the reporter who eased your way to the front row during every one of his speeches. When his speeches were over, you pointed out mistakes in what he said and wrote unfavorable newspaper stories about him. You did not believe the President was correct in his plans for the country, and your newspaper stories said so. You were becoming famous for the stories you wrote.

About the fifth week of the campaign, as the President was about to speak, it began to rain. As soon as the rain began, the President moved to the front of the platform. He looked across the crowd and caught your eyes. He must have noticed that you did not wear your raincoat because he politely took off his raincoat, leaned over the rail, and handed the coat to you.

Stop reading.

Ask yourself: "What would I have said or done now if I had been the reporter?" Write here what you would have done:

———————————————————————————————————————

———————————————————————————————————————

———————————————————————————————————————

———————————————————————————————————————

———————————————————————————————————————

———————————————————————————————————————

———————————————————————————————————————

———————————————————————————————————————

———————————————————————————————————————

———————————————————————————————————————

LEARNING TO ASK QUESTIONS

PART 2

Stunned, the reporter took the coat. Then he asked a question: "Mr. President, you know I am your biggest critic. Why do you want me to have your coat?"

The President looked very directly at the reporter and with a kind voice said, "I know how smart you are. I know how strong you are in your opinions. I respect that. I'm also sure that if you could feel what it is like to be President you would better understand me and my positions. You may also see that some of your opinions are not correct. I thought if you wore my coat you might understand what it feels like to be President."

Soon after this incident, President Roosevelt and the reporter grew to become close friends. Upon his reelection, the President gave the reporter the job of Press Secretary. The Press Secretary became very successful. He and the President worked closely together until the President died.

THINKING GUIDE
WHEN I DON'T KNOW A WORD

Check to see whether the word is on my sight word list.

the

Sound it out if the word follows a regular English pattern.

lĭ ŏn s
lioness!

Use structural analysis if it is a long word.

school house

Look at other words in the sentence. Does that help me?

Quietly ask a friend.

Ask the teacher.

Lion
Lioness

Look in the dictionary.

Use the word in a sentence.

My huge schoolhouse is the biggest building on the street.

THINKING GUIDE
COMPARING AND CONTRASTING

NAME _____ DATE _____

I'm confused about _____

I now understand that _____

_____

A.   B.   C.

_____

_____

THINKING GUIDE
COMPARING AND CONTRASTING

NAME _____ DATE _____

I'm confused about _____

I now understand that __I shouldn't be__
__deceived by appearances__

A. Whales
1. warm blooded
2. have hair
3. complex respiratory system
4. have lungs
5. get oxygen from air
6. carry babies

B. Commonalities
1. live in water

C. Fish
1. cold blooded
2. no hair
3. gills are simple respiratory system
4. no lungs
5. gets oxygen from water
6. hatch eggs

READING

AN AMERICAN INDIAN LEGEND:
WHY THE WOODPECKER HAS A LONG BEAK

In the days of long ago the Great Spirit came down from the sky and talked with men. Once as he went up and down the earth, he came to the wigwam of a woman. He went into the wigwam and sat down by the fire, but he looked like an old man, and the woman did not know who he was.

"I have fasted for many days," said the Great Spirit to the woman. "Will you give me some food?" The woman made a very little cake and put it on the fire. "You can have this cake," she said, "if you will wait for it to bake." "I will wait," he said.

When the cake was baked, the woman stood and looked at it. She thought, "It is very large. I thought it was small. I will not give him so large a cake as that." So she put it away and made a small one. "If you will wait, I will give you this when it is baked," she said, and the Great Spirit said, "I will wait."

When the cake was baked, it was larger than the first one. "It is so large that I will keep it for a feast," she thought. So she said to her guest, "I will not give you this cake, but if you will wait, I will make another one." "I will wait," said the Great Spirit again.

Then the woman made another cake. It was still smaller than the others had been at first, but when she went to the fire for it, she found it the largest of all. She did not know that the Great Spirit's magic had made each cake larger, and she thought, "This is a marvel, but I will not give away the largest cake of all." So she said to her guest. I have no food for you. Go to the forest and look there for your food. You can find it in the bark of the trees, if you will."

The Great Spirit was angry when he heard the words of the woman. He rose up from where he sat and threw back his cloak. "A woman must be good and gentle," he said, "and you are cruel. You shall no longer be a woman and live in a wigwam. You shall go out into the forests and hunt for your food in the bark of trees."

The Great Spirit stamped his foot on the earth, and the woman grew smaller and smaller. Wings started from her body and feathers grew upon her. With a loud cry she rose from the earth and flew away to the forest.

And to this day all woodpeckers live in the forest and hunt for their food in the bark of trees.

—from Florence Holbrook, *The Book of Nature Myths* (Boston: Houghton Mifflin Company, 1930)

READING

A ROMANIAN LEGEND:
WHY THE WOODPECKER HAS A LONG BEAK

Know that the woodpecker was originally not a bird but an old woman with a very long nose, which she put into everybody's pots and pans, sniffing about, eavesdropping, inquisitive, and curious about whether it belonged to her or not, adding a little in her talebearing and taking off a bit from another tale, and so making mischief among her neighbors. When God saw her doings, he took a huge sack and filled it with midges, beetles, ants, and all kinds of insects, and tying it tightly, gave it to the old woman, and said to her: "Now, take this sack and carry it home, but beware of opening it, for if your curiosity makes you put your nose into it, you will find more than you care for, and you will have trouble without end."

"Heaven forbid," replied the old hag, "that I should do such a thing; I am not going against the will of God. I shall be careful."

So she took the sack on her back and started trotting home, but whilst she was carrying it her fingers were already twitching, and she could scarcely restrain herself, so no sooner did she find herself a short distance away than she sat down in a meadow and opened the sack. That was just what the insects wanted, for no sooner did she open it than they started scrambling out and scampered about the field, each one its own way as fast as its little legs would carry it. Some hid themselves in the earth, others scrambled under the grass; others, again, went up the trees, and all ran away as fast as they could.

When the old woman saw what had happened, she got mightily frightened, and tried to gather the insects to pack them up again, and put them back into the sack, and tied it up. Then came the voice of God, who asked her what she had done, and if that was the way she kept promises.

"Where are the insects, beetles, and midges, which I gave you to carry? From this moment you shall change into a bird and go about picking up all those insects until you get my sack full again, and only then can you become a human being again." And so she changed into a woodpecker; the long beak is the long nose of the old woman, and she goes about hunting for these midges, beetles, and ants in the hope of filling up the sack, so she can again resume her human shape. But to this very day she has not completed her task, and has remained the woodpecker.

READING
DIFFERENT VERSIONS OF FAIRY TALES
YOU CAN SELECT TO READ

The Three Little Pigs

The Three Little Pigs by Eric Blegvad

Walt Disney's The Three Little Pigs by B. Brenner

The Three Little Pigs by Paul Galdone

The Three Little Hawaiian Pigs and the Magic Shark by Laird and Laird

The True Story of The Three Little Pigs by J. Scieszka

The Three Little Pigs by M. Zemach

Little Red Riding Hood

Little Red Riding Hood by P. Galdone

Little Red Cap by J. Grimm

Little Red Riding Hood by J. Goodall

Little Red Riding Hood by J. Marshall

Lon Po Po: A Red Riding Hood Story from China, translated by Ed Young

Jack and the Beanstalk

Jim and the Beanstalk by R. Briggs

Jack and the Beanstalk by L. Cauley

Jack and the Beanstalk by Walter de la Mare

Jack and the Beanstalk by B. deRegniers

Jack and the Bean Tree by G. Haley

Jack and the Beanstalk by Joseph Jacobs

Jack and the Beanstalk by D. W. Johnson

Jack and the Wonder Beans by J. Still

The Old Lady Who Swallowed a Fly

I Know an Old Lady Who Swallowed a Fly by E. Adams

There Was an Old Woman by S. Kellog

I Know an Old Lady Who Swallowed a Fly by N. B. Westcott

The Gingerbread Boy

The Runaway Pancake by A. Asogojornsen and J. Moe

The Bun: A Tale from Russia by M. Brown

The Gingerbread Boy by Paul Galdone

Johnny-Cake by J. Jacob

The Gingerbread Rabbit by R. Jarrel

The Pancake by A. Lobel

Journey Cake, Ho! by R. Sawyer

The Hare and the Tortoise

The Hare and the Tortoise by C. Castle

The Hare and the Tortoise by P. Galdone

The Hare and the Tortoise by J. Stevens

The Hare and the Tortoise by B. Wildsmith

Cinderella

Cinderella by M. Brown

Cinderella by A. Ehrlich

Cinderella by P. Galdone

Cinderella by J. Grimm

Cinderella by C. Perrault

The Paper Bag Princess by R. Munson

Sydneyrella and the Glass Slipper by B. Myers

Yeh-Shen by A. Louie

The Egyptian Cinderella by S. Climo

Korean Cinderella by E. Adams

Princess Furball by C. Huck

Tatterhood and Other Tales by E. J. Phelps

Moss Grown by W. Hooks

The Rough-Face Girl by R. Martin

SIGNAL WORDS

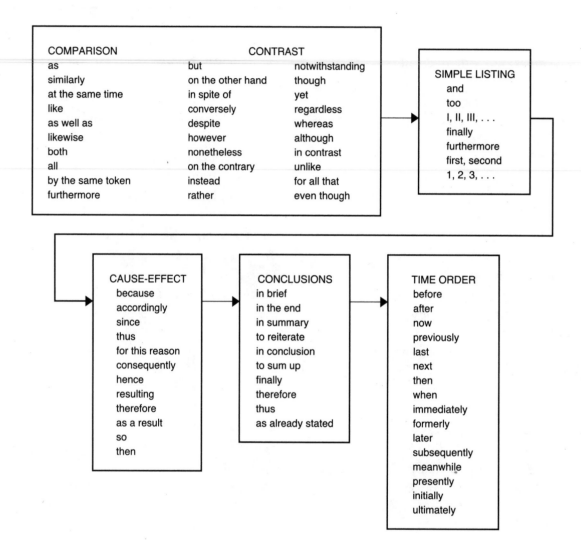

COMPARISON
as
similarly
at the same time
like
as well as
likewise
both
all
by the same token
furthermore

CONTRAST
but
on the other hand
in spite of
conversely
despite
however
nonetheless
on the contrary
instead
rather

notwithstanding
though
yet
regardless
whereas
although
in contrast
unlike
for all that
even though

SIMPLE LISTING
and
too
I, II, III, . . .
finally
furthermore
first, second
1, 2, 3, . . .

CAUSE-EFFECT
because
accordingly
since
thus
for this reason
consequently
hence
resulting
therefore
as a result
so
then

CONCLUSIONS
in brief
in the end
in summary
to reiterate
in conclusion
to sum up
finally
therefore
thus
as already stated

TIME ORDER
before
after
now
previously
last
next
then
when
immediately
formerly
later
subsequently
meanwhile
presently
initially
ultimately

THINKING GUIDE
COMPARING AND CONTRASTING

NAME _____ DATE _____

I'm confused about _____

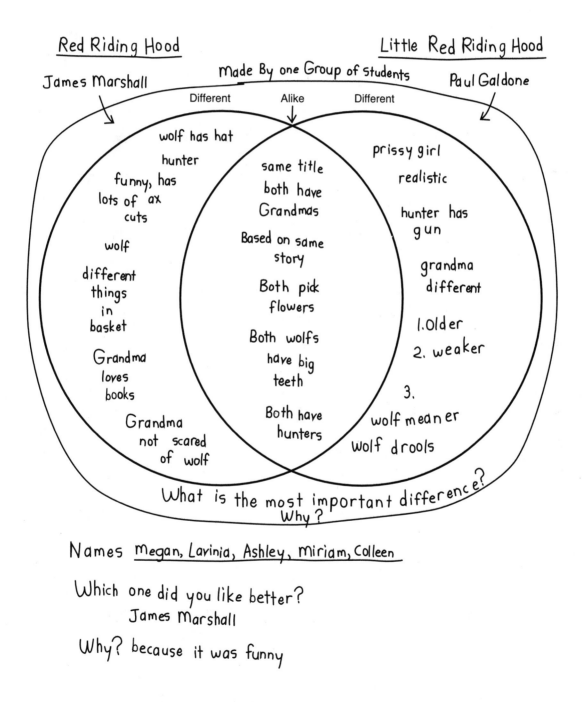

Red Riding Hood

James Marshall

Little Red Riding Hood

Paul Galdone

Made By one Group of students

Different   Alike   Different

wolf has hat

hunter

funny, has lots of ax cuts

wolf

different things in basket

Grandma loves books

Grandma not scared of wolf

same title
both have Grandmas

Based on same story

Both pick flowers

Both wolfs have big teeth

Both have hunters

prissy girl

realistic

hunter has gun

grandma different

1. Older
2. weaker

3.
wolf meaner

Wolf drools

What is the most important difference? Why?

Names Megan, Lavinia, Ashley, Miriam, Colleen

Which one did you like better?
    James Marshall

Why? because it was funny

EDITING CHECKLIST

DATE _____

WRITER'S NAME _____

REVIEWER'S NAME _____

■ *Directions: Read to check your classmate's information and to evaluate the clarity of thinking and reading.*

What is the paper mainly about? _____

What part do you like best? Put an asterisk next to the part you like best and describe your reasons.

_____

_____

What parts are not clear? Put a question mark next to the unclear parts and describe your reasons.

_____

_____

Is the paper interesting? Why or why not? _____

■ *Questions to check organization (circle your response):*

Did the author use comparative words to describe complex or confusing objects, qualities, or ideas?

    Yes   Somewhat   No

Did the author tell how two things are alike?

    Yes   Somewhat   No

Did the author tell how two things are different?

    Yes   Somewhat   No

Did the author use key words clearly?

    Yes   Somewhat   No

■ *Revision plan:*

What two parts do you think should be changed or revised? Give suggestions for the revision.

    1. _____

    2. _____

READING

"They worshipped courage, those early Polynesians. The spirit which had urged them across the Pacific in their sailing canoes, before the dawn of recorded history, not knowing where they were going nor caring what their fate might be, still sang its song of danger in their blood. There was only courage. A man who was afraid—what place had he in their midst? And the boy Mafatu—son of Tavana Nui, the Great Chief of Hikueru—always had been afraid, so the people drove him forth. Not by violence, but by indifference.

Mafatu went out alone to face the thing he feared the most. And the people of Hikueru still sing his story in their chants and tell it over the evening fires.

It was the sea that Mafatu feared. He had been surrounded by it ever since he was born. The thunder of it filled his ears; the crash of it upon the reef, the mutter of it at sunset, the threat and fury of its storms—on every hand, wherever he turned—the sea."

© Addison-Wesley Publishing Company, Inc.

NAME _____ DATE _____

I'm confused about _____

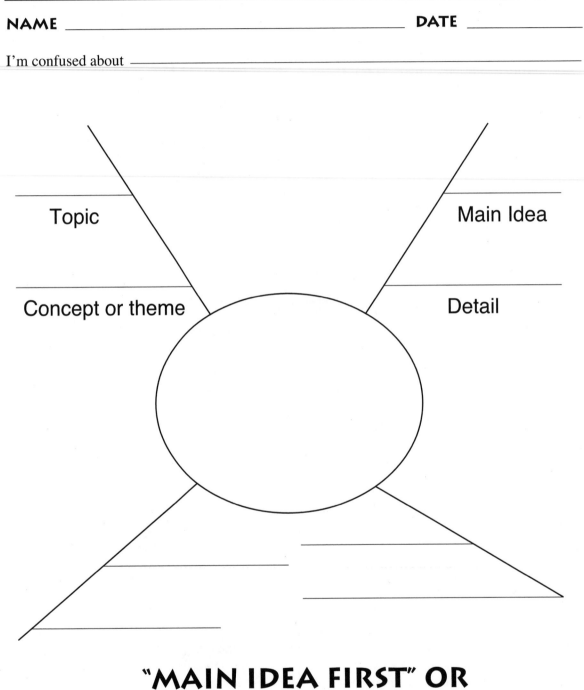

Topic

Main Idea

Concept or theme

Detail

"MAIN IDEA FIRST" OR CONCEPT PATTERN

NAME _____ **DATE** _____

I'm confused about _____

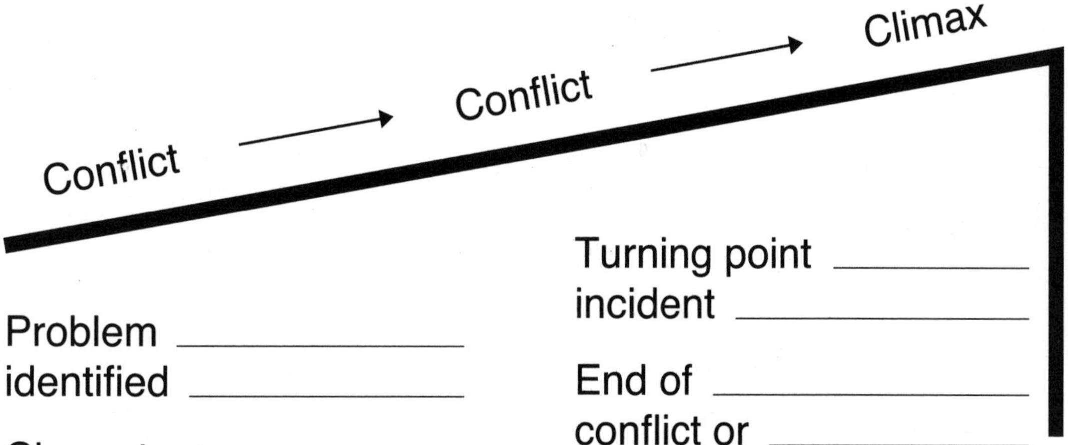

Climax

Conflict

Conflict

Conflict

Turning point _____
incident _____

Problem _____
identified _____

End of _____
conflict or _____
resolution _____

Character _____
introduced _____

Setting _____
described _____

Problem Statement:

_____

_____

_____

Solution:

_____

_____

_____

"PLOT IN STORIES" OR
PROBLEM/SOLUTION PATTERN

NAME _____ **DATE** _____

I'm confused about _____

Initiating Event

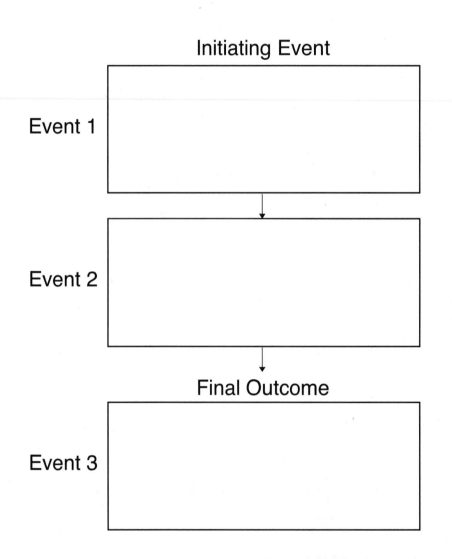

Event 1

Event 2

Final Outcome

Event 3

"TELLING THINGS IN ORDER" OR SEQUENCE PATTERN

NAME _____ **DATE** _____

I'm confused about _____

	Name 1	Name 2
Attribute 1		
Attribute 2		
Attribute 3		

"TELLING BOTH SIDES" OR
SIMILARITY/DIFFERENCE PATTERN

PATTERN GAME

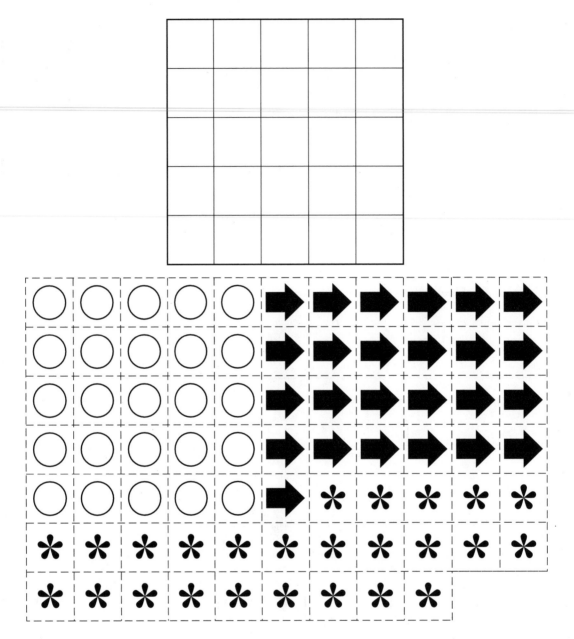

How to Play: This game is for three people. Each group receives one game board and players cut out the square marker pieces. Player 1 designs a secret pattern and places no more than 5 of his or her symbols in the squares to represent that pattern. Players 2 and 3 try to guess the pattern by taking turns placing their own markers in squares. If Player 1 says that a marker is in the correct place, it stays. If not, it is removed. Continue until the secret pattern is complete. Then let another player design a secret pattern, and continue playing until all players have had the same number of turns. Keeping score: Keep track of each player's guesses. Subtract the incorrect guesses from the correct ones. There may often be negative scores. The player with the most points wins.

RECOGNIZING PATTERNS

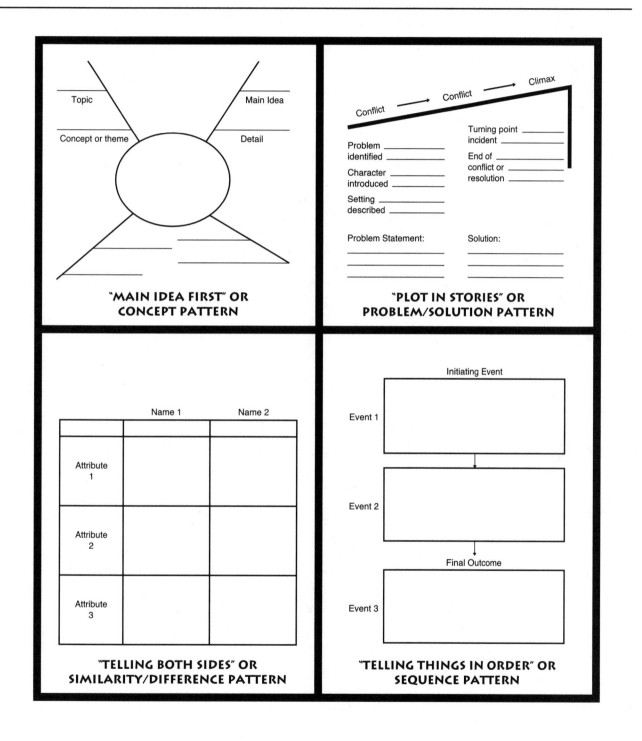

"MAIN IDEA FIRST" OR CONCEPT PATTERN

Topic

Main Idea

Concept or theme

Detail

"PLOT IN STORIES" OR PROBLEM/SOLUTION PATTERN

Conflict → Conflict → Climax

Problem identified _____

Character introduced _____

Setting described _____

Turning point incident _____

End of conflict or resolution _____

Problem Statement:
_____
_____
_____

Solution:
_____
_____
_____

"TELLING BOTH SIDES" OR SIMILARITY/DIFFERENCE PATTERN

	Name 1	Name 2
Attribute 1		
Attribute 2		
Attribute 3		

"TELLING THINGS IN ORDER" OR SEQUENCE PATTERN

Event 1 — Initiating Event

Event 2

Event 3 — Final Outcome

These are structures of four basic patterns you will find in nature, literature, and your life. When you find other patterns you can draw pictures of them on the back of this Thinking Guide.

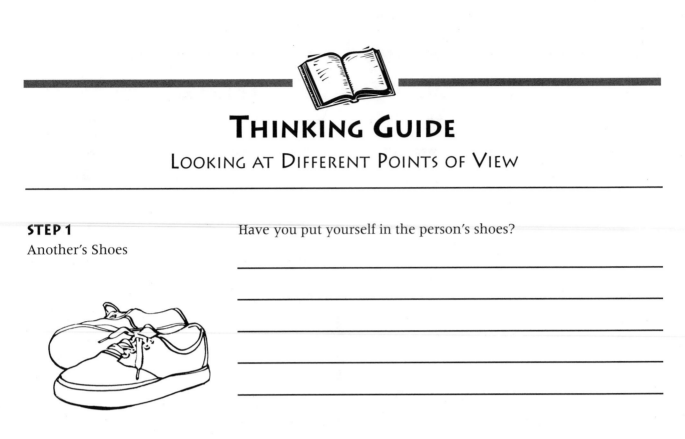

THINKING GUIDE

LOOKING AT DIFFERENT POINTS OF VIEW

STEP 1
Another's Shoes

Have you put yourself in the person's shoes?

_____

_____

_____

_____

_____

STEP 2
Use Details

Are there details, opinions, and values that suggest the person's point of view?

_____

_____

_____

_____

STEP 3
People Think Differently

Have you viewed the situation from the person's perspective to understand the different point of view?

_____

_____

_____

_____

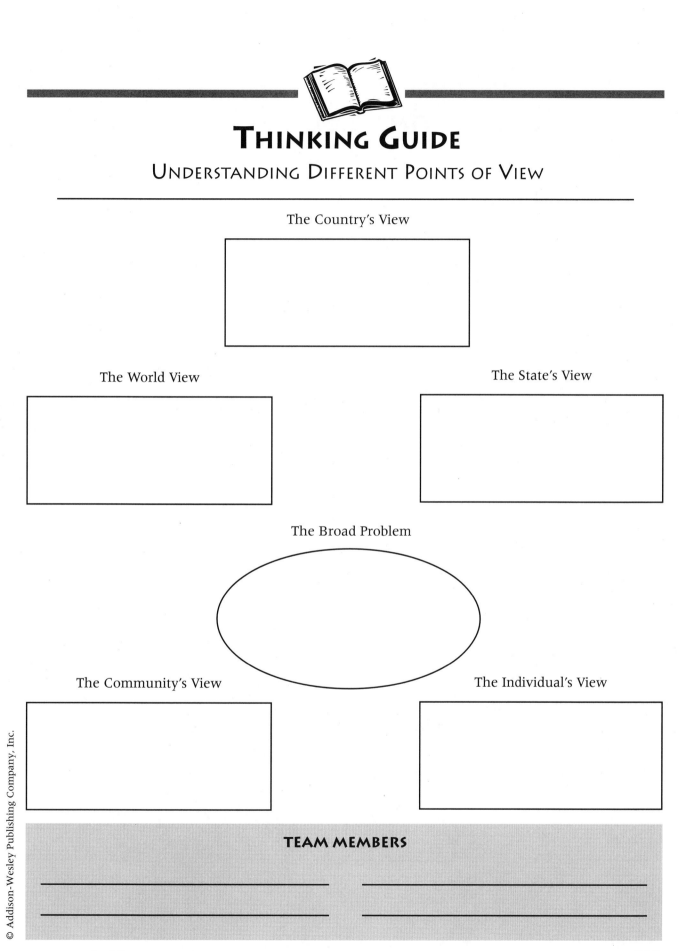

THINKING GUIDE

UNDERSTANDING DIFFERENT POINTS OF VIEW

The Country's View

The World View

The State's View

The Broad Problem

The Community's View

The Individual's View

TEAM MEMBERS

 # PUTTING YOURSELF IN SOMEONE ELSE'S SHOES

1. What is a conflict you have/have had with another person (parent, classmate, brother, sister, etc.?)

2. What is/was that other person's point of view about the conflict?

3. What is/was the best resolution of your conflict from the other person's point of view?

4. What can you learn from considering the conflict from that other point of view?

THINKING GUIDE

RECOGNIZING PROPAGANDA

DEVICE	EXAMPLE/ DESCRIPTION	DID AUTHOR USE?		EVIDENCE
		Yes	No	
1. Bandwagon	claiming everyone is doing it: "Is your house the only one on the block not protected by Alpha Alarm?"	☐	☐	_____ _____
2. Repetition	repeating favorable words: "bargain," "best," "first," "sale"	☐	☐	_____ _____
3. Transfer	transferring of feelings about one thing to another: "If you like your mother, you'll like our pie."	☐	☐	_____ _____
4. Testimonial	famous person promoting something: "I'm a famous basketball star and to stay strong I eat Sugar Flakes cereal every morning."	☐	☐	_____ _____
5. "Better Hurry" or "It's Free"	trying to make you think there is a good reason to take action immediately or within a definite time period or that you can get something for nothing: "Better hurry, only a limited supply available."	☐	☐	_____ _____ _____
6. Glittering Generality	using glowing words or phrases to draw your attention: "Patriotic citizens will agree. . ."	☐	☐	_____ _____
7. Name Calling	referring to something as undesirable or desirable by choosing a word that has either a positive or negative emotional appeal: "The greedy crooks at the other store just want your money. We want to help you."	☐	☐	_____ _____ _____ _____

READING

THE COSTS TO THE COMMUNITY

Smoking is a major health problem, causing misery to those affected by smoking-related diseases, but its costs are enormous in other ways.

Millions of working days are lost each year because of absences caused by smoker's diseases. Workers who smoke more than twenty cigarettes each day have to take at least twice as much time off work because of illness as do non-smokers. The other costs to the community are just as great. Many of the diseases which can be caused by smoking, such as bronchitis and emphysema, require long periods of medical and nursing care, which are very expensive. In addition there are the social security and insurance payments which have to be made to the sufferers or their relatives.

Smoking is also directly expensive to the smoker. Especially in the Third World, the cost of tobacco may form a large part of the smoker's income—money which could be better spent on food and housing. If smokers become ill, they lose money because they are unable to work, and they may suffer premature retirement or early death.

Many lung conditions associated with smoking involve lengthy and expensive medical and nursing care. Hospital beds are therefore occupied by patients who could have avoided ill health.

Taken from *Smoking and Health,* by Brian R. Ward, 1986, Franklin Watts Publisher

Thinking Guide Answer Key

Recognizing Propaganda

DEVICE	EXAMPLE/ DESCRIPTION	DID AUTHOR USE?		EVIDENCE
		Yes	No	
1. Bandwagon	claiming everyone is doing it: "Is your house the only one on the block not protected by Alpha Alarm?"	☑	☐	costs, expensive, health deficits
2. Repetition	repeating favorable words: "bargain," "best," "first," "sale"	☐	☑	
3. Transfer	transferring of feelings about one object to another: "If you like your mother, you'll like our pie."	☐	☑	
4. Testimonial	famous person promoting something: "I'm a famous basketball star and to stay strong I eat Sugar Flakes cereal every morning."	☐	☑	
5. "Better Hurry" or "It's Free"	speaker trying to make you think there is a good reason to take action immediately or within a definite time period or that you can get something for nothing: "Better hurry, only a limited supply available."	☐	☑	
6. Glittering Generality	using glowing words or phrases to draw your attention: "Patriotic citizens will agree. . ."	☑	☐	major, misery, enormous, expensive
7. Name Calling	referring to something as undesirable or desirable by choosing a word that has either a positive or negative emotional appeal: "The greedy crooks at the other store just want your money. We want to help you."	☑	☐	never really says or states "Don't Smoke"

THINKING GUIDE
MAKING REASONED JUDGMENTS

NAME _____ DATE _____

BOX 1	FACTS

from encyclopedia, atlas, almanac, math text, other people's statements, your own statements

$+$

BOX 2	OPINIONS

from newspapers, advertisements, other people's statements, your own statements

$+$

BOX 3	YOU

what you already know and what you think are the strongest facts and opinions from boxes 1and 2

$=$

BOX 4	REASONED JUDGMENT

State the reasoning behind your statement.

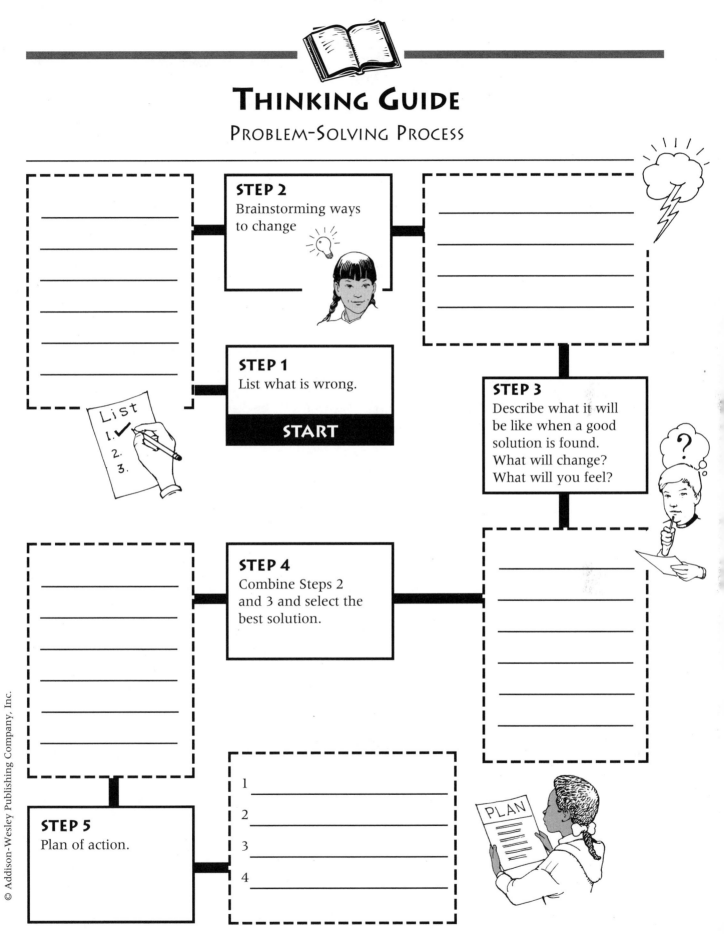

THINKING GUIDE

PROBLEM-SOLVING PROCESS

STEP 2
Brainstorming ways
to change

STEP 1
List what is wrong.

START

STEP 3
Describe what it will
be like when a good
solution is found.
What will change?
What will you feel?

STEP 4
Combine Steps 2
and 3 and select the
best solution.

STEP 5
Plan of action.

1 _____
2 _____
3 _____
4 _____

PLAN

THINKING GUIDE
SELECTING MY OWN PROBLEM-SOLVING STRATEGY

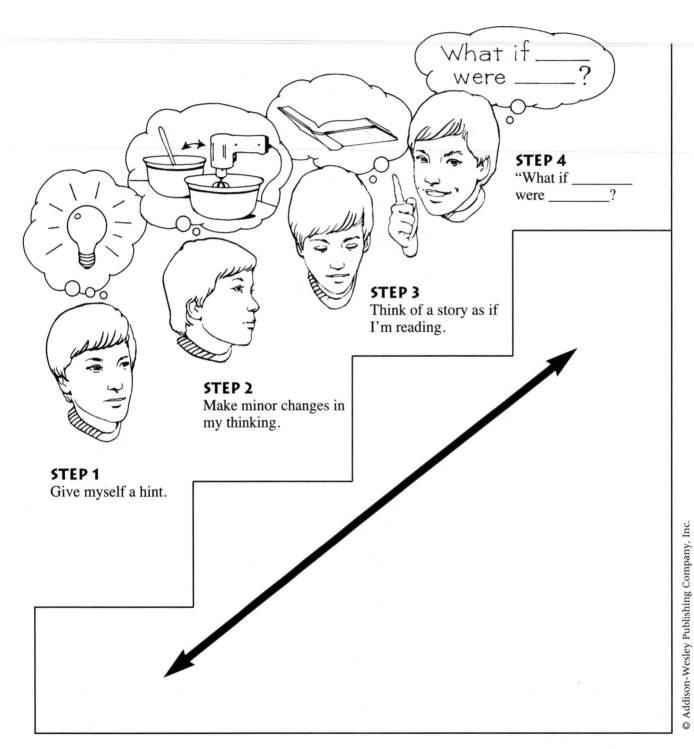

What if _____ were _____?

STEP 4
"What if _____ were _____?

STEP 3
Think of a story as if I'm reading.

STEP 2
Make minor changes in my thinking.

STEP 1
Give myself a hint.

THINKING GUIDE

RECOGNIZING WHAT I DO WELL

STEP 1: WHAT DO I DO WELL?

What have my parents or other adults told me I do well?

STEP 2: SEEING MYSELF IN OTHER PEOPLE

What characters in books are like me?

STEP 3: MY STRENGTHS SHOW IN ACTIVITIES I ENJOY DOING.

What activities do I enjoy?

STEP 4: USE A STRENGTH TO IMPROVE A WEAKNESS.

What can I do to use my strengths to improve my weaknesses?

DESCRIBING MY STRENGTHS AND WEAKNESSES

Using your own ideas and some of the ideas discussed by the group, make a list of your strengths and weaknesses, how you know they are strengths, and how you want to overcome your weaknesses.

MY STRENGTHS

An example of how these strengths can be observed:

1 _____   _____

2 _____   _____

3 _____   _____

4 _____   _____

5 _____   _____

6 _____   _____

7 _____   _____

MY WEAKNESSES

How I can overcome these weaknesses:

1 _____   _____

2 _____   _____

3 _____   _____

4 _____   _____

5 _____   _____

THINKING GUIDE
DO I UNDERSTAND?

?	**☆**	

I DON'T KNOW IF I KNOW

It could be that I'm confused.
(go to Step 1)

It could be that I don't have enough information.
(go to Step 2)

It could be I lack confidence in my understanding.
(go to Step 3)

I KNOW I DON'T KNOW

I know I'm confused and I think it's because:

I don't have enough information.
(go to Step 2)

I lack confidence.
(go to Step 3)

I KNOW I KNOW

I'm not confused.

I have enough information.

I'm confident in my ability to understand.

		☆☆☆

STEP 1	**STEP 2**	**STEP 3**

Why am I confused?

- Is there a word I don't understand?
- Do I lack background in this area?
- Is a sentence too long?
- Was my concentration broken?
- Did I have to figure out unknown words?
- Did I understand the author's purpose?

Why don't I have enough information?
- I can get more by asking myself if I know:

  Who?

  What?

  Where?

  When?

  Why?

  How?

To trust my ability to put new information together to comprehend, I assess:

- Whether I know I have enough information about what I'm reading;
- Whether I put together all the words correctly to be sure I didn't confuse any ideas;
- If I have done both items above I can test my understanding by reading or thinking about the next part to see if that part logically connects to what I understand right now.

STEP 1 + STEP 2 + STEP 3 = COMPREHENSION

READING

THE CASE OF THE HITCHHIKER

"Boy, thanks for the lift," exclaimed the young man as he slid off his knapsack and climbed into the front seat of the air-conditioned patrol car beside Sheriff Monahan. "Aren't you going to arrest me for bumming a ride?"

"Not today," replied the sheriff. "Too busy."

The young man grinned in relief. He took a chocolate bar from his knapsack, broke off a piece, and offered the rest to the sheriff. "No, thanks," said the police officer, accelerating the car.

"You chasing someone?" asked the hitchhiker.

"Four men just held up the First National Bank. They escaped in a big black sedan."

"Hey," gasped the hitchhiker. "I saw a black sedan about ten minutes ago. It had four men in it. They nearly ran me off the road. First car I saw in hour. But they took a left turn. They're headed west, not north."

Sheriff Monahan braked the patrol car and swung it around. The young man began peeling an orange, putting the rinds tidily into a paper bag,

"Look at the heat shining off the road ahead," said the sheriff. "Must be eighty-five in the shade today."

"Must be," agreed the hitchhiker. "Wait—you passed the turn off—where're you going?"

"To the police station," snapped the sheriff— a decision to which Haledjian heartily agreed upon hearing the hitchhiker's story.

How come?

from *Two-Minute Mysteries* and *More Two-Minute Mysteries* by Donald J. Sobel.
Reprinted by permission of Scholastic, Inc., copyright © 1967 and 1971.

READING

THE CASE OF THE LINCOLN LETTER

"It might be genuine," murmured Dr. Fry, chief of the crime lab.

Inspector Winters peered through a magnifying glass at the ragged sheet of foolscap. He read the writing, from which part had been torn:

" '. . . in Gettysburg at the Wills home facing the public square. Bands blared, serenading whomever spoke. I begged to be excused. The crowd was little pleased. The band played the national anthem and moved on to Seward's . . .' "

The last sentence ran into a tear. However, the signature was unmarred—"A. Lincoln"

It might be worth tens of thousands of dollars," said Dr. Fry.

"For an incomplete letter of President Lincoln's?" inquired the inspector. "Are they that rare?"

"Look at the reverse side," advised Dr. Fry.

The inspector released a low whistle of astonishment. On the other side of the sheet was scrawled a partial draft of the Gettysburg address!

"I found it by accident in the old Bible my sister keeps in the attic," said Sy "The Weasel" McCloskey.

"Wasn't that where you found the counterfeit tens last year?" put in the inspector sarcastically.

Dr. Fry interrupted. "I'll run some chemical tests on the paper. It'll take a couple of days."

"The paper turned out to be the right age," a surprised Inspector Winters reported to Dr. Haledjian. "I'll wager you'll never guess the value of that one little sheet!"

"About 10 cents—to a police museum," replied Haledjian. "It is obviously a forgery."

What was the weasel's error?

from *Two-Minute Mysteries* and *More Two-Minute Mysteries* by Donald J. Sobel.
Reprinted by permission of Scholastic, Inc., copyright © 1967 and 1971.

READING

THE CASE OF DEATH AT SUNRISE

Inspector Winters raised the tattered window shade, letting morning light into the dingy room of Nick the Nose.

In the courtyard four stories below, policemen were gathered around the shattered body of a young woman.

"Let's hear it again," the inspector said to Nick.

Nick, who hadn't sold one of his phony tips to the police in months, shifted nervously.

"About sunrise I'm sitting in this chair reading the racing form," began the greasy little informer. "I got the insomnia, see? Suddenly I hear scuffling and I see Mrs. Clark. She lives right across the court on the fourth floor.

"Well, she's struggling with a man in a uniform. He gives her a shove toward the window, and whammy, out she goes!

"The first thing I think of is you—maybe you'll figure it's suicide instead of murder. So I run down to the drugstore to telephone you. I stayed with the body till we came up here, just to keep everything like it was for you."

Nick licked his lips. "I seen the killer's face. I figure I can identify him or at least tell you what kind of uniform he had on. That ought to be worth something."

"It is—this!" growled the inspector, delivering his foot to the seat of Nick's pants.

"Quite the appropriate payment," commented Haledjian when he heard of Nick's latest attempt at a payday.

Why did Nick get the boot instead of cash?

from *Two-Minute Mysteries* and *More Two-Minute Mysteries* by Donald J. Sobel.
Reprinted by permission of Scholastic, Inc., copyright © 1967 and 1971.

READING

THE CASE OF THE STOLEN BIBLE

Dr. Haledjian put the telephone receiver to his ear and heard the frantic voice of Ted Petrie, a rare-book collector.

"A thief took the hinges off the door of one of my book cabinets and made off with a 16th-century Bible," explained Petrie. "Can you come right over to my place?"

Half an hour later, Haledjian stood on the second floor of Petrie's home and examined the small, empty book cabinet. The glass door, unhinged, lay on the carpet.

"I was downstairs watching television," said Petrie. "I went to the kitchen for a bite to eat and suddenly a man dashed down the stairs and out the front door. He was carrying the Bible.

"Of course I chased him. At the corner of Vine and Davis lost him in the crowd watching the St. Patrick's Day parade. I stopped at the first pay telephone and called you.

"I always keep the cabinet locked. I expect the noise of the television kept me from hearing the thief at work upstairs."

"The Bible is insured?" asked Haledjian.

"Yes, for a fortune," answered Petrie. "But money can't replace such a book!"

"Then I suggest you put it back," said Haledjian. "I don't believe a word of your story! "

Why not?

from *Two-Minute Mysteries* and *More Two-Minute Mysteries* by Donald J. Sobel.
Reprinted by permission of Scholastic, Inc., copyright © 1967 and 1971.

ANSWERS TO MYSTERIES

THE CASE OF THE HITCHHIKER

The hitchhiker quickly confessed to being one of the hold-up gang, left behind to misdirect pursuit. His story was obviously phony, since he "broke off a piece" of chocolate. Standing for more than an hour in eighty-five-degree heat, as he claimed, the chocolate bar would have been soupy.

THE CASE OF THE LINCOLN LETTER

The two words, "national anthem."

While "The Star Spangled Banner" was the foremost patriotic song of Lincoln's day, it did not officially become our national anthem until 1931. During his presidency there was no national anthem.

THE CASE OF DEATH AT SUNRISE

The inspector surmised that Nick had discovered the body while entering the building and concocted the murder angle for a buck.

He couldn't have seen from the window of his room what he described. The shade was drawn, remember?

THE CASE OF THE STOLEN BIBLE

At the time he telephoned Haledjian, Petrie had no way of knowing exactly how the cabinet on the second floor had been opened.

from *Two-Minute Mysteries* and *More Two-Minute Mysteries* by Donald J. Sobel. Reprinted by permission of Scholastic, Inc., copyright © 1967 and 1971.

READING LOG

NAME _____ DATE _____

BEFORE READING

What is the topic? _____

_____

What do I know about the topic? _____

_____

What do I expect to find out about the topic? _____

_____

DURING READING

What do I want to remember and talk about later? _____

_____

AFTER READING

Did I find the answers to my questions? _____

_____

What didn't I find the answers to? _____

_____

What else did I learn that I didn't know? _____

_____

What was the most surprising or interesting thing I learned? _____

_____

What did I learn by doing this? _____

_____

NOT ENOUGH INFORMATION

KEEP TRACK OF WHY YOU DON'T HAVE ENOUGH INFORMATION

NAME _____ DATE _____

PAGE	WHO	WHAT	WHERE	WHEN	WHY	HOW

Lesson 10 Blackline Master 38

IT'S OK NOT TO KNOW

■ **LIST.**

1. Is it a word?

2. Is it my lack of background?

3. Is the sentence too long?

4. Was my concentration broken?

5. Do I need to go back and reread?

6. What is the author's purpose?

■ **KEEP TRACK OF WHY YOU DON'T KNOW.**

BOOK READ	PAGE	WHO	WHAT	WHERE	WHEN	WHY	HOW

THINKING GUIDE

CREATING MENTAL IMAGES TO KEEP MY MIND FOCUSED
WHEN I READ AND LISTEN

Listen carefully to the story being told to you or read it carefully yourself. Tie the sentences together in your mind to "see" what they mean.

Close your eyes and try to picture the story.

Picture yourself in the story.

or

Think about what you would do in the story.

Draw or remember the picture you have created in your mind when you need to remember what you heard or read.

THINKING GUIDE

BRAINSTORMING

STEP 1
All ideas are welcome.

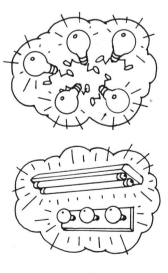

STEP 2
Give as many ideas as you can.

STEP 3
Add to one another's ideas.

STEP 4
Think of crazy and new ideas.

STEP 5
Combine all ideas until the best idea is created.

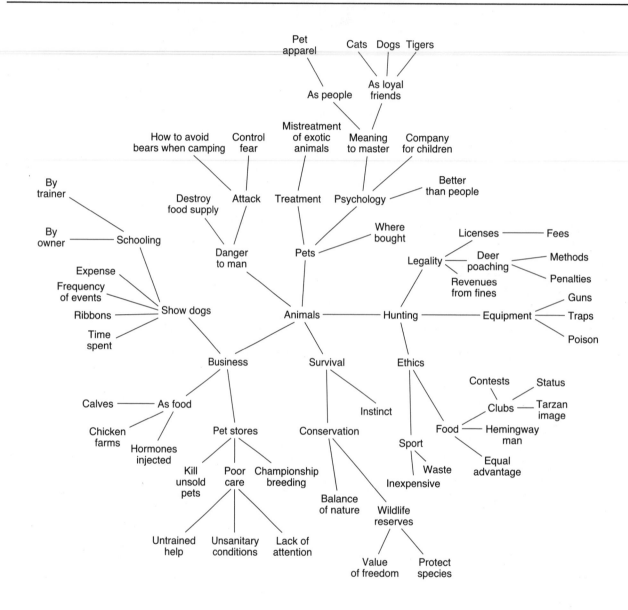

READING

LETTER FROM A BIRMINGHAM JAIL

■

MARTIN LUTHER KING, JR.

(King's letter is a response to a public statement signed by eight prominent white Birmingham clergymen. The letter appeared in Birmingham newspapers on April 12, 1963. It urges the demonstrators to cease their activities and observe the "principles of law and order and common sense.)

April 16, 1963

My Dear Fellow Clergymen:

While confined here in the Birmingham city jail, I came across your recent statement calling my present activities "unwise and untimely." Seldom do I pause to answer criticism of my work and ideas. If I sought to answer all the criticisms that cross my desk, my secretaries would have little time for anything other than such correspondence in the course of the day, and I would have no time for constructive work. But since I feel that you are men of genuine good will and that your criticisms are sincerely set forth, I want to try to answer your statement in what I hope will be patient and reasonable terms.

I think I should indicate why I am here in Birmingham, since you have been influenced by the view which argues against "outsiders coming in." I have the honor of serving as president of the Southern Christian Leadership Conference, an organization operating in every southern state, with headquarters in Atlanta, Georgia. We have some eighty-five affiliated organizations across the South, and one of them is the Alabama Christian Movement for Human Rights. Frequently we share staff, educational and financial resources with our affiliates. Several months ago the affiliate here in Birmingham asked us to be on call to engage in a nonviolent direct-action program if such were deemed necessary. We readily consented, and when the hour came we lived up to our promise. So I, along with several members of my staff, am here because I was invited here. I am here because I have organizational ties here.

But more basically, I am in Birmingham because injustice is here. Just as the prophets of the eighth century left their villages and carried their "thus saith the Lord" far beyond the boundaries of their home towns, and just as the Apostle Paul left his village of Tarsus and carried the gospel of Jesus Christ to the far corners of the Greco-Roman world, so am I compelled to carry the gospel of freedom beyond my own home town. Like Paul, I must constantly respond to the Macedonian call for aid.

Moreover, I am cognizant of the interrelatedness of all communities and states. I cannot sit idly by in Atlanta and not be concerned about what happens in Birmingham. Injustice anywhere is a threat to justice everywhere. We are caught in an inescapable network of mutuality, tied in a single garment of destiny. Whatever affects one directly, affects all indirectly. Never again can we afford to live with the narrow, provincial "outside agitator" idea. Anyone who lives inside the United States can never be considered an outsider anywhere within its bounds.

You deplore the demonstrations taking place in Birmingham. But your statement, I am sorry to say, fails to express a similar concern for the conditions that brought about the demonstrations. I am sure that none of you would want to rest content with the superficial kind of social analysis that deals merely with effects and does not grapple with underlying causes. It is unfortunate that demonstrations are taking place in Birmingham, but it is even more unfortunate that the city's white power structure left the Negro community with no alternative.

In any nonviolent campaign there are four basic steps: collection of the facts to determine whether injustices exist; negotiation; self-purification; and direct action. We have gone through all these steps in Birmingham. There can be no gain saying the fact that racial injustice engulfs this community. Birmingham is probably the most thoroughly segregated city in the United States. Its ugly record of brutality is widely known. Negroes have experienced grossly unjust treatment in the courts. There have been more unsolved bombings of Negro homes and churches in Birmingham than in any other city in the nation. These are the hard, brutal facts of the case. On the basis of these conditions, Negro leaders sought to negotiate with the city fathers. But the latter consistently refused to engage in good-faith negotiation.

Then, last September, came the opportunity to talk with leaders of Birmingham's economic community. In the course of the negotiations, certain promises were made by the merchants—for example, to remove the stores' humiliating racial signs. On the basis of these promises, the Reverend Fred Shuttlesworth and the leaders of the Alabama Christian Movement for Human Rights agreed to a moratorium on all demonstrations. As the weeks and months went by, we realized that we were the victims of a broken promise. A few signs, briefly removed, returned; the others remained.

As in so many past experiences, our hopes had been blasted, and the shadow of deep disappointment settled upon us. We had no alternative except to prepare for direct action, whereby we would present our very bodies as a means of laying our case before the conscience of the local and the national community. Mindful of the difficulties involved, we decided to undertake a process of self-purification. We began a series of workshops on nonviolence, and we repeatedly asked ourselves: "Are you able to accept blows without retaliating?" "Are you able to endure the ordeal of jail?" We decided to schedule our direct-action program for the Easter season, realizing that, except for Christmas, this is the main shopping period of the year. Knowing that a strong economic-withdrawal program would be the by-product of direct action, we felt that this would be the best time to bring pressure to bear on the merchants for the needed change. . . .

You may well ask: "Why direct action? Why sit-ins, marches and so forth? Isn't negotiation a better path?" You are quite right in calling for negotiation. Indeed, this is the very purpose of direct action. Nonviolent direct action seeks to create such a crisis and foster such a tension that a community which has constantly refused to negotiate is forced to confront the issue. It seeks so to dramatize the issue that it can no longer be ignored. My citing the creation of tension as part of the work of the nonviolent-resister may sound rather shocking. But I must confess that I am not afraid of the word "tension." I have earnestly opposed violent tension, but there is a type of constructive, nonviolent tension which is necessary for growth. Just as Socrates felt that it was necessary to create a tension in the minds so that individuals could rise from the bondage of myths and half-truths to the unfettered realm of creative analysis and objective appraisal, so must we see the need for nonviolent gadflies to create the kind of tension in society that will help men rise from the dark depths of prejudice and racism to the majestic heights of understanding and brotherhood.

The purpose of our direct-action program is to create a situation so crisis-packed that it will inevitably open the door to negotiation. I therefore concur with you in your call for negotiation. Too long has our beloved Southland been bogged down in a tragic effort to live in monologue rather than dialogue.

Letters to the Editor

Dear Editor:

Today, everybody is concerned about violence at school.

People used to think school was a safe place to let your kids go to learn. Think again.

Nowadays, kids everywhere are carrying guns and knives to school.

A lot of kids have been stabbed and shot because of violence at school. Not long ago, my cousin was shot in the back of his head at point blank range in an Irving school.

The pain his family had to go through was very sad. No family should ever have to go through this.

That is why I want something to be done about the violence going on at school. All schools should install metal detectors to deter the violence in our schools.

Erica Valderas
Rosemont Middle

Dear Editor:

I don't think there should be so much violence in the movies.

Kids should be able to go to the movies without seeing a lot of violence.

I also think there should be more kid movies.

Whitney Newton, 10
All Saints Episcopal

Dear Editor:

Even though I like it, rap music is pointless.

I like it because it's cool and energetic.

Most of the rappers have good voices, but some of the music is too noisy and pointless. I don't like the cursing either.

Diana Calvilla
Haltom Middle

Dear Editor:

The State Fair of Texas is a tradition in our family. My parents went every year after they were married and they even started taking me and my brother when we were still in strollers.

We don't miss a thing. My dad's favorites are the car exhibits; my mom likes crafts; and my brother and I like the food. It seems like we never stop eating.

We all look forward to this family outing. Try it with your family and I guarantee you'll have a great time. Don't forget, our State Fair is the best one in America.

James Walker
Monnig Middle

Q: I got a bad report card. My teacher asked me if I have good study habits. I'm not sure if I do or not. What are some good study habits anyway?

A: Planning: Try to plan to study the same time each day. This time should be before you get too tired and give you enough time to finish all of your assignments. Divide your time between your different subjects. Talk on the phone, watch TV and be with your friends at a time other than your study time.

Location: Be sure to pick a "study spot" that has good light

IF LIFE IS A BOWL OF CHERRIES, HOW DO YOU HANDLE THE PITS?

and a comfortable temperature. If you must have noise, be sure the volume is very low.

Preparation: Take good notes in class and review often to avoid cramming for a test. It may help to take reading notes when an assignment requires answering study questions. Keep study materials neatly organized.

Breaks: Some students find it helpful to take breaks during their study time to eat a snack and move around. Others find it helpful to study with a friend, parent or tutor. These are just a few tips. I hope you will be writing soon to say your grades have improved!

Good Luck!

Have a problem? Need some advice? Call or write to us…

from "Class Acts," *Fort Worth Star Telegram*, October 19, 1993, Section F, page 2

SHOWBIZ

MOVIES   MUSIC   TELEVISION   TOP SINGLES   VIDEOS   FUN

Movies

RUDY

What's it about? Sean Astin is Rudy Ruettiger, a small, self-driven schoolboy who works against all odds to achieve his dream: To become a member of the Notre Dame football team.

Is it worth seeing? Sean Astin is always engaging and the story avoids most sports pictures' play-by-play adherence to formula. Terrific supporting players Ned Beatty and Charles S. Dutton should also make it worth checking out.

Does it earn its rating? The PG is for mature subject matter and some profanity.

THE BEVERLY HILLBILLIES

What's it about? More movie ideas from re-run land…can *Gilligan's Island: The Movie* be far off? This time its TV's richest hicks, the Clampetts, a backwards Ozark family turned billionaires, relocate to California when oil is discovered on their property. The film pits the wealthy yokels against a pair of shady bank underlings out to cheat the Clampetts out of their fortune.

Is it worth seeing? Well, sort of. Lily Tomlin alone is worth the price of admission as the lovelorn, ever dependable Miss Hathaway. Cloris Leachman is Granny to a "T" and Jim Varney gives a pleasant, understated reading of Jed, but the whole thing is so darn silly. Kids would get a kick out of the slapstick if it weren't for a bunch of unnecessary vulgarities sprinkled throughout.

Does it earn its rating? The PG is pretty loose considering the wealth of vulgar gags and rude gestures. There's some violence for comic effects and some adult subject matter, so the younger crowd should steer clear.

Todd Camp's 1-10 rating: 5

from "Class Acts," *Fort Worth Star Telegram*, October 19, 1993, Section F, page 2

TOP MOVIES

1 *Demolition Man,* $10 million, Rated R

2 *The Beverly Hillbillies,* $8.6 million, Rated PG

3 *Cool Runnings,* $7.2 million, Rated PG

4 *Malice,* $5.5 million, Rated R

5 *Judgment Night,* $4 million, Rated R

6 *The Good Son,* $3.3 million, Rated R

7 *The Joy Luck Club,* $3 million, Rated R

8 *The Age of Innocence,* $2.7 million, Rated PG

9 *Mr. Jones,* $1.8 million, Rated R

10 *A Bronx Tale,* $1.7 million, Rated R

SOURCE: The Associated Press

© Addison-Wesley Publishing Company, Inc.

174   Lesson 12 Blackline Master 46

SPORTS

PROFESSIONAL   COLLEGE   HIGH SCHOOL   PERSONALITIES

Michael Jordan

BASKETBALL STAR LEAVES THE COURT

Michael Jordan's sudden retirement from basketball left many people, especially young fans, stunned and speechless.

Michael, 30, announced last week that he was stepping away from the Chicago Bulls after nine years. He has won three National Basketball Association championships, two Olympic gold medals, several scoring titles and many other awards.

But the superstar said he has lost his drive.

"It's not because I don't love the game," he said at a news conference. "I love the game of basketball. I always will. I just feel that at this particular time in my career, I've reached the pinnacle. It's time for me to move away."

Recent times have been tough for Michael. He has been pounded by negative publicity because of gambling. His father, James, was murdered this summer. Two teens have been charged in his death.

Michael has many supporters among North Texas students. He is an idol to many people, and young players have tried to model their game after his.

"I thought it was surprising. I'm going to miss him,"

said John Mentzer, third-grader at Pope Elementary. "I love the way he played, but I thought it was time to retire since his dad died."

Although many youths see the reasoning behind his decision, they don't understand it.

"I don't think he should let two 18-year-old kids run his life," said Craig Keaton, Shackelford Junior High freshman. "I think he should have had a career year for his dad (rather than retiring)."

To many sports critics, Michael was considered the best to have ever played the game. Pro basketball fans around the world miss him.

—Chris Mycoskie
Shackelford Junior High

from "Class Acts," *Fort Worth Star Telegram,* October 19, 1993, Section F, page 5

© Addison-Wesley Publishing Company, Inc.

REVIEWS

TV Notes

AFTERSCHOOL FUN

Now that school's back in full swing, the *Schoolbreak Special* returns with more series that tackle issues affecting the youth of today. The newest special, *Other Mothers*, airs at 4 p.m. Tuesday, Oct. 2, on CBS (KDFW/Channel 4)

Justin Whalin, Meredith Baxter and Joanna Cassidy star in this one-hour drama about a boy who must come to grips with being in a new school and the opinions of his peers and teachers when they find out his parents are lesbians.

FREE YOUR MIND

MTV explores the state of many social problems in our nation. The *Free Your Mind Forum* airs at 9 p.m. Wednesday, Oct. 13.

MTV News correspondent Tabitha Soren hosts this discussion about the racial, religious and sexual discrimination that continues to plague our society.

BASEBALL FRIDAY

As the road to the World Series continues, several networks are devoting time on Friday, Oct. 15, to programs about that great American pastime.

Baseball Relief: An All-Star Salute airs at 8 p.m. on Fox (KDAF/Channel 33). This first ever baseball-themed comedy/variety special features appearances by Sharon Stone, Jerry Seinfeld, Dennis Miller, Boyz II Men, Rita Rudner, Willie Mays and Michael Richards in a benefit for the Comic Relief's Pediatric Care Program for Homeless Children.

When It Was A Game airs at 8 p.m. on PBS (KERA/Channel 13).

Baseball legend Mickey Mantle reflects on his life and career in *Mickey Mantle: The American Dream Comes To Life*, which airs at 9:30 p.m. on Channel 13. This 1988 biography looks at Mantle's life on and off the field with game footage and memorabilia.

—JENNIFER LAND
Class Acts Correspondent

CHOOSING A CAT

Many kids are overjoyed when they find a stray kitten.

The cat may be the perfect pet—but then again maybe not.

Certain breeds of cats do not make great pets for families, according to Harper's Illustrated Handbook of Cats, by Dr. Robert W. Kirk, a New York veterinarian.

Cat breeds have specific temperaments, Kirk indicates. He recommends adopting an adult cat rather than a kitten because its

personality is already established.

Many people judge a cat by appearance, but the personality determines how well it shares the families' home and lifestyle. Almost all kittens are cute, active and sociable. Without knowing its background, the kitten could grow up to be nervous, shy, indifferent or aggressive, Kirk warns.

from "Class Acts," *Fort Worth Star Telegram*, October 19, 1993, Section F, pages 3 and 4

THINKING GUIDE

WORKING COOPERATIVELY IN GROUPS

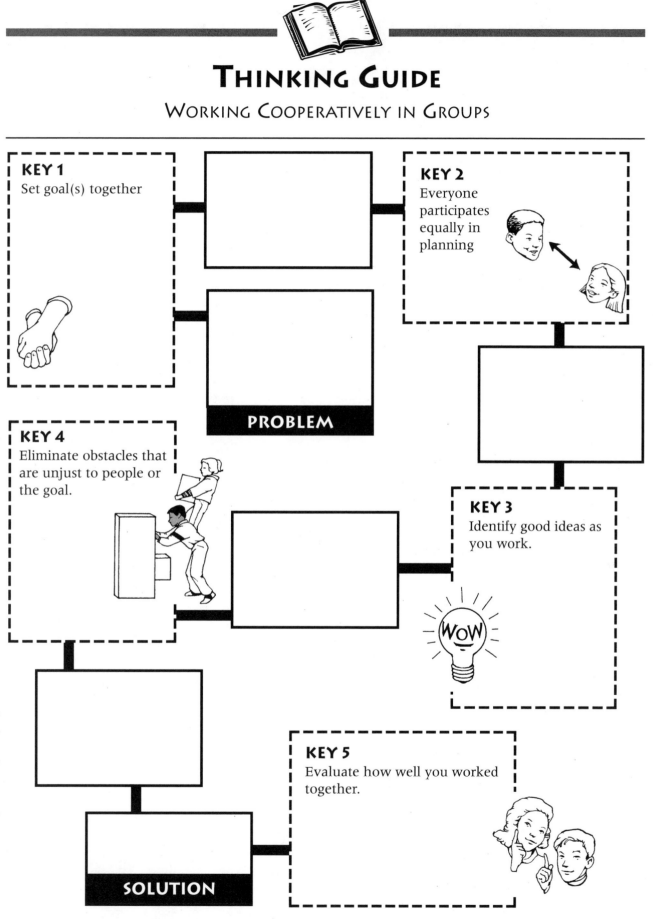

KEY 1
Set goal(s) together

KEY 2
Everyone participates equally in planning

PROBLEM

KEY 4
Eliminate obstacles that are unjust to people or the goal.

KEY 3
Identify good ideas as you work.

WoW

KEY 5
Evaluate how well you worked together.

SOLUTION

READING

IF I WERE IN CHARGE OF THE WORLD

BY MARGO A. HARABAR

GRADE 4, SUNNYSIDE SCHOOL, PITTSBURGH, PENNSYLVANIA

If I were in charge of the world

I would make sure everyone had a home.

I'd made sure everyone had food and clothing.

Everyone would go to school to learn

If I were in charge of the world.

Everyone would be healthy.

I would make sure everyone was happy where they lived.

If I was in charge of the world

I would make sure there was peace and love.

WHY DO I SIT HERE ALL ALONE?

BY LESLIE SANDERS

GRADE 4, FRANKLIN PUBLIC SCHOOLS, FRANKLIN, TENNESEE

Why do I sit here all

alone?

While all the girls play.

They like to sing, dance,

and swing.

Oh, why do I sit here

all alone?

READING

CHRISTMAS EVE

BY GREGORY M. SAVRAN
GRADE 5, PORT WASHINGTON SCHOOL DISTRICT, PORT WASHINGTON, NY

A young girl looks out a church window for Santa,

Focuses her eyes on the stars in the night sky.

The stars are glistening and dancing in the moonlight.

She pictures an old barn,

Children are playing.

Everything is as it had been.

She stares at the stars.

Slowly stars start to fall one by one.

Turning into snowflakes,

Drifting down to the ground,

Meeting their friends. She looks at the snowflakes,

Like baby stars,

Sung Christmas lullabyes,

By angels formed from the clouds in the night sky.

She looks away and back.

It is Christmas night,

Anything is possible on Christmas.

DAILY EVALUATION

GROUP NAME _____ DATE _____

GROUP MEMBERS _____

CONTENT GOALS ACHIEVED	GROUP WORK SKILLS DEMONSTRATED
DAY 1	DAY 1
DAY 2	DAY 2
DAY 3	DAY 3
DAY 4	DAY 4
DAY 5	DAY 5

Lesson 13 Blackline Master 52

RULES TO HELP US WORK TOGETHER IN GROUPS

GROUP NAME

 Group Goals

 Everyone participates

 Everyone has good ideas

 What we did best

 Problems we had

IDEAS OF TYPES OF MATERIALS THAT CAN BE USED IN PUPPETS

Stick Puppets

Finger Puppets

Rod Puppets

Hand Puppets

Sock Puppet

Styrofoam Puppet

Paper Plate Puppet

Finger Puppet (with tabs)

Finger Puppet (from glove finger)

Cloth Puppet

Stick Puppet

Paper Bag Puppet

Cylinder Puppet

Humanettes

from Block, C.C. (1993). *Teaching the Language Arts*. Boston, MA: Allyn & Bacon, p. 360.

THINKING GUIDE

TAKING RESPONSIBILITY

TO GET WORK DONE AND NOT PUT IT OFF

Set a deadline. You may want it to be ahead of schedule.

Break the task into parts and do similar parts together.

Select an easy part of a difficult task to do first so you can begin without procrastinating.

Reward yourself when you have finished.

Get up early to give yourself more time.

When there is a choice, sign up to be first.

Remove yourself from distractions. Put yourself in an environment that makes it easy to study and learn.

WHEN SOMETHING GOES WRONG OR HURTS SOMEONE

Say "I'm sorry. I should have told you when you asked."

I realize now that I could have helped by taking some responsibility sooner.

I'm responsible!

I can help by taking some responsibility sooner.

I can recognize what needs to be done.

I can work out a plan of action.

We wish to thank Ms. Juliana Glover and Ms. Margaret Cupaiolli for their assistance on the design of the field-test version of this lesson.

READING

THE TORTOISE AND THE HARE

There once was a hare who was unkind to a tortoise, ran very fast, and was a show-off. He made fun of the poor tortoise's slow pace, and tortoise tried not to listen to the hare.

One day the tortoise got tired of being teased. "I'm going to put a stop to this teasing," he thought. He said to the hare, "Let's have a race."

The hare was surprised. He replied, "That's silly, because I can run much faster than you." Still the hare agreed to the race because the other animals were listening.

All the animals set the course for the race and elected the fox to be the judge. The fox said, "On your mark, get set, go!" Immediately, the hare sped off. The tortoise slowly plodded along. He did not hurry but kept right on moving. The hare decided that he was so far ahead he could take it easy. He lay down in some tall grass and fell asleep. The tortoise passed the sleeping hare on his way to the finish line. Suddenly, the surprised hare awoke with a start when he heard clapping and cheers. Because of his slow and steady pace, the tortoise had won the race. The tortoise used one of the steps in taking responsibility to "get the job done right!"

MORAL: SLOW AND STEADY WINS THE RACE.

READING

THE GARDENER AND HIS DOG

One hot summer day a gardener went to get water from the well. His little dog went with him. The dog barked and jumped up and down to try to see what was in the well. As the gardener was watering his plants, he heard a loud splash. His dog was gone. The dog had fallen into the well.

The gardener quickly went down into the well to save his dog. Just as he came to the top again, however, the dog bit his hand.

The man was surprised and angry. He said, "Why did you do that? Is that how you say thanks? I feed you and treat you kindly. If this is how you act, then pull yourself out of the well." Then he dropped the dog right back into the well.

MORAL: DON'T BITE THE HAND THAT FEEDS YOU.

READING

THE FOX AND THE CAT

One day a fox and a cat were talking about clever ways to keep from harm. "Why, I have a bag of more than one hundred tricks for escaping from my enemies," boasted the fox.

"I have only one way," said the cat, " but it always works!"

Just at that moment they heard the cry of a pack of hounds. The cat quickly climbed a tree and hid herself in the branches. "This is the way I escape!" she said. "What are you going to do?"

The fox thought one way and then another. As he tried to decide, the barking became louder. The dogs kept coming nearer and nearer and they surrounded the fox. He was easily killed by the huntsmen.

MORAL: ONE SURE PLAN IS BETTER THAN A HUNDRED ON WHICH YOU CANNOT DEPEND.

READING

THE LAZY LION
BY MICHELLE HERRING

Once there was a very lazy lion. He went to Forestville Elementary School. One day his teacher, Mrs. Bear, assigned a book report. The lion did not like book reports, but he had to do it or his mother would be angry with him. So the lazy lion went home and started working. After he had worked for about ten minutes, he got a phone call from his friend the tiger. "Hi, Lion. Can you come over and stay the weekend?" said the tiger. "I don't know," said the lion. "I will go ask my mom." So the lion went to ask his mom. "Mom, can I spend the weekend at Tiger's house?" asked the lion. "Well . . . yes, but you have to work on your book report while you're there," said his mother. The lazy lion did not want to, but he said, "OK," and rushed off to his friend's house.

That weekend the lazy lion and his friend, the tiger, had so much fun that the lion forgot all about his book report. Before he knew it, Monday came and the teacher was collecting the reports. The lion did not have his, so the teacher called his mom. When the lion got home, his mother was very angry. "You will not be able to go to visit your friends for two weeks," said the lion's mother. " I am very sorry," said the lion. "I will never do that again."

MORAL: SET YOURSELF AWAY FROM DISTRACTIONS AND ALWAYS DO YOUR WORK FIRST, THEN REWARD YOURSELF BY PLAYING.

• •

THE DOG AND THE REPORT
BY ASHLEY KIRCHNER

Once there was a dog that was told he had to do a report on a person that he didn't want to do a report on. His teacher told him that he had to do that person because he took so long trying to figure out which person he wanted, so she just assigned him one. He went home to his mother and said, "Mom, will you help me with my report because my teacher said I took too long deciding, so she gave me one I didn't want." The dog's mom said, "No, because you took so long." So he ended up doing a report that he didn't want to do.

MORAL: WHEN THERE IS A CHOICE TO SIGN UP, BE THE FIRST.

TAKING RESPONSIBILITY IN GROUPS

DATE _____

NAME _____

In the first chart, list ten items that would show that you are taking responsibility as you work in a group. Then read the list of items in the second chart and write an idea from the Thinking Guide that could change each of these negative actions to a positive one.

TAKING RESPONSIBILITY IN GROUP WORK

Looks Like:	Sounds Like:

NOT TAKING RESPONSIBILITY IN GROUP WORK

Looks Like:	Sounds Like:
leaves group	interrupt others
scribbles bare minimum	"She's copying."
taps on desk or watches other groups	"I didn't know it was due."
waves hand to give funny and wrong answer	jokes to get group off-track
is late or misses meetings	"Do I have to?"

THINKING GUIDE

SETTING GOALS

NAME _____ DATE _____

Goal _____

WRITE IT DOWN!

PLAN OF ACTION:

1 _____

2 _____

3 _____

How you will know when you reach your goal:

_____

_____

Picture how you will feel:

When?   calendar

ASSESSMENT INSTRUCTIONS

The assessment instruments for *Reason to Read*, Volume One, are divided into three types. Five assessments evaluate students' self-initiated use and integration of thinking strategies into their daily lives and language-arts activities. Eleven performance assessments are related to the reading and language-arts competencies in the program. A variety of other performance assessments determine how well students can initiate individual strategies at appropriate times in their lives and in school-related tasks.

A description of these assessment instruments follows.

ASSESSMENTS OF THINKING STRATEGIES

The following five assessments evaluate students' application of the thinking strategies in this program.

The Class Monitoring Record (Blackline Master 62) assesses the degree to which students achieve the objectives in each lesson. Student names are written at the top of this evaluation form. In the space that intersects with a student's name and the strategy printed in the left-hand column, one of the following symbols is written to describe that student's achievement level relative to that strategy. The Class Monitoring Record is designed to be used at the end of each lesson. It can also be updated at the end of the year by recording times when students demonstrated a prompted or self-initiated use of the strategies at some point during the school year.

SI/[date]: If a student demonstrates use of the strategy through his or her own self-iniation, you will record "SI" (self-initated use) and the date the strategy was first used without your prompting.

P/[date]: If a student demonstrates use of the strategy after you prompt him or her to do so, or if a student employs the strategy effectively during the lesson, you will record "P" (prompted use) and the date the strategy was first employed effectively when prompted to do so.

Blank: When a space is left blank, it indicates that a student has not yet demonstrated effective use of the strategy.

Running Record of Language Arts and Thinking Strategies (Blackline Master 63) is designed as a self-evaluation. It encourages student reflection. After each lesson students describe a time when they will use the strategies without being asked to use them. In addition, some teachers return the Running Record at the end of the year. Students use this instrument to determine how often they self-initated each strategy.

Journal Writing Assessment: Student Self-Evaluation (Blackline Master 64) can be used in one-to-one student conferences and in lessons in which writing projects are completed. With this form students evaluate their writing abilities and thinking according to four criteria.

Journal Writing Assessment: Teacher Evaluation (Blackline Master 65) is designed as a grading scale for student writings. After 12 writing samples have been collected, you assess each entry by four criteria. Individual assessments can be combined to identify specific improvements students have made during the grading period.

Conference Log (Blackline Master 66) can be used to record information gained in conferences with individual students. This form is unique in that students also record the insights they gained during the conference. While you meet, you and the student can complete the form together. The Conference Log enables you to list topics discussed, goals established, future teaching needs, written work assessed, and anecdotal records.

ASSESSMENTS OF READING AND LANGUAGE ARTS COMPETENCIES

The following assessments enable students to demonstrate how much they have increased their reading, writing, speaking, and listening abilities as a result of this program.

Genres Introduced in *Reason to Read* (Blackline Master 67) reinforces students' knowledge of literary genres. Students either define each genre and give examples that they have read from each or write the titles from each genre they read during this program. This assessment can also be used as a reference tool if you ask students to write about the knowledge they gained and appreciations they have for various genres.

Attitude/Interest Inventory (Blackline Master 68) can be used as a pre- and postassessment. Pretest scores will provide individual and collective baseline data about students. Posttest scores will indicate changes in students' attitudes toward reading during the period in which this program was used. This instrument will also detect changes in students' reading interests.

The Reading Wheel (Blackline Masters 69 and 70) is a book-record form whereby students list all books they read in a year. Alternatively, students can use this instrument to record what they have learned and appreciated about each genre.

Oral-Language Needs Monitor (Blackline Master 71) assesses 12 dimensions of effective speaking abilities in this program. Students assess their own abilities and state new goals they have in each dimension.

Speech Critique (Blackline Master 72) can be used by classmates to assess peers' oral presentations during lessons in this program. This assessment enables students to analyze 18 qualities in oral presentations and to write specific strengths they noticed. Students also suggest an improvement and method to accomplish that improvement.

Informal Checklist for Usage (Blackline Master 73) assists students who experience difficulties in expressing themselves orally. You can complete this instrument at two points in the school year and compare the first to the second to note improvements. The second assessment occurs after students have used strategies in this program to implement a plan of action to correct their specific problems. After you complete the assessments, discuss them with individual students during conferences.

Story Map (Blackline Master 74) assesses students' recognition of story grammar. It can also be used as a guide when students create their own stories orally or in writing.

Editing Checklist (Blackline Master 75) enables students to evaluate writings of their own or their peers. The assessment enables students to use markings that professional editors use and to isolate eight conventions that could interfere with written messages.

Writing Overview (Blackline Master 76) can be used as an individual student or whole-class record form. If used as an individual student assessment document, each student would receive a copy. On the rows at the top of the form students write the titles of individual writings they complete in *Reason to Read*. In the row that reflects each title, students place a checkmark in the column that best reports the level of competence displayed in organization, meaning, conventions, thought quality, word selection, and story structure. After several writings have been evaluated, this form enables students to identify strategies that would improve their writings.

Alternatively, if used as a whole-class record form, student names are written across the rows at the top of the evaluation. Students' writings are evaluated on the same criteria as above. After a writing sample from each student has been assessed, instructional groups can be formed to eliminate student needs.

Clues to Improving Handwriting (Blackline Master 77) assesses students' handwriting. Individual students can also use the assessment to develop an individual plan of action to improve their handwriting.

ASSESSMENTS OF SELF-INITIATED APPLICATION OF THINKING STRATEGIES

The following assessments enable you and students to judge the degree to which individual thinking strategies in *Reason to Read* are applied in students' everyday lives.

Assessing Thinking Abilities (Blackline Master 78) is designed to assess the ways in which students have used the strategies in this program in their lives. On this form, students can either write the names of one or two strategies they learned within each category of thinking ability or write the title of a written or oral presentation where they have used or will have used a specific strategy.

Student Self-Assessment of Thinking Abilities (Blackline Master 79) is used as a student self-assessment form. Students identify specific incidents in which they have used 20 strategies from *Reason to Read*. Space is also provided for students to select strategies they want to improve in the coming weeks.

Student Self-Assessment of Cooperative Groups (Blackline Master 80) enables students to evaluate how well they work cooperatively in groups and how well they use the strategies in this program to advance group goals.

Student Self-Assessment for Group Work During Consensus Building (Blackline Master 81) assesses students' use of eight strategies for consensus building.

Problem-Solving Assessment (Blackline Master 82) can be used as a question to which students write a response. Answers should evidence that students employ several strategies from this program when they solve problems.

Associative Word Test of Creative Thinking (Blackline Master 83) is designed to assess students' growth in creative thinking strategies. It can be used as a pre- and posttest to identify increases in students' creativity as a result of their use of the strategies within this program.

Portfolio Assessment (Blackline Master 84) lists criteria that can be used to evaluate students' increased thinking abilities as evidenced in the portfolios they create.

CLASS MONITORING RECORD

CLASS _____

DATE _____

NAME

- Asking questions while reading, thinking, and listening
- Comparing and contrasting (after asking questions) to overcome confusion
- Recognizing patterns to increase retention
- Understanding different points of view
- Eliminating propaganda before making a decision
- Making decisions by recognizing facts, opinions, and reasoned judgments
- Solving problems using PSP
- Solving small problems independently
- Recognizing strengths and weaknesses
- Monitoring understanding and increasing comprehension
- Creating mental images to stay focused
- Brainstorming to become more creative
- Working cooperatively in groups
- Gaining confidence and becoming more responsible
- Setting achievable goals

Assessment Blackline Master 62

RUNNING RECORD OF LANGUAGE ARTS AND THINKING STRATEGIES

NAME _____

Directions: On the line after the title of the lesson you just finished, describe a time when you used or will use the strategy without having to be told to use it.

1   Asking Questions While Reading, Thinking, and Listening _____

2   Comparing and Contrasting (After Asking Questions) to Overcome Confusion _____

    _____

3   Recognizing Patterns to Increase Retention _____

4   Understanding Different Points of View _____

5   Eliminating Propaganda Before Making a Decision _____

6   Making Decisions by Recognizing Facts, Opinions, and Reasoned Judgments _____

    _____

7   Solving Problems Using PSP _____

8   Solving Small Problems Independently _____

9   Recognizing Strengths and Weaknesses _____

10 Monitoring Understanding and Increasing Comprehension _____

11 Creating Mental Images to Stay Focused _____

12 Brainstorming to Become More Creative _____

13 Working Cooperatively in Groups _____

14 Gaining Confidence and Becoming More Responsible _____

15 Setting Achievable Goals _____

JOURNAL WRITING ASSESSMENT
STUDENT SELF-EVALUATION[1]

NAME _____ DATE _____

1. Name four ways you have improved the quality of your thinking and writing in journal entries.

_____

_____

_____

_____

2. List four ways you have used thoughts about the material you read recently in your journal entries during the last few weeks.

_____

_____

_____

_____

3. How have you used new thinking strategies to better express your opinions, emotions, ideas, and experiences in your journal entries during the last few weeks?

_____

_____

_____

4. Have you reached the goals we set during our last conference? How do you know that you did or didn't reach the goals we set? _____

_____

_____

_____

[1]Created in consultation with Brandt, C., Gore, L., Hatfield, S., Moore, S., and Oglesby, K., Texas Christian University, Fort Worth, Texas.

Journal Writing Assessment
Teacher Evaluation[1]

NAME _____ **DATE** _____

A. QUANTITY:

12 journal entries (2 per week) required each 6 weeks with clear and understandable ideas.

Possible score of 12 (1 point per entry).   _____

B. USE OF WRITING FORMAT:

Mechanics (punctuation and spelling) and use of sentence formation (correct grammar and variety of sentence types). For each of the 12 entries, if mechanics and sentence formation are above the class average or above the student's last level of capability, student receives one point.

Possible score of 12 points (1 point per entry).   _____

C. QUALITY:

a) Writing evidences of use of strategies taught.

b) Organization has a special flair.

c) Quality and richness of language: word selection is evocative, precise, and/or vivid.

d) Story structure is smooth, effective, and/or captivating.

e) Writing uses examples or expressions of the student's own opinions, emotions, ideas, and experiences as specific examples or to support reasoned judgments.

(Possible score is 1 point per entry for each of the five dimensions of quality.   _____
Possible total score of 60.)

D. RESPONSES TO SELF-EVALUATION:

Student receives 1 point for answering accurately each of the four sections of the *Journal Writing Assessment: Student Self-Evaluation* form.

(Possible score is 1 point per section for accuracy in self-report and 1 point for improvement in ability to self-assess. Possible score is 8: 2 points per each of the four sections on the *Journal Writing Assessment: Student Self-Evaluation* form.)

                                                    TOTAL _____

TEACHER COMMENTS: (Set goals for next journal writing assignment period.)

_____

_____

[1]Created in consultation with Brandt, C., Gore, L., Hatfield, S., Moore, S., and Oglesby, K., Texas Christian University, Fort Worth, Texas.

Conference Log

NAME _____

DATE _____

CONFERENCE TOPICS

1
2
3
4
5
6

GOALS ESTABLISHED FOR NEXT CONFERENCE

1
2
3
4
5
6

SMALL TEACHING GROUPS NEEDED

1
2
3
4
5
6

WRITTEN WORK CHECKED AND NEW GOALS FOR NEXT CONFERENCE

1
2
3
4
5
6

TEACHER COMMENTS AND INSIGHTS

1
2
3
4
5
6

STUDENT COMMENTS AND INSIGHTS

1
2
3
4
5
6

GENRES INTRODUCED IN <u>REASON TO READ</u>

NARRATIVE

GENRES: FICTION

Short Stories _____

Drama _____

Historical Fiction _____

Science Fiction _____

Realistic Fiction _____

Folk Literature _____

Myths _____

Fables _____

Mysteries _____

Sports Stories _____

EXPOSITORY

GENRES: NONFICTION

Contemporary and Historical Nonfiction _____

Articles _____

Book Reviews _____

Proverbs _____

Essays _____

Editorials _____

Informational Texts _____

Reference Books _____

Biographies and Autobiographies _____

Current Event Periodicals _____

Hobby Books and How-To Books _____

Sports Stories _____

POETIC

GENRES: POETRY

Sonnets _____

Pastoral Poems _____

Blank Verse _____

Lyric Poems _____

Free Verse _____

Narrative Poems _____

ATTITUDE/INTEREST INVENTORY

NAME _____ **DATE** _____

1. Does anyone read to you at home? How often?_____

2. Do you like reading by yourself?_____

3. Finish this sentence: "When I read, I feel . . ."_____

4. Make up a title for what would be the most exciting book you have ever read. _____

_____

5. Name your favorite book or story. What makes it your favorite? _____

6. Do you have a hero or favorite person? Who is it and why do you admire this person? _____

_____

7. What do you want to do or be when you grow up? _____

8. If you could live anywhere in the world, where would it be? _____

9. Is reading important to you? Why or why not? _____

10. What kind of stories make you feel bored? _____

11. Tell about a favorite story you've written. _____

12. Which types of stories do you like to read?

Historical Fiction	1	2	3	4
Animal Stories	1	2	3	4
Mysteries	1	2	3	4
Newspapers	1	2	3	4
Sports Stories	1	2	3	4
Science Fiction	1	2	3	4
Fairy Tales, Fables	1	2	3	4
Poetry	1	2	3	4
Humorous Stories	1	2	3	4
Biographies	1	2	3	4

> **1 = a lot**
> **2 = sometimes**
> **3 = not usually**
> **4 = never**

Additional comments about your reading abilities and interests (Use the back of this paper.):

Created by Ms. Sara Falstad, graduate student, TCU

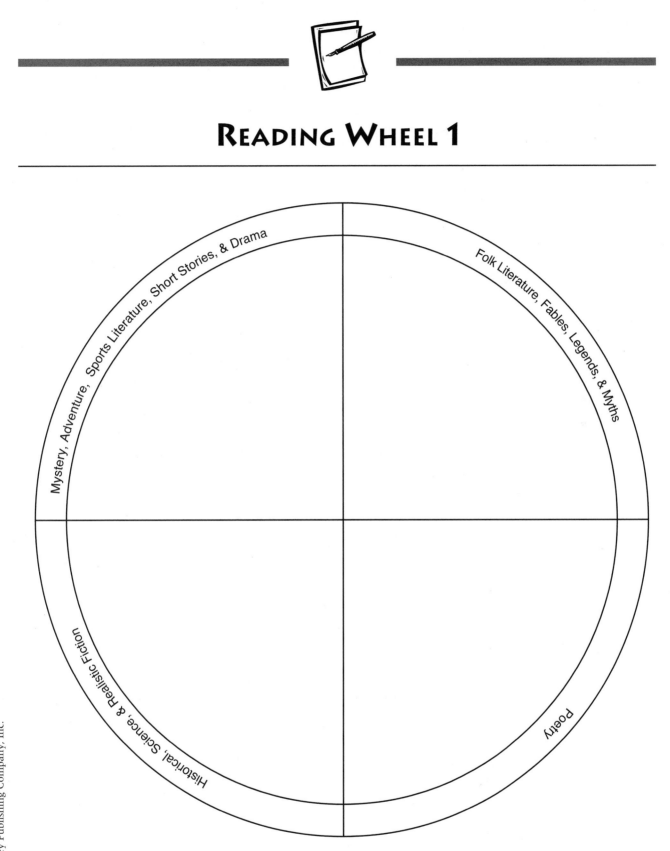

Mystery, Adventure, Sports Literature, Short Stories, & Drama

Folk Literature, Fables, Legends, & Myths

Historical, Science, & Realistic Fiction

Poetry

READING WHEEL 2

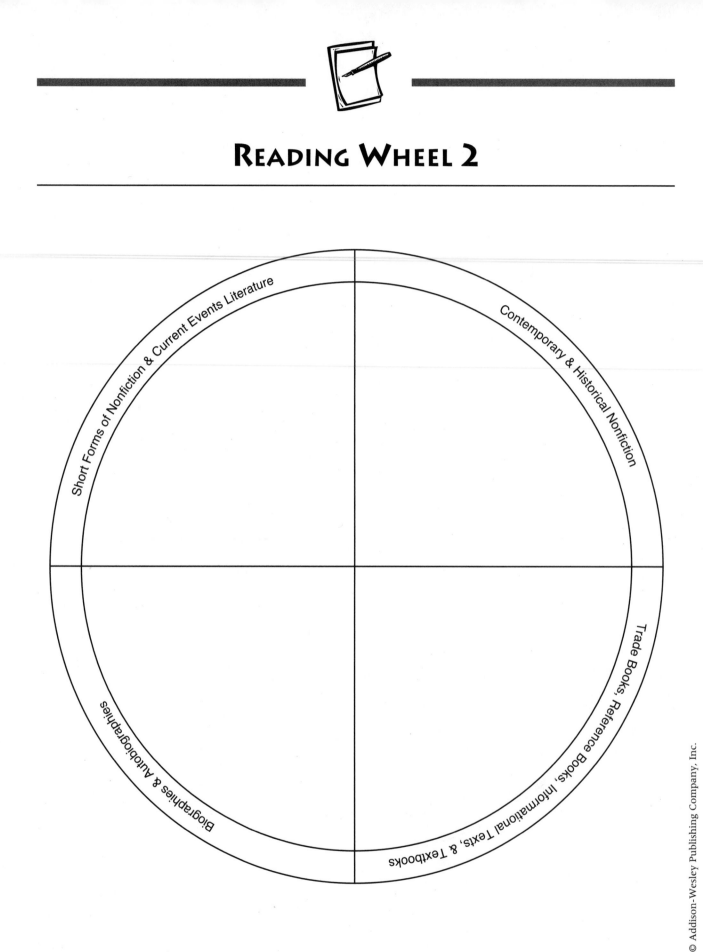

Short Forms of Nonfiction & Current Events Literature

Contemporary & Historical Nonfiction

Trade Books, Reference Books, Informational Texts, & Textbooks

Biographies & Autobiographies

ORAL-LANGUAGE NEEDS MONITOR

NAME _____ **DATE** _____

Directions: In the blank before each number write today's date if you think you do that item well. If you know a way you want to improve on an item, leave the blank before the item empty and describe what you want to improve on the line after that item. Later in the year, when you have improved that ability, write the date when you achieve this goal in the blank.

_____ 1. Pronounce words well: recognize and correct substitutions ("w" for "v"), omissions ("member" for "remember"), insertions, and distortions _____

_____

_____ 2. Use good pitch and tone of speaking. _____

_____ 3. Give reasoned judgments, support my opinions, and speak concisely and effectively.

_____

_____ 4. Use appropriate speed. _____

_____ 5. Use adequate volume. _____

_____ 6. Do not use crutch words. _____

_____ 7. Extend small-group discussions without coaxing. _____

_____ 8. Check for accuracy of spoken statements. _____

_____ 9. Ask questions for clarification. _____

_____ 10. State novel but probable points. _____

_____ 11. Give solutions or compromises for conflicting data. _____

_____ 12. Do not let dialect interfere with meaning. _____

SPEECH CRITIQUE

NAME _____ DATE _____

Place a check in each blank that describes the speech.

❐ Spoke loud enough.

❐ Spoke slow enough.

❐ Looked at audience.

❐ Related enough details to keep interest but not too many.

❐ Appeared to be relaxed.

❐ Appeared to have confidence and to know the subject.

❐ Presented good introduction that made me want to listen.

❐ Presented good closing that helped me remember the main points.

❐ Did not read notecards.

❐ Had practiced the speech enough and had good expression.

❐ Tone of voice was good.

❐ Voice was easy to listen to.

❐ Didn't have nervous gestures, such as using hands in distracting ways or repeating a word or phrase over and over ("uh," "O.K.,"

"Do you understand?" and so on)

❐ Speech met its purpose of informing, persuading, or entertaining.

❐ Speaker seemed to have a special style or talent in giving speeches and that special talent was _____.

❐ Speech was just the right length.

❐ Speech was well organized and the speaker stuck to the important points.

❐ Voice was clear and strong.

Strengths and special qualities of the speaker:

Suggested Improvements:

Suggested methods of improvement:

_____
Student's Signature

© Addison-Wesley Publishing Company, Inc.

Assessment Blackline Master 72

INFORMAL CHECKLIST FOR USAGE

NAME _____   DATE _____

	CORRECT	INCORRECT	SOMETIMES CORRECT
1. Understands there is more than one level of appropriate usage.	☐	☐	☐
2. Is able to change level of spoken usage according to occasion, audience, and purpose.	☐	☐	☐
3. Is able to change level of written usage according to occasion, audience, and purpose.	☐	☐	☐
4. Has eliminated baby talk.	☐	☐	☐
5. Uses correct form of *I, me, he, him, she, they, them.*	☐	☐	☐
6. Uses correct form of *is, are, was, were.*	☐	☐	☐
7. Uses correct past tense of irregular verbs.	☐	☐	
8. Uses correct past participle.	☐	☐	☐
9. Does not use double negatives.	☐	☐	☐
10. Does not use *ain't, hisn, hern,* etc.	☐	☐	☐
11. Uses correct possessive pronoun.	☐	☐	☐
12. Uses *it's* and *its* correctly.	☐	☐	☐
13. Does not use *them* as a demonstrative pronoun.	☐	☐	☐
14. Does not use *this here* and *that there.*	☐	☐	☐
15. Uses *a* and *an* correctly.	☐	☐	☐
16. Uses the correct personal pronoun in compound constructions.	☐	☐	☐
17. Uses *we* (subject) and *us* (object) correctly.	☐	☐	☐
18. Does not use *he don't, she don't, it don't.*	☐	☐	☐
19. Uses number agreement in *there is, there are, there was, there were.*	☐	☐	☐
	☐	☐	☐
20. Uses *learn* and *teach,* and *leave* and *let* correctly.	☐	☐	☐
21. Does not use *my brother he,* etc.	☐	☐	☐
22. Uses proper agreement with antecedent pronouns.	☐	☐	☐
23. Uses *said* in past tense.	☐	☐	☐
24. Uses *good* as adjective and *well* as adverb.	☐	☐	☐

Most critical usage problems are: _____

_____

_____

(From *The Effective Teaching of Language Arts* (2nd ed.) by Donna Norton, 1985, Charles E. Merrill Publisher, p. 228)

STORY MAP

NAME _____ DATE _____

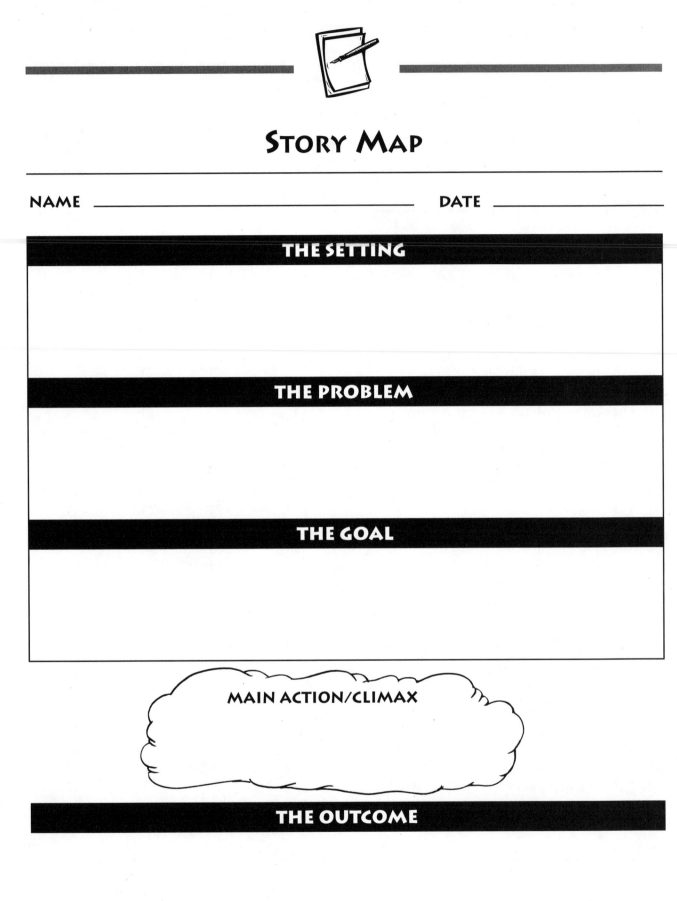

THE SETTING

THE PROBLEM

THE GOAL

MAIN ACTION/CLIMAX

THE OUTCOME

Assessment Blackline Master 74

EDITING CHECKLIST

NAME _____ DATE _____

AUTHOR _____ TITLE _____

❑ Spelling
(It was a (specel) shirt.)   *special*
(Watch for homonyms: (Wear) should I (where) it?)   *Where*   *wear*

❑ Capitalization
(I looked good. let's go! I'm ready to visit doctor collins.)
(Watch for out-of-place capitals: We went to the School.)

❑ Punctuation
(The sentences all end with punctuation marks, I've checked for appropriate use of commas, for example, in listing and for sentence clarity. Apostrophes are used to show possession and as part of a contraction.)

❑ Paragraph indentation
(and that is the best . . .
¶   Another idea for . . .)

❑ Margins
(then . . .
    and so . . .)

❑ Complete sentences
(Then went home.)   *we*

❑ Clear Meaning
(They went out for hamburgers after practice.)   *band*

❑ What could make this paper better?

_____
_____

⬭ Spelling or word choice	⊙ Add period	¶ New paragraph
= Capitalize	∧ Add comma	∧ Insert
/ Don't capitalize	∨ Add apostrophe	⌐ Delete

WRITING OVERVIEW

ORGANIZATION	Special flair																					
	Very clear																					
	Gaps in meaning																					
	Confusing																					
MEANING	Effective																					
	Appropriate																					
	Irrelevant																					
	No focus																					
CONVENTIONS	Additional meaning																					
	Correct mechanics																					
	Several errors																					
	Errors interfere																					
THOUGHT QUALITY	Accurate																					
	Logical																					
	Illogical																					
	Innacurate																					
WORD SELECTION	Evocative																					
	Complete																					
	Some precision																					
	Lacks precision																					
STORY SELECTION	Captivating																					
	Smooth																					
	Some confusion																					
	Lacks structure																					

CLUES TO IMPROVING HANDWRITING

NAME _____ DATE _____

1 RATE THE QUALITY OF YOUR HANDWRITING

Excellent = 1   Good = 2   Average = 3   Fair = 4   Poor = 5

☐ Neatness

☐ Arrangement (margins, indentations)

☐ Legibility

2 LOCATE THE TROUBLE SPOTS IN YOUR HANDWRITING

Check one or two areas in which you need special practice:

☐ **SLANT:** Do all your letters lean the same way and are your down strokes straight?

☐ **SPACE:** Are the spaces between letters and words even?

☐ **SIZE:** Are your tall letters (*l, h, k, b,* and *f*) about three times as tall as the small letters, the middle-sized letters (*t, d, p*) about twice the height of small letters, and the lower-loop letters one-half space below the writing line?)

☐ **ALIGNMENT:** Are all tall letters evenly tall, all small letters evenly small, and all letters resting on the line?

☐ **LINE QUALITY:** Is the thickness of the line about the same throughout the page?

☐ **ENDING STROKES:** Are the endings simple, without unnecessary strokes, and long enough to guide the spacing between words?

☐ **LETTER FORMATION:** Are the loops open and equal in size? Are the letters *m, n, h,* and *u* rounded? Are the letters *o, d, a, g, p,* and *q* closed? Have you made long retraces in *t, d,* and *p*? Are your capital letters well formed?

ASSESSING THINKING ABILITIES

NAME ———————————————————— DATE ————————————————

Basic Strategies, such as asking questions and making comparisons when confused
example: _____

_____

_____

Strategic Processes, such as recognizing patterns and understanding different points of view
example: _____

_____

_____

Making Decisions by eliminating propaganda and using reasoned judgments
example: _____

_____

_____

Using Metacognitive Skills by recognizing my strengths and monitoring my understanding
example: _____

_____

_____

THINKING, READING, WRITING, SPEAKING, AND LISTENING STRATEGIES

Problem Solving using PSP hints, corrections, storytelling, and "What if _____ were _____?"
example: _____

_____

_____

Using Creative Thinking Strategies, such as images and brainstorming
example: _____

_____

_____

Strategies for Group Work, such as 5 steps of working collaboratively
example: _____

_____

_____

Strategies for Working Effectively Alone, such as becoming more responsible and setting achievable goals
example: _____

_____

_____

STUDENT SELF-ASSESSMENT OF THINKING ABILITIES

NAME —————————————————————————— DATE ——————————————

THE STRATEGIES I USED OR IMPROVED THIS WEEK ARE:

☐ Communication: Listening, as shown by _____

☐ Asking questions, as shown by_____

☐ Speaking simply and clearly, as shown by _____

☐ Explaining by comparing and contrasting, as shown by _____

☐ Recognizing patterns, as shown by _____

☐ Understanding different points of view, as shown by _____

GROUP PROCESS:

☐ Keeping the attention of the group, as shown by _____

☐ Asking others their opinions, as shown by _____

☐ Making good contributions, as shown by _____

☐ Moving the work of the group ahead, as shown by _____

☐ Finding out if the group is ready to make a decision, as shown by _____

☐ Helping to make a decision, as shown by _____

☐ Assessing our work, as shown by _____

☐ Other _____

THINKING:

☐ Considering what has been said by recognizing propaganda, opinions, facts, and reasoned judgments, as shown by_____

☐ Recognizing my strengths and weaknesses, as shown by _____

☐ Coming up with possible explanations or solutions using PSP, hints, making minor corrections, storytelling, and using "What if ____ were ____?"

_____

☐ Monitoring my understanding, as shown by _____

☐ Becoming more creative by using mental images and brainstorming, as shown by

_____

☐ Becoming more responsible and setting attainable goals, as shown by

_____

☐ The skills I want to improve next week are: _____

STUDENT SELF-ASSESSMENT OF COOPERATIVE GROUPS

DATE —————————— PROJECT ——————————————

NAMES OF GROUP MEMBERS ———————————— ——————————

———————————— ——————————

Please evaluate your group work by answering the questions below:

1 What did your group do well?

2 What problems did your group have?

3 How did your group solve its problems?

4 What social skills does your group need to work on in your next cooperative group activity?

from Block, C.C. (1993). *Teaching the Language Arts: Expanding Thinking Through Student-Centered Instruction*. Needham Heights, MA: Allyn and Bacon, p. 394.

Assessment Blackline Master 80

STUDENT SELF-ASSESSMENT FOR GROUP WORK DURING CONSENSUS BUILDING

NAME ——————————————————————— DATE ———————————————

Put an "x" on the line at the point that best describes your involvement today in your group. 5 means "the whole time" and 1 means "not at all."

1. I offered my opinion to the group.

5 4 3 2 1

2. I listened to others' opinions and statements.

5 4 3 2 1

3. I responded to others' statements or opinions.

5 4 3 2 1

4. I compromised on some of my opinions in order to reach a group decision.

5 4 3 2 1

5. I helped someone else add to the discussion by asking them for their opinion or statement.

5 4 3 2 1

6. I feel that I need to work on _____.

7. A group skill I think I am good at is _____.

8. Overall, the grade I think I deserve today is: _____.

O = outstanding   S = satisfactory   N = needs improvement

PROBLEM-SOLVING ASSESSMENT

Place yourself in the following situation and write about all that you would think and do.

A friend comes to you with a problem about school. Your friend does not know how to solve the problem. You do not know how to solve it either. Describe in essay form what the problem is and what you and your friend will do together to try to solve the problem.

_____

_____

_____

_____

_____

_____

_____

_____

_____

_____

_____

_____

_____

_____

_____

_____

_____

ASSOCIATIVE WORD TEST OF CREATIVE THINKING

Read the three words in each line and think of a fourth that when added gives new meaning or is related to each of the words: e. g., river note blood _____ .
The fourth word may come before or after the given words.

This "associative" word answer is "bank." Now think of a word that fits with the three others in each row.

1. board   duck   dollar   _____

2. file   head   toe   _____

3. boiled   lid   flower   _____

4. chicken   malaria   butter   _____

5. class   stage   soccer   _____

Answers to the Associative Word Test are:

1. bill

2. nail

3. pot

4. yellow

5. coach

PORTFOLIO ASSESSMENT

Directions: Use one sheet for each portfolio to be evaluated. Circle the number in each of the five categories that best describes the level of quality contained in the portfolio. Five is the highest ranking. Total the rankings to derive a total possible score. If you want to place this score on a 91–100 scale, multiply the total portfolio score by 4.

VERSATILITY

Wide variety of reading and writing across genre.	Some variety.	Little or no variety. Collection shows little breadth or depth.	
5	4	3	2 1

STRATEGIC THINKING

Samples reveal discoveries and pivotal strategy use.	Illustrates in inflexible or mechanistic ways of thinking.	Minimal use of process to reflect on achievements and no application of lessons and strategies in this program.	
5	4	3	2 1

RESPONSE

Engaged with content. Discusses key issues. Evidence of critical questioning.	Personal reflection, but focus is narrow.	Brief retelling of isolated events in content.	
5	4	3	2 1

SELF-EVALUATIONS

Multidimensional evaluations using a wide variety of justifications. Establishes meaningful goals and notes improvements.	Developing insights; some specifics are noted. Limited goal setting. Vague assessment of improvements.	Single focused and too global in evaluations. Goal setting too broad or nonexistent.	
5	4	3	2 1

INDIVIDUAL PIECES

Strong control of a variety of elements: ideas, organization, cohesion, surface features, etc.	Growing command evidenced. Some flaws, but major ideas are clear.	Needs to improve sophistication of ideas, text features, and surface features.	
5	4	3	2 1

TOTAL SCORE: ———

✗ 4: ———

Assessment Blackline Master 84

1. Why?

2. Is the most important point _____ or _____?

3. What do you mean by "_____"?

4. If I understand, you mean _____.

5. Where will the point you are making not apply? How does ___ relate to _____?

6. If your idea is accepted, what is the greatest change that will occur?

7. Would you say more about _____?

8. What is the difference between _____ and _____?

9. Would this be an example?

10. Is it possible that _____? What else could we do?

11. If _____ happened, what would be the result.

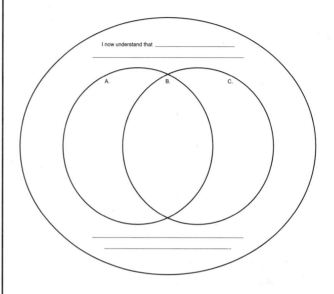

I now understand that _____

A.   B.   C.

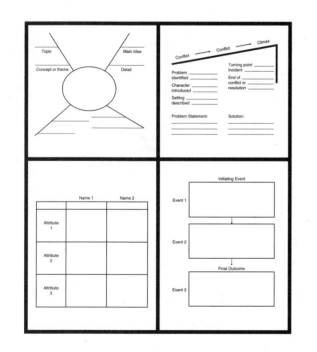

STEP 1
Another's Shoes

Have you put yourself in the person's shoes?

STEP 2
Use Details

Are there details, opinions, and values that suggest the person's point of view?

STEP 3
People Think Differently

Have you viewed the situation from the person's perspective to understand the different point of view?

Assessment Blackline Master 85

Top-left: Views diagram

The Country's View

[ ]

The World View

[ ]

The State's View

[ ]

The Broad Problem

( )

The Community's View

[ ]

The Individual's View

[ ]

TEAM MEMBERS

_____   _____

_____   _____

Top-right: Propaganda devices table

DEVICE	EXAMPLE/ DESCRIPTION	DID AUTHOR USE?		EVIDENCE
1. Bandwagon	claiming everyone is doing it: "Is your house the only one on the block not protected by Alpha Alarm?"	Yes ☐	No ☐	_____ _____
2. Repetition	repeating favorable words: "bargain," "best," "first," "sale"	Yes ☐	No ☐	_____ _____
3. Transfer	transferring of feelings about one thing to another: "If you like your mother, you'll like our pie."	Yes ☐	No ☐	_____ _____
4. Testimonial	famous person promoting something: "I'm a famous basketball star and to stay strong I eat Sugar Flakes cereal every morning."	Yes ☐	No ☐	_____ _____ _____
5. "Better Hurry" or "It's Free"	trying to make you think there is a good reason to take action immediately or within a definite time period or that you can get something for nothing: "Better hurry, only a limited supply available."	Yes ☐	No ☐	_____ _____ _____ _____
6. Glittering Generality	using glowing words or phrases to draw your attention: "Patriotic citizens will agree. . ."	Yes ☐	No ☐	_____ _____
7. Name Calling	referring to something as undesirable or desirable by choosing a word that has either a positive or negative emotional appeal: "The greedy crooks at the other store just want your money. We want to help you."	Yes ☐	No ☐	_____ _____ _____ _____

Bottom-left: Facts/Opinions equation

BOX 1   FACTS

from encyclopedia, atlas, almanac, math text, other people's statements, your own statements

+

BOX 2   OPINIONS

from newspapers, advertisements, other people's statements, your own statements

+

BOX 3   YOU

what you already know and what you think are the strongest facts and opinions from boxes 1 and 2

=

BOX 4   REASONED JUDGMENT

State the reasoning behind your statement.

Bottom-right: Steps flowchart

STEP 2
Brainstorming ways to change

STEP 1
List what is wrong.

START

STEP 3
Describe what it will be like when a good solution is found. What will change? What will you feel?

STEP 4
Combine Steps 2 and 3 and select the best solution.

STEP 5
Plan of action.

1 _____
2 _____
3 _____
4 _____

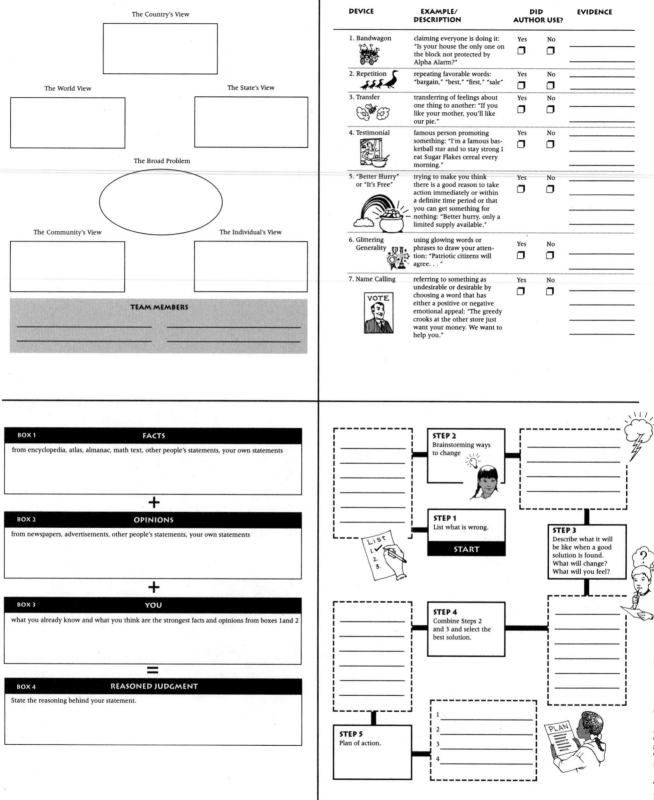

Assessment Blackline Master 86

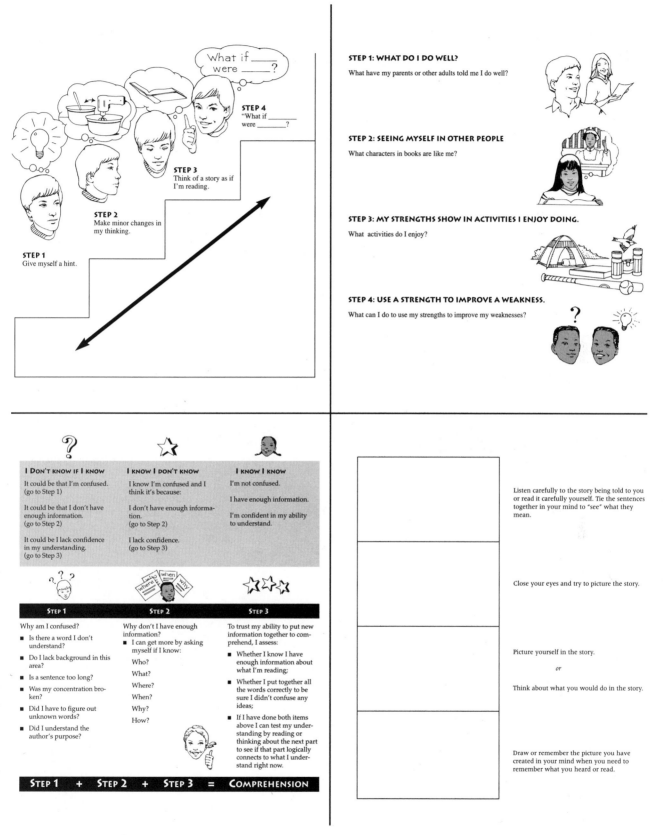

What if _____ were _____?

STEP 4
"What if _____ were _____?"

STEP 3
Think of a story as if I'm reading.

STEP 2
Make minor changes in my thinking.

STEP 1
Give myself a hint.

STEP 1: WHAT DO I DO WELL?

What have my parents or other adults told me I do well?

STEP 2: SEEING MYSELF IN OTHER PEOPLE

What characters in books are like me?

STEP 3: MY STRENGTHS SHOW IN ACTIVITIES I ENJOY DOING.

What activities do I enjoy?

STEP 4: USE A STRENGTH TO IMPROVE A WEAKNESS.

What can I do to use my strengths to improve my weaknesses?

I DON'T KNOW IF I KNOW	I KNOW I DON'T KNOW	I KNOW I KNOW
It could be that I'm confused. (go to Step 1)	I know I'm confused and I think it's because:	I'm not confused.
It could be that I don't have enough information. (go to Step 2)	I don't have enough information. (go to Step 2)	I have enough information.
It could be I lack confidence in my understanding. (go to Step 3)	I lack confidence. (go to Step 3)	I'm confident in my ability to understand.

STEP 1

Why am I confused?

- Is there a word I don't understand?
- Do I lack background in this area?
- Is a sentence too long?
- Was my concentration broken?
- Did I have to figure out unknown words?
- Did I understand the author's purpose?

STEP 2

Why don't I have enough information?

- I can get more by asking myself if I know:

Who?

What?

Where?

When?

Why?

How?

STEP 3

To trust my ability to put new information together to comprehend, I assess:

- Whether I know I have enough information about what I'm reading;
- Whether I put together all the words correctly to be sure I didn't confuse any ideas;
- If I have done both items above I can test my understanding by reading or thinking about the next part to see if that part logically connects to what I understand right now.

STEP 1 + STEP 2 + STEP 3 = COMPREHENSION

Listen carefully to the story being told to you or read it carefully yourself. Tie the sentences together in your mind to "see" what they mean.

Close your eyes and try to picture the story.

Picture yourself in the story.

or

Think about what you would do in the story.

Draw or remember the picture you have created in your mind when you need to remember what you heard or read.

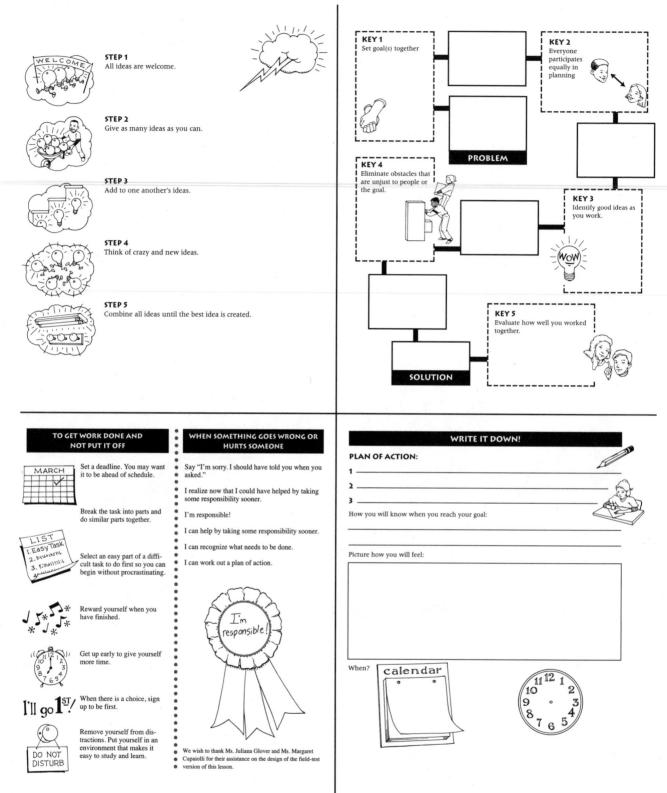

STEP 1
All ideas are welcome.

STEP 2
Give as many ideas as you can.

STEP 3
Add to one another's ideas.

STEP 4
Think of crazy and new ideas.

STEP 5
Combine all ideas until the best idea is created.

KEY 1
Set goal(s) together

KEY 2
Everyone participates equally in planning

PROBLEM

KEY 4
Eliminate obstacles that are unjust to people or the goal.

KEY 3
Identify good ideas as you work.

KEY 5
Evaluate how well you worked together.

SOLUTION

TO GET WORK DONE AND NOT PUT IT OFF

Set a deadline. You may want it to be ahead of schedule.

Break the task into parts and do similar parts together.

Select an easy part of a difficult task to do first so you can begin without procrastinating.

Reward yourself when you have finished.

Get up early to give yourself more time.

When there is a choice, sign up to be first.

Remove yourself from distractions. Put yourself in an environment that makes it easy to study and learn.

WHEN SOMETHING GOES WRONG OR HURTS SOMEONE

Say "I'm sorry. I should have told you when you asked."

I realize now that I could have helped by taking some responsibility sooner.

I'm responsible!

I can help by taking some responsibility sooner.

I can recognize what needs to be done.

I can work out a plan of action.

I'm responsible!

We wish to thank Ms. Juliana Glover and Ms. Margaret Cupaiolli for their assistance on the design of the field-test version of this lesson.

WRITE IT DOWN!

PLAN OF ACTION:

1 _____
2 _____
3 _____

How you will know when you reach your goal:
_____

Picture how you will feel:

When? calendar

© Addison-Wesley Publishing Company, Inc.

HOMESTRETCH

Pages 222–238 contain fifteen letters and two forms that can be sent home to parents. Each letter is designed to accompany one of the fifteen lessons in *Reason to Read*. The purpose of each letter is to create for students a stronger connection between home and school. Each letter contains suggestions for building on the activities the student does at school relative to each lesson's objective. The first and last letters are each accompanied by a form. While the forms can be sent home at any time in the school year, the descriptions for their use appear in the first and last letters. The purpose of the Observation Guide, page 222, is to gather information about each student's reading and writing abilities from the parent's perspective. This form is designed to make the parent's observational data available to you for use in planning future instruction for individual students. The purpose of the calendar, page 238, is to help the parent organize the work she or he is doing with the student at home.

OBSERVATION GUIDE

Student's Name_____Parent's Name_____

Date_____

Please circle the responses and complete the sentences with statements that best reflect your child's abilities to read and write. Your observations will assist me in teaching your child new strategies at school.

My child:

1. Reads from a wide variety of materials, including books, magazines, and newspapers:

   at least once a day   once a week   rarely

2. Takes time during the evening to read or write

   each day   once a week   rarely

3. Tells me about the things he or she enjoys at school

   each day   once a week   rarely

4. Seeks out reading for information without having to be told to do so

   sometimes   rarely

5. Brings home (and reads or responds to) books and other materials from the library

   each week   once a month   rarely

6. Seems to have improved the ability to think deeply and understand what he or she reads since beginning this program

   very much   somewhat   no change

7. Seems to be using a wider vocabulary in spoken and written communications since beginning this program

   very much   somewhat   no change

8. Is solving problems for self and in groups more effectively

   often   sometimes   no change

My child would be a better reader, in my opinion, if: _____

My child would be a better writer, in my opinion, if:_____

My child's greatest growth in reading and writing has been: _____

The instruction he or she has most enjoyed was:_____

By the next time I complete this "Observation Guide" I would like for my child to have improved in

   the following abilities: _____

Date_____

Dear Parent,

Our class is beginning the first lesson in *Reason to Read*, a program that combines learning better reading comprehension with increasingly higher-level thinking. With each lesson, I will send home a letter providing ways you can practice a new reading and thinking strategy with your child.

In this first lesson, students are learning how to ask questions to understand more. The following are examples of questions your child is learning to ask while reading and listening:

Why?

Is the most important point ___ or ____?

What do you mean by "_____"?

Where will _____not apply?

How does ____ relate to _____?

If I understand, you mean _____. Is that right?

Would this be an example:_____?

What else could we do?

Would you say more about_____?

If _____ happened, what would be the result?

I encourage you to notice when your child asks questions to gain more information. You can add to what your child is learning in the following enjoyable and easy ways.

1. Your child will enjoy telling you about questions asked in school.

2. Your child will benefit from hearing your stories about times when asking one of the above questions helped you. Share with each other the best question you asked or heard someone else ask during the day.

3. Ask your child some of the above questions. Tell how they helped you understand what he or she said.

4. Point out the good questions television or book characters ask.

5. Take turns describing situations in which it is difficult for you or your child to ask questions. Together develop a plan for asking one of the above questions when that situation arises again.

I have also attached an "Observation Guide" on which you can describe your child's reading and writing behaviors at home. I appreciate the time you take to complete the "Observation Guide" and return it to me. If you would like to tell me specific growths your child has as a result of your work together, or if you would like to ask me any questions about your child's questioning abilities, please feel free to contact me by note or telephone.

Sincerely,

Date_____

Dear Parent,

Our class is beginning the second lesson in *Reason to Read*, a program that combines learning better reading comprehension with increasingly higher-level thinking. In this lesson, students are learning how to make comparisons between things they know and things that confuse them. In class your child will select two books about the same subject and identify ways in which the books are similar and different. Your child will also use a diagram to make comparisons. Have your child draw the diagram for you and explain how it assists thinking and eliminates confusion.

Encourage your child to compare new information with previous experiences. Such thinking will increase your child's ability to consider more than one point of view. You can also use the following everyday experiences to increase your child's ability to compare and contrast while reading, listening, and thinking.

1. Whenever your child says, "I don't understand," ask him or her to describe the type of thinking to do whenever confusion exists. If your child says to begin by comparing and contrasting new information to what is known, offer praise and assistance in doing so. If your child does not know what to do, draw the above diagram and ask how it can help.

2. Whenever your child disagrees with a brother, sister, or friend, encourage her or him to use the above diagram to resolve the conflict and to identify points of agreement. If the disagreement is resolved, ask your child how comparative thinking helped achieve a solution. If the disagreement is not resolved, ask your child to compare and contrast this disagreement to one that was resolved successfully. Did this comparison help your child to understand why a resolution was not reached?

3. To have fun with this strategy, compare and contrast qualities of villains and heroes in books, movies, or television shows. Ask your child what makes a person a hero and compare those points to ones you would select.

If you would like to tell me specific growths your child has as a result of your work together, or if you would like to know more about comparative thinking, please feel free to contact me by note or telephone.

Sincerely,

Blackline Master 91

Date_____

Dear Parent,

Our class is beginning the third lesson in *Reason to Read*, a program that combines learning better reading comprehension with increasingly higher-level thinking. In this lesson your child will learn four patterns authors and speakers use to communicate their ideas. This letter tells ways you can practice pattern recognition with your child.

Ask your child to describe and diagram the four types of patterns we have explored in class: Main Idea or Concept Pattern; Plots in Stories or Problem/Solution Pattern; Telling Things in Order or Sequence Pattern; and Telling Both Sides or Similarity/Difference Pattern. Then, ask your child to describe the pattern his or her favorite author uses to write.

You may also enjoy asking your child to identify the pattern you use most often when you speak. For example, your child should be able to determine which of the above patterns you most frequently use by telling you that you usually:

- start your conversations by telling the main point and then giving details (Main Idea or Concept Pattern);

- state a problem and tell all the events that need to occur (or did occur) to solve that problem (Plots in Stories or Problem/Solution Pattern);

- tell things in order (Sequence Pattern); or

- state both sides of an issue (Telling Both Sides or Similarity/Difference Pattern).

An activity you may enjoy is to ask your child to draw a concept map with his or her name in the center. This activity will demonstrate the parts of your child's life that she or he considers important.

Throughout the coming weeks, as you read books with your child, ask him or her to identify the type of pattern the author used to organize his or her thoughts. Such practice will greatly enhance your child's ability to predict upcoming events and remember what he or she reads.

If you would like to tell me specific growths your child has as a result of your work together, or if you would like to ask me any questions about your child's ability to recognize patterns, please feel free to contact me by note or telephone.

Sincerely,

Date_____

Dear Parent,

Our class is beginning the fourth lesson in *Reason to Read*, a program that combines learning better reading comprehension with increasingly higher-level thinking. In this lesson, students are learning how to understand different points of view in writing and conversations. Your child is learning to take three steps in his or her thinking to understand a person's point of view. Ask your child to tell you what these three steps are. You can add to what your child is learning in the following enjoyable and easy ways.

1. Whenever you are watching or listening to a television or radio news broadcast together and an expert on a topic is interviewed, ask your child to tell you what that person's point of view is and how your child recognized it.

2. When you read with your child or your child tells you about a book he or she is reading, ask how the book would be different if the author had written from another character's point of view.

3. If your child describes a disagreement he or she had with a brother, sister, or friend, ask what your child could do to better understand the other person's point of view.

4. Discuss the types of words people have used in the past that have persuaded you to change your point of view about something of interest to your child.

I encourage you to notice when your child understands points of view different from his or her own. Praising this ability and asking how he or she understood the different point of view will increase your child's ability to continue this high-level thinking.

If you would like to tell me specific growths your child has as a result of your work together, or if you would like to ask me any questions about your child's abilities to understand different points of view while reading and discussing, please feel free to contact me by note or telephone.

Sincerely,

Date_____

Dear Parent,

Our class is beginning the fifth lesson in *Reason to Read*, a program that combines learning better reading comprehension with increasingly higher-level thinking. In this lesson, students are learning how to recognize propaganda in information they read and hear. They are also learning how to eliminate the persuasive effects of propaganda devices before they make decisions about written and spoken information.

I encourage you to notice when your child points out different types of propaganda in advertisements, editorials, conversations, and nonfiction writings such as magazines and newspapers. The types of devices we are studying include: (1) Bandwagon: claiming everyone is doing it; (2) Repetition: repeating favorable words; (3) Transfer: transferring a good feeling about one thing to another; (4) Testimonial: a famous person promoting something; (5) Better Hurry: a speaker insisting there is a good reason to take action immediately; (6) Glittering Generality: using glowing words or phrases to draw attention; and (7) Namecalling: referring to something as undesirable or desirable by choosing a word that has either a positive or negative emotional appeal. You can add to what your child is learning in the following enjoyable and easy ways.

1. Your child will enjoy telling you about the seven types of propaganda devices he or she is learning in school and pointing them out in television commercials. Ask what types of devices are being used in some of the most frequently appearing commercials and how the manufacturer is using that device to increase the sales of the product.

2. When your child is interested in a current event, have him or her watch news broadcasts on two different television stations and describe to you whether either broadcast tried to slant the event using any propaganda device.

3. Tell about times in which you were or were not swayed by a propaganda device and the effect it had upon your actions.

4. When you are reading, point out to your child the types of propaganda devices that are used to sway adults to take certain actions.

If you would like to tell me specific growths your child has as a result of your work together, or if you would like to ask me questions about your child's abilities to recognize propaganda, please feel free to contact me by note or telephone.

Sincerely,

Date_____

Dear Parent,

Our class is beginning the sixth lesson in *Reason to Read*, a program that combines learning better reading comprehension with increasingly higher-level thinking. In this lesson, students are learning strategies for distinguishing between fact and opinion and for combining facts and opinions with what they already know to make reasoned judgments as they read, listen, and think.

I encourage you to praise your child when he or she makes a good judgment and recognizes the differences between facts and opinions while reading and listening. You can add to what your child is learning in the following enjoyable and easy ways.

1. You may enjoy reading one of the books in the series entitled *You Be the Jury*. In these books, you and your child will read four or five pages that present a court case containing facts and opinions. Your child can describe how he or she separated the two types of statements to make the best reasoned judgment concerning the verdict in each case.

2. Your child will benefit from hearing stories about times in which you had to separate facts from opinions and combine the best information you had with your past experiences to make the very best judgment you could.

3. Ask your child to apply what he or she has learned in this lesson to experiences he or she had in the past when two friends disagreed and asked your child to solve the disagreement.

If you would like to tell me specific growths your child has as a result of your work together, or if you would like to ask questions about your child's abilities to make reasoned judgments about material he or she reads, please feel free to contact me by note or telephone.

Sincerely,

Blackline Master 95

Date_____

Dear Parent,

Our class is beginning the seventh lesson in *Reason to Read*, a program that combines learning better reading comprehension with increasingly higher-level thinking. In this lesson, students are learning how to apply the Problem-Solving Process to reading and to situations in their lives. The four steps in the process are (1) sorting out the problem to understand clearly what is wrong; (2) brainstorming ways to change; (3) describing what it will be like when a good solution is found; (4) combining the information in steps 2 and 3 to select the best solution; and (5) implementing a plan of action.

I encourage you to notice when your child solves problems successfully at home. You can ask your child to describe the thinking strategies he or she used to solve the problem and praise him or her for doing so. Also, you can add to what your child is learning in the following enjoyable and easy ways.

1. Your child may enjoy telling you about some of the ways the main characters in books did and did not use the Problem-Solving Process to solve problems they faced. Such "storytelling" experiences will strengthen your child's ability to apply this problem-solving process in situations he or she faces.

2. You and your child may enjoy using the Problem-Solving Process to solve everyday problems. Perhaps your child feels as if he or she does not have as many friends at school as desired; perhaps your child has trouble turning in homework or has difficulty being organized or keeping his or her room and belongings neat. Ask your child what problem he or she would like to try to solve using the Problem-Solving Process.

If you would like to tell me specific growths your child has as a result of your work together, or if you would like to ask questions about your child's abilities to ask solve problems at school and to understand the problems described in books he or she reads, please feel free to contact me by note or telephone.

Sincerely,

Date_____

Dear Parent,

Our class is beginning the eighth lesson in *Reason to Read*, a program that combines learning better reading comprehension with increasingly higher-level thinking. In this lesson, students are learning how to (1) give themselves hints when they have a small problem to solve; (2) make repeated minor changes; (3) share stories from books and their own lives in which similar problems were solved effectively; and, (4) ask "What if _____ were _____?" whenever they get stuck in their thinking.

I encourage you remind your child to use one of these strategies when he or she faces problems. You can add to what your child is learning in the following enjoyable and easy ways.

1. Your child may enjoy telling you about problems he or she solved at school and how he or she used one of the above strategies to do so.

2. Your child will benefit from telling you about the main characters in books and the strategies they used to solve their problems. Your child will also enjoy hearing stories you tell about times in which you used one of the above strategies to solve a problem you faced.

3. You may enjoy discussing with your child ways groups of people can use the above strategies to solve prominent world problems such as hunger, the deterioration of the ozone layer, or the increasing deficit.

If you would like to tell me specific growths your child has as a result of your work together, or if you would like to ask questions about your child's abilities to use the above strategies at school, please feel free to contact me by note or telephone.

Sincerely,

Date_____

Dear Parent,

Our class is beginning the ninth lesson in *Reason to Read*, a program that combines learning better reading comprehension with increasingly higher-level thinking. In this lesson, students are learning to identify strengths and weaknesses they have in reading, speaking, listening, writing, and thinking. One of the strategies students learned to use in identifying their communication strengths was to recall what other adults have told them they do well. I encourage you to tell your child the specific strengths you appreciate about your his or her reading, speaking, listening, writing, and thinking abilities and to point out when you notice new strengths developing. You can add to what your child is learning in the following enjoyable and easy ways.

1. Ask your child to describe a strength he or she recognizes in his or her reading, speaking, writing, listening, or thinking. You may also want to extend the discussion by asking your child to describe a weakness in any of these areas and what you can do together to overcome this weakness.

2. Have your child describe a book he or she has read in class recently and how he or she gained ideas about himself or herself by recognizing the main character's strengths.

3. Ask your child how he or she could use a strength to overcome a weakness in reading, speaking, writing, listening, or thinking.

4. As you watch television together, you might ask your child to give advice to one of the characters on the screen based on a strength or weakness of that character.

If you would like to tell me specific growths your child has as a result of your work together, or if you would like to ask any questions about your child's abilities to recognize his or her strengths and weaknesses in reading, speaking, writing, listening, or thinking, please feel free to contact me by note or telephone.

Sincerely,

Date_____

Dear Parent,

Our class is beginning the tenth lesson in *Reason to Read*, a program that combines learning better reading comprehension with increasingly higher-level thinking. In this lesson, students are learning how to pay attention to their thinking and to monitor whether words are making sense when they are reading. I encourage you to ask your child what he or she has learned to do to make sense of reading material. You can add to what your child is learning in the following enjoyable and easy ways.

1. Take turns with your child reading a few pages aloud and then telling the other what you were thinking while reading.

2. If your child becomes confused while reading, remind him or her to ask:
   - Is it a word I don't understand?
   - Is it my lack of background knowledge?
   - Is a sentence too long?
   - Was my concentration broken?

3. Your child can describe to you what to do when he or she does not have enough information or lacks confidence in putting new information together. He or she will describe how to use the "who, what, where, when, why, and how" questions while reading and how to strengthen confidence by thinking about what will happen next in the reading. Confidence in reading ability builds by reading to see if the next part of the material connects to what is understood right now and whether predictions will occur.

4. Ask your child what is the most frequent cause of his or her confusion and lack of comprehension when reading. Is it difficult words, lack of background experience with the topic, long sentences, broken concentration, not going back and rereading, not being able to find the author's purpose, not finding "who, what, where, when, or how" details while reading? As you read with your child, stop at difficult points and ask what your child is thinking.

If you would like to tell me specific growths your child has as a result of your work together, or if you would like to ask questions about your child's abilities to think about the reading process, please feel free to contact me by note or telephone.

Sincerely,

Date_____

Dear Parent,

Our class is beginning the eleventh lesson in *Reason to Read*, a program that combines learning better reading comprehension with increasingly higher-level thinking. In this lesson, students are learning how to form mental pictures while they read, listen, and think so they can increase their comprehension. You can add to what your child is learning in the following enjoyable and easy ways.

1. Have your child fill a glass container with a colored liquid (which you mixed in advance from 1/2 cup vinegar and 5 drops food coloring). Then ask your child to sprinkle a magical powder (1 tablespoon of baking soda) into the liquid. (You have placed the baking soda in a small, unmarked bowl so your child will not know the contents.) The liquid will bubble, foam, and expand until it erupts over the sides of the container. Then, ask your child to create a mental picture to answer the following questions. After your child has answered each question, you can provide an answer as well, based on a mental picture you create:

   Who first created this potion and what does this person look like?

   Why did this person create it?

   What does this potion do?

   What consequences might result from its use?

2. Describe to your child how many people picture themselves successfully engaged in important upcoming events. These mental pictures help them develop the confidence to succeed in that event. Ask your child to think about a goal and to describe a mental picture of him or herself successfully reaching that goal. Then describe your own goal and mental picture about an upcoming event in your life.

If you would like to tell me specific growths your child has as a result of your work together, or if you would like to ask any questions about your child's abilities to use mental images to improve his or her reading, please feel free to contact me by note or telephone.

Sincerely,

Date_____

Dear Parent,

Our class is beginning the twelfth lesson in *Reason to Read*, a program that combines learning better reading comprehension with increasingly higher-level thinking. In this lesson, students are learning the brainstorming strategy to increase their creativity, broaden their thinking, and expand their abilities to apply what they read and hear to novel situations. Ask your child to describe the steps in the brainstorming process and the ways we have used it in class. I encourage you to remind your child to "brainstorm" whenever he or she is seeking new ideas and solutions. You can add to what your child is learning in the following enjoyable and easy ways.

1. Your child studied essays, book reviews, movie reviews, and editorials in this lesson. Ask your child to describe the type of writing he or she did and to describe what he or she learned about these types of writings.

2. Your child was a part of a group that wrote an editorial to suggest ways to improve the classroom. Ask your child to show you how to brainstorm by using the topic: "How to improve the way my bedroom is arranged."

3. Your child will benefit from brainstorming with you. Whenever you and your child have a decision to make, sit together with a sheet of paper to brainstorm as many ideas as possible about that decision. Write all ideas on the paper as they are said. Try to continue the brainstorming for ten minutes, since often the best ideas occur after several minutes have elapsed. Then review the brainstorming list and combine ideas until the best decision has been identified.

If you would like to tell me specific growths your child has as a result of your work together, or if you would like to ask any questions about your child's abilities to brainstorm or tie his or her readings to novel situations, or about your child's level of creativity, please feel free to contact me by note or telephone.

Sincerely,

Date_____

Dear Parent,

Our class is beginning the thirteenth lesson in *Reason to Read*, a program that combines learning better reading comprehension with increasingly higher-level thinking. In this lesson, students are learning how to work cooperatively and effectively in groups. I encourage you to notice when your child works well in groups and to compliment specific actions he or she takes to increase the group's effectiveness. You can add to what your child is learning in the following enjoyable and easy ways.

1. Ask your child to describe the following strategies:

    ■ contributing equally

    ■ volunteering to contribute a talent or resource to the group goal

    ■ "wraparound strategy"

    ■ seeking a first, second, and third alternative plan of action

2. In this lesson, your child studied poetry and wrote a poem individually or in a group. You may enjoy discussing your child's response to poetry and asking your child to share with you the poem he or she wrote.

3. Your child will benefit from hearing what you do in group situations whenever disagreements arise. Describe which of the following strategies you use to resolve disagreements:

    ■ Discuss or stand firm on your position.

    ■ Persuade by justifying and reasoning about your position.

    ■ Ask for a vote and let the majority rule.

    ■ Compromise by combining and modifying.

    ■ Try to mediate between others.

    ■ Ask people not to decide now but to wait until tomorrow.

    ■ Give in or play the martyr.

    ■ Use humor to move away from confrontation.

    ■ Ignore a difficult item or try to postpone it indefinitely.

If you would like to tell me specific growths your child has as a result of your work together, or if you would like to ask any questions about your child's abilities to work cooperatively in groups, please feel free to contact me by note or telephone.

Sincerely,

Date_____

Dear Parent,

Our class is beginning the fourteenth lesson in *Reason to Read*, a program that combines learning better reading comprehension with increasingly higher-level thinking. In this lesson, students are learning strategies to gain confidence and to become more responsible in setting their own language arts goals as well as goals in other areas of their life. I encourage you to notice when your child assumes responsibility for schoolwork and other tasks at home and to compliment him or her for using the strategies. The strategies your child was taught in this lesson include:

- Set a deadline.

- Break tasks into parts and do similar parts together.

- Do an easy part of a difficult task first so you can begin the difficult task without procrastinating.

- Reward yourself when you are finished.

- Get up early to give yourself more time.

- When there is a choice, sign up to be first.

- Remove yourself from distractions.

- Say "I'm sorry" if you have made a mistake.

You can add to what your child is learning in the following enjoyable and easy ways.

1. Ask your child to tell you the strategies that helped to increase confidence in his or her own abilities and to assume more responsibilities in learning.

2. Review the above list of specific strategies. Then share other strategies you use to accomplish difficult tasks and to correct something that goes wrong.

3. In this lesson students read several fables and even wrote one of their own. Ask your child about fables, the fable and moral he or she wrote, and where the idea for them arose.

If you would like to tell me specific growths your child has as a result of your work together, or if you would like to ask questions about your child's abilities to take responsibilities in his or her learning, please feel free to contact me by note or telephone.

Sincerely,

Blackline Master 103

Date_____

Dear Parent,

Our class is beginning the last lesson in *Reason to Read*, a program that combines learning better reading comprehension with increasingly higher-level thinking. In this lesson, students are learning how to set achievable goals for their reading and writing. I encourage you to notice when your child sets a goal for at home. Point out to your child the effective things he or she does to reach that goal. In class, your child learned the following goal-setting strategies : (a) write down your goals; (b) develop a plan of action that has several steps; and (c) picture how you will feel when the goal is reached. You can add to what your child is learning in the following enjoyable and easy ways.

1. In this lesson, your child chose a famous person to learn more about. Ask who your child studied and what he or she learned about setting goals from reading about that person's life.

2. In this lesson, your child also established a one-week action plan to achieve a goal related to school-work. Ask your child what that plan was and which parts were most successful.

3. Your child may have also identified a language-arts skill that he or she wanted to improve. If your child selected a skill, ask him or her to identify the level of improvement in that area and to be realistic about his or her own abilities to assume responsibility. If your child did not select an area to improve at school, you may ask him or her to work for 15 minutes with you each night on a subject area. Before you begin the nightly work, ask your child to complete the strategies from this lesson: writing the goal, developing a plan of action that has several steps, and picturing how it will feel to reach the goal. After one week's work, ask your child to assess his or her progress.

If you would like to tell me specific growths your child has as a result of your work together, or if you would like to ask any questions about your child's abilities to establish effective goals, please feel free to contact me by note or telephone. I have attached a blank calendar to this letter. It can be used to set goals with your child, to assist your child in assuming daily responsibilities, or to record other types of activities your child selects to complete.

Thank you for all you have done during our reading program to build upon our school lessons.

Sincerely,

MONTH

SUNDAY	MONDAY	TUESDAY	WEDNESDAY	THURSDAY	FRIDAY	SATURDAY

APPENDIX A

THINKING STRATEGIES INCLUDED IN <u>REASON TO READ</u>

There are eight domains of thinking strategies that are amenable to instruction (Baron and Sternberg, 1987; Beyer, 1987; Collins and Mangieri, 1992; deBono, 1970). These strategies affect the quality of students' reading abilities. Each volume of *Reason to Read* contains two strategies from each of the Domains 1–6 and three strategies each from Domains 7 and 8.

Domain 1 contains *basic cognitive strategies,* including the ability to clarify ideas, examine relationships, see errors, summarize, and remember. Domain 2 includes *strategic-thinking processes and higher-level comprehension processes.* Strategies in Domain 2 call upon more than one strategic ability, such as inferencing, making connections between ideas, elaborating, interpreting, thinking like a content expert, and making multiple comparisons and contrasts.

Domain 3 consists of *decision-making strategies,* with which students learn how to select from competing alternatives, use decision-making tools, and develop positive decision-making attitudes, such as drive and persistence. Domain 4 is comprised of *problem-solving strategies,* such as resolving perplexing situations, assessing the quality of ideas, eliminating biases, establishing criteria, and judging the credibility of sources. Domain 5 includes *metacognitive strategies,* such as assessing one's current knowledge relative to task

demands and identifying barriers that interfere with talents, projects, and goals.

Domain 6 is comprised of *creative and innovative strategies,* including shifting frames of reference; using "USUL" "AREA" processes; forecasting; brainstorming; and eliminating blocks to creativity. Domain 7 includes *strategies for thinking effectively in groups,* such as understanding the nature and quality of thinking in group settings, exercising power/authority/influence appropriately, using talents interactively, and achieving group goals cooperatively. Domain 8 consists of *strategies to think effectively when working alone,* such as setting goals, establishing redirection, taking action, and eliciting self-motivation to increase productivity.

The specific language arts competencies included in *Reason to Read* appear on pages 241–243 (Appendix B).

THINKING DOMAINS AMENABLE TO INSTRUCTION

Domain 1:   Basic thinking skills

Domain 2:   Fundamental thinking processes

Domain 3:   Decision-making tools

Domain 4:   Problem-solving strategies

Domain 5:   Metacognitive strategies

Domain 6: Creative and innovative thinking processes

Domain 7: Thinking effectively when working in groups

Domain 8: Thinking effectively when working alone

Domain 1: *basic cognitive operations,* including the ability to clarify ideas, examine relationships, see errors, summarize, and remember.

Domain 2: *thinking processes* that call upon more than one mental operation, including inferencing, interpreting, thinking like experts, and making multiple comparisons. In Domain 2, concepts, literal elaborations, and connections are formed.

Domain 3: *decision-making abilities* with which one must select from competing alternatives that may or may not be obvious to the decision maker, using decision-making tools, and recognizing critical points when making a decision to eliminate problems before beginning.

Domain 4: *ability to solve problems,* including resolving perplexing situations, assessing the quality of ideas, eliminating biases, establishing criteria, and judging the credibility of sources.

Domain 5: *metacognitive thinking,* involving control of self; assessing one's current knowledge relative to individual tasks; and identifying barriers that interfere with one's talents, projects, and goals.

Domain 6: *creative and innovative thinking,* including shifting frames of reference and using models, metaphors, substitutions, humor, risk-taking, and curiosity, as well as forecasting to create new thoughts and products.

Domain 7: *thinking effectively in groups,* understanding the nature and quality of thinking in a group setting; exercising power/authority/influence appropriately; using talents interactively; and developing analytical listening abilities.

Domain 8: *ability to think effectively when alone,* set goals, establish redirection, take action, and elicit self-motivation to increase productivity.

READING/LANGUAGE ARTS COMPETENCIES DEVELOPED IN REASON TO READ

The specific reading/language arts competencies instructed in *Reason to Read* reflect the reading/language arts abilities specified by departments of education in North American states and provinces. Curriculum guides designed for states and provinces in North America were consulted as *Reason to Read* lessons were written. These guides included the Chapter 76 Curriculum, Subchapter B, Essential Elements in English Language Arts, Kindergarten through Grades 9 for the Texas State Department of Education; and the California State Board of Education *English-Language Arts Framework*. The objectives as well as the lessons in which they appear are listed below. Objective numbers 26, 29, 31, 32, 34, 38, 43, 44, 45, 48, 49, 50, 63, 65, 66 are developed in all lessons.

LANGUAGE ARTS COMPETENCIES DEVELOPED IN LESSONS

Reading and language arts objectives for *Reason to Read* are as follows:

1) Introduction to eight word-recognition strategies, Lesson 1, 15

2) Sight word instruction, Lessons 1,15

3) Phonic analysis and comparing word families, Lesson 1

4) Structural analysis, Lessons 1, 3

5) Semantic context clues, Lessons 1, 2, 15

6) Syntactic context clues, Lessons 1, 2, 15

7) Dictionary skills, Lesson 1

8) Appropriate incidents for skipping words, Lessons 1, 15

9) Asking for word meanings, Lessons 1, 15

10) Vocabulary developmental activities, Lesson 3

11) Reviewing and refining decoding strategies while reading personal and school-related materials, Lesson 5

12) Introduction of one of the components of literal comprehension abilities, Lessons 1, 4, 8, 14

13) Identifying main idea statements, Lessons 10, 15,

14) Identifying sequential clue words, Lessons 3, 4

15) Relating supporting sentences to main topic sentences, Lessons 3, 12, 13

16) Identifying important and less important details, Lessons 6, 9

17) Strengthening interpretive comprehension, Lessons 1, 5, 10, 11, 14

18) Relating experiences using appropriate vocabulary in complete sentences, Lessons 7, 9, 13, 14

19) Arranging events in sequential order, including time and degree of importance, Lesson 13

20) Recognizing various persuasive devices, Lessons 5, 13

21) Understanding cause-and-effect relationships, Lesson 6

22) Predicting probable outcomes or actions, Lesson 12

23) Making generalizations, Lesson 6

24) Evaluating and making judgments, Lesson 6

25) Developing facility in oral reading for an audience, Lessons 9, 12, 13, 14

26) Using periodicals, card catalogs, and reference works to locate information, Lessons 1–15

27) Comparing information on charts, graphs, tables, and lists, Lesson 3

28) Adjusting the method and rate of reading to the purpose and type of material including study-type reading, Lesson 7

29) Developing literary appreciation skills to provide personal enjoyment, Lessons 1–15

30) Recognizing and using personification as a literary device, Lesson 11

31) Appreciating, recognizing, and responding to various forms of literature, Lessons 1–16

32) Becoming acquainted with a variety of selections, characters, and themes of our literary heritage, Lessons 1–15

33) Activating prior knowledge, Lesson 11

34) Selecting books for individual needs and interests, Lesson 1–15

35) Recognizing differences in first-, second-, and third-person points of view, Lesson 4

36) Describing the time and setting of a story, Lesson 11

37) Explaining and relating to the feelings and emotions of characters, Lessons 4, 12

38) Selecting topics and generating materials about which to write, talk, and reflect, Lessons 1–15

39) Selecting and narrowing a topic for a specific purpose, Lesson 12

40) Varying word choice to accommodate the purpose and audience, Lesson 5

41) Using sequential clue words, chronological and spatial order, and order of importance, Lesson 3

42) Participating in rewriting conferences, Lesson 2

43) Spelling increasingly complex words, Lessons 1–15

44) Applying increasing complex conventions of punctuation and capitalization, Lessons 1–15

45) Writing legible cursive letters, Lessons 1–15

46) Including in paragraphs various kinds of complete sentences, Lesson 9

47) Using conventional formats (letters and commonly used forms), Lesson 12

48) Using correct agreement between pronouns and antecedents, Lessons 1–15

49) Using correct subject-verb agreement with personal pronouns, indefinite pronouns, and compound subjects, Lessons 1–15

50) Using modifiers (adjective and adverbs) and all other parts of speech correctly, Lessons 1–15

51) Producing coordinating and subordinating sentence elements to construct meaning, Lesson 11

52) Using semantic mapping to increase vocabulary and improve comprehension, Lesson 3

53) Recognizing paragraph structure, Lesson 3

54) Strengthening reading and listening retention, Lessons 3, 4, 11

55) Understanding authors' and speakers' use of comparisons and contrasts to inform, persuade, and entertain, Lesson 2

56) Distinguishing facts from opinions, Lessons 5, 6, 12

57) Strengthening inferential comprehension, Lesson 6

58) Recognizing persuasive writings and speeches, Lessons 5, 6, 12

59) Recognizing problems and solutions in fiction, Lessons 7, 8

60) Strengthening applied comprehension, Lessons 1, 7, 12, 13

61) Discovering that fiction can be an information gaining resource, Lesson 9

62) Increasing awareness of how different cultures face similar problems, Lesson 7

63) Building listening skills, Lessons 1–15

64) Relating unknown to known information by constructing a mental image, Lesson 11

65) Building group-work skills, Lessons 1–15

66) Increasing recall, Lessons 1–15

67) Developing creative thinking abilities, Lessons 11, 12, 13

68) Recognizing sequential words that signal comparative and contrasting statements, Lesson 2

69) Strengthening comprehension of complex concepts through the use of comparative and contrasting thinking, Lesson 2

70) Increasing metacognitive thinking, Lessons 9, 10

APPENDIX C

EFFECTS OF <u>REASON TO READ</u> UPON STUDENTS' COMPREHENSION AND THINKING DEVELOPMENT

A description of the research base for *Reason to Read* follows. If you wish more extensive reports of the program's effectiveness, please refer to the following publications.

Block, C. (1993). "Strategy Instruction in a Literature-Rich Reading Program." *The Elementary School Journal,* November, 135–153.

Collins, C. (1992). "Improving reading and thinking: From teaching or not teaching skills to interactive interventions." In Pressley, M., Harris, K. and Guthrie, J. (Eds.). *Promoting Academic Competence and Literacy in Schools.* San Diego, CA: Academic Press.

Collins, C. and Mangieri, J. (1992). *Teaching Thinking: An Agenda for the Twenty-first Century.* Hillsdale, NJ: Erlbaum.

Collins, C. (1991). "Reading instruction that increases students' thinking abilities." *Journal of Reading, 42,* 557–565.

Collins, C. (1990). "The thinking development movement gains momentum." *Teaching Thinking and Problem Solving,* 11, pp. 3, 5.

Collins, C. (1990). "Administrators can promote higher-level thinking skills." *National Association of Secondary School Principals Bulletin,* 74, pp. 102–109.

Collins, C. (1988). "Principals: Taking the lead in thinking skills development." *Reach:* Vol. 3. Austin, TX: Texas Education Agency.

Mangieri, J. and Block, C. C. (1994) *Creating Powerful Thinking in Teachers and Students: Diverse Perspectives.* Fort Worth, TX: Harcourt Brace College Publishers.

RESEARCH BASE

My problems seem less complicated now that I know problem-solving techniques. I did not expect to list my problems on paper and figure out an answer, but I do. Because of you [my reading teacher] I make decisions now instead of beating around the bush. Thank you very much! Thank you for teaching me how to think.

—Jason, a seventh grader's unsolicited note to a teacher using *Reason to Read*

The purpose of this section is to report data from studies of the effects of *Reason to Read*. We began our research with four premises. First, if *Reason to Read* can assist students to think consistently and reflectively as they read, they will improve their comprehension and use more information from printed sources in their daily lives. Second, students who have trouble comprehending may need more than improved schema and decoding competencies. These students' thinking processes may be immature and need guidance to grow. Therefore *Reason to Read* develops a capacity to strengthen thinking processes and helps reduce reading problems. Third, when students become confused about important concepts, inferences, and relationships in reading, their repertoire of thinking abilities may be so limited that they have never encountered (nor can they replicate) an author's reasonings and problem-solving processes. Because *Reason to Read* expands students' repertoires, they should become less confused. Last, if we want students to address their decoding and comprehension problems independently we need to provide extensive opportunities for them to practice problem solving and to self-select from a repertoire of thinking guides. *Reason to Read* provides students with these opportunities.

To develop this series we reviewed taxonomies and descriptions of thinking competencies. Thinking abilities that are amenable to instruction were categorized into eight dimensions, as shown in Appendix A (Baron Sternberg, l987; Beyer, 1987; Collins, 1989a, l990a; deBono, 1970; Marzano, Jones and Brandt, 1988; Paul,1990).

Prior to publication, several research studies involving *Reason to Read* were completed. The first took place from 1989–1990, the second from January–April 1990, and the third began in 1991 and continues to the present.

The first study field-tested several lesson formats in kindergarten through eleventh-grade classrooms. These field tests involved 32 teachers in 9 schools and 643 Anglo, African American, and Latino students. Several impor-

tant findings from this study guided construction of the present lesson plan format. First we asked students what skills they felt they needed in order to think better. The attributes most frequently expressed were stimulation of intellect through cognitive challenges, advanced information on topics, positive thinking models/instruction, decision-making tools, and a classroom environment that offered autonomy (Collins, 1990a).

The students in the field test went on to describe that our best lessons included student self-selection of reading material; contained dense but sequential information; allowed high-level, small group discussions; and incorporated individual goal-setting activities and assessments that pushed them to exceed their past performances. Students also reported the best teachers praised them specifically for their thinking and modeled, also through think-alouds, the "hard-won" thinking habits they had developed. They believed these lessons gave them the direction, autonomy, and courage to think through their own problems (Collins, 1989b).

When the lessons that resulted from our first study were incorporated into the reading curriculum in our second study, **experimental subjects significantly outperformed untrained subjects in many ways.** First, experimental subjects scored significantly higher on the post-test for reading comprehension (RCOMP) of the Iowa Test of Basic Skills, $F= 91.49$, $p < .001$. The experimental group also scored significantly higher than the control group on vocabulary (VOCAB), and total battery scores (TOTAL), $F=42.47$, $p <.001$, and $F=12.65$, $p>.001$, respectively. The means and standard deviations between groups appear in Table 1.

Table 1 Middle school students' mean scores and standard deviations on the Iowa Test of Basic Skills after lessons in eight domains of thinking skills

Subscales of the ITBS				
Student group	RCOMP	VOCAB	LANGTOT[†]	Total
Control	27.52	15.71	75.23	255.91
	(8.1)	(7.3)	(24.0)	(65.24)
Experimental	51.08*	29.62*	81.39	328.23*
	(4.8)	(3.3)	(14.0)	(42.90)

[†]Tests of spelling capitalization, punctuation, and usage
*p<.001

Another effect of *Reason to Read* was demonstrated in post-experimental writing samples. Without being told that their responses were a part of a study, subjects were asked to "Describe some important things you learned this year." **Experimental subjects used all domains of thinking in their writing;** control subjects used only the lowest two domains. A statistically significant association existed between thought categories used in writing and experimental control groups (F=258.52, p<.0001), as shown on page 245. The following are the categorizations we used for this analysis:

> Noting facts
> Content elaborations
> Personal elaborations
> Evaluative thinking
> Metacognition
> Expressing a lack of understanding
> Asking questions
> Confirming beliefs and transferring content learned
> Expressing attitudes/values about content learned
> Expressing attitudes about instruction received
> Changing classroom practices
> Evaluating one's own thinking
> Drawing analogies and making abstract comparisons

To analyze whether students transferred their reasoning skills to life, all subjects were asked to respond to the question, "Have you used anything you learned at school this month to help you with problems outside of school?" While 0% of control subjects answered affirmatively, 92% **of the experimental group used their new thinking tools outside of school** and related specific incidents, such as:

> "When I get home the first thing I do is plan or sketch out the next day so that I will be prepared."

> "My older brother lost his license and I helped him find it by asking him what he was doing the last time he saw it and together we used backward reasoning."

> "I recently used the backward reasoning skills with my grades."

> "I think about what I need to get accomplished that day. I organize my things to do that day better."

> "I used backward reasoning when I lost a grooming brush at the stables."

> "Prediction skills I've been using, and I've been getting into less trouble."

> "Because of my reading teacher, I make decisions now instead of beating around the bush."

> "I feel more confident to ask someone something in a strange environment without feeling like a nerd."

The fact that experimental subjects self-selected all levels of thought is educationally significant. The differences in slopes between groups was also statistically significant. (See the diagram on page 247.)

In the third measure of this study, the self-esteem scores of the experimental subjects in social competence, behavior in groups, appearance, and physical competence (as measured by the Harter Self-Perception Profile for children, 1985) were compared to self-esteem scores in control groups. Although there were no significant differences between groups on pretest measures, **experimental subjects scored significantly above control subjects on post-tests of their self-perception** of social competence, behavior in groups, appearance, and physical competence (Collins, 1991).

Finally, five raters viewed tapes of the last lesson taught in experimental and control classes. All **raters ranked subjects in experimental classes as better thinkers than subjects in control classes.** These raters also identified 12 differences between interactions that occurred in experimental versus control groups. Experimental subjects:

- did not interrupt the person talking;

- asked each other questions;

- made fewer random comments during discussion;

- built upon each others' answers;

- volunteered ideas, evidence, and rationale to help classmates' thinking;

- gave each other sufficient time to answer questions;
- were more interested in the class and their tasks until the end of the period;
- used terms to describe their thinking;
- used jargon less frequently;
- had lower noise levels; and
- had teachers who engaged a greater number of students in discussions.

These very positive results emanated from only thirty-three days of instruction, in only one curriculum area. Their success certainly would justify incorporating thinking intervention lessons into a year-long curriculum.

The third study began in September 1991 and will continue for five years. This study will involve 1,708 subjects, as shown on the next page.

In this study, after 11 weeks of instruction with *Reason to Read* we assessed experimental subjects' ability to generate ideas and to think with reflectivity. Experimental subjects significantly increased their ability to generate plausible solutions to problems. (For example, six ideas in a seven-minute period were generated in four-member groups prior to instruction; and fifteen ideas per group of four were generated following instruction.) Likewise, **experimental subjects significantly increased their reflectivity.** The test of reflectivity was to read a first-person narrative in which the narrator was identified only as "I."

Students were to determine who the narrator was using one to six clues. On the pretest, eighty-eight percent of the experimental and control subjects could not identify the narrator. These subjects' reflection time (time from point of beginning to read until selection of narrator) was one minute and fourteen seconds. Of the twelve percent who eventually identified the narrator, all made at least one inaccurate identity within the same one-minute-and-fourteen-second reflection time. On the posttest, ninety-six percent of experimental subjects identified the narrator of a first-person narrative (with Forms A and B being counterbalanced in pre-testing and post-testing). The subjects identified this narrator on their first attempt and increased their reflective time. They averaged three minutes and forty-six seconds before stating an answer.

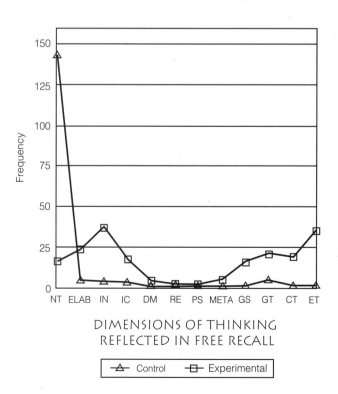

DIMENSIONS OF THINKING
REFLECTED IN FREE RECALL

Control —△— Experimental —☐—

LEGEND
DIMENSIONS OF THINKING

NT = Notetaking (Level 1—Recall)

ELAB = Elaboration (Level 1—Clarifying)

IN = Producing Inferences (Level 2—Processing and Producing New Interpretations)

IC = Interpreting Content (Level 2—Making Comparisons and Analyzing Concepts)

DM = Decision Making (Level 3—Selecting Information To Use in Life)

RE = Research (Level 4—Establishing Criteria and Solving Problems)

PS = Problem Solving (Level 4—Judging Credibility of Sources)

META = Metacognitive Thinking (Level 5—Assessing One's Own Knowledge Relative to Tasks)

GS = Goal Setting and Establishing Redirection When Alone (Level 8—Ability to Think Productively When Alone)

GT = Thinking Effectively In Groups (Level 7—Using Talents Interactively)

CT = Creative and Innovative Thinking (Level 6—Specific Actions for Improving)

ET = Evaluating One's Own Thinking Ability (Level 5—Metacognitive Thinking)

EXPERIMENTAL SUBJECTS AND CONTROL SUBJECTS FOR 1991–1996 RESEARCH STUDY

Experimental Subjects	Control Subjects
K–43	43
12	12
1–22	22
2–21	21
3–22	22
–23	23
4–22	22
–19	19
–18	18
5–20	20
6–130	130
7–250	250
8–210	210
Honor 7–20	20
Honor 8–22	22
854	854

In the present study we have also analyzed data concerning 433 middle school students' abilities to solve problems, think critically, and generate alternatives. The assessment instrument was a test designed by Irving Sigel of Education Testing Service. Students' problem-solving abilities were analyzed by three criteria: number of thinking strategies stated, precision of thought in statements made, and number of alternative solutions stated. A significant effect was found between groups concerning the number of thinking strategies used to solve a problem (t = -11.15, p < .0001). The **experimental groups also included significantly more thinking strategies to solve the problem** than control subjects (M = 2, SD = 1.40 for experimental and M = .5, SD .69 for control subjects). Similarly, a significant effect was found between groups concerning the precision of thought and number of alternative solutions cited (x_2 = 14.61, df = 2, p < .001; and t = –7.69, p < .0001 respectively) as shown in the next column.

The ability to reason was assessed through comparison of student answers to two questions of reasoning ability from the California State Department of Education Statewide Assessment Test. A significant relationship was found between groups and their selection of the most valid reason for a stated judgment (x_2 = 361.98, df = 4, p< .0001). Experimental subjects significantly outscored controls.

We are pleased with the results derived from *Reason to Read* to date. We are confident that such positive results will continue to occur as it is used in more United States classrooms.

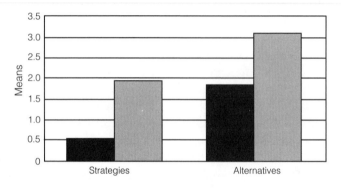

MEAN THINKING STRATEGIES & ALTERNATIVE SOLUTIONS GENERATED ON ESSAY TEST

■ Control (n = 153) ▨ Experimental (n = 187)

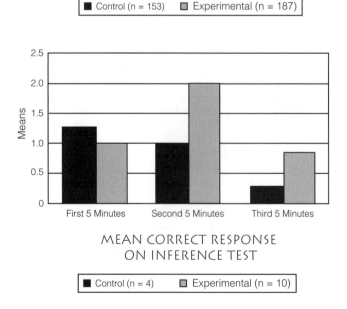

MEAN CORRECT RESPONSE ON INFERENCE TEST

■ Control (n = 4) ▨ Experimental (n = 10)

SUMMARY AND CONCLUSION

Through our studies we are more convinced that thinking abilities can be increased, and that reading lessons are a valuable section of the curriculum in which they can be developed. Reading comprehension abilities increase through *Reason to Read* lessons. We also know that teacher direction and student selection interact to expand thinking. We have evidence that teacher scaffolding and thinking guides provide the support and opportunities for increased thinking, reading achievement, and positive self-esteem. Moreover, data was produced to support the hypotheses that *Reason to Read* lessons develop reasoning abilities, reflectivity, and problem-solving skills. Two types of thinking/reading objectives interact to produce greater gains than instruction to build one at a time. Further, activities that purposely integrate reading/thinking objectives with listening, writing, and speaking have a positive effect upon thinking/reading development. Authentic instruction, as we have defined it, also enhances students' reasoning and problem-solving abilities. As Sternberg (1991) stated:

> Nature enjoys playing an occasional trick on humans, and one of her favorite tricks is to make an important discovery or principle too simple to be recognized as important. However, a growing body of educational research seems to have caught nature at this game. It suggest that one of the most important lessons teachers can impart to students is simple: "Be extremely thorough and careful in your thinking." For years we urged students not to count on their fingers, not

to move their lips when they read, and to try to read faster. Research has now shown that there are engineers who count on their fingers, lawyers who move their lips while reading, and literary figures like William Buckley who admit they read "painfully slowly." What we have not done is stressed emphatically to students that the core of academic success is systematic, accurate thought. Newton modestly observed: "If I have succeeded in my inquiries more than others, I owe it less to any superior strength of mind, than to a habit of patient thinking."

We look forward to conducting additional tests of *Reason to Read* in our future work. Our goal is to assist students to contribute more productively to our world through their thoughts, words, and deeds. We believe the first step is to help them to think more clearly and consistently as they read and to think more effectively in general. *Reason to Read* has demonstrated how students can reach this goal.

While we are unable to predict the problems our youth will face in the future, we have learned that teaching young adolescents to think through *Reason to Read* increases their thinking repertoires, helps them gain more control in their lives, and enables them to meet new challenges more successfully. We encourage teachers to take a first step to better prepare our students for the cognitive demands in their future. We can begin by using the lessons in this book to increase students' thinking and communication abilities simultaneously.

REFERENCES

Anderson, R. C., Hiebert, E. H., Scott, J. A. and Wilkerson, I. A. G. (1985). *Becoming a Nation of Readers: The Report of the Commission on Reading.* Washington, DC: National Institute of Education.

Baron, J. and Sternberg, R. (1987). *Teaching Thinking Skills: Theory and Practice.* New York: Freeman.

Beck, I. and Dole, J.(1992). "Reading and thinking with history and science text." In C. Collins and J. Mangieri (Eds.) *Teaching Thinking: An Agenda for the Twenty-first Century.* Hillsdale, NJ: Erlbaum.

Beck, I. (1989). "Reading and reasoning." *The Reading Teacher, 42* (9), 676–684.

Beyer, B. (1987). *Practical Strategies for the Teaching of Thinking.* Boston, MA: Allyn & Bacon.

Block, C. (1993). "Strategic Instruction in a Literature-Rich Classroom." *Elementary School Journal,* November, 135–153.

Block, C. (1993a, April). "Effects of Strategy Instruction Upon Students of Above Average, Average, and Below Average Reading Achievement." Paper presented at the annual meeting of the American Educational Research Association, Atlanta.

Block,C. (1993c). *Teaching the Language Arts: Expanding Thinking Through Student-Centered Instruction.* Boston, MA: Allyn & Bacon.

Bonds, C. W. and Bonds, L. T. (1984). "Reading and the Gifted Student. *Roeper Review, 5,* 4–6.

Borick, G. (1979). Implications for Developing Teacher Competencies from Processes and Procedure Research." *Journal of Teacher Education, 30,* 77–86.

Brophy, J. and Evertson, C. (1974). *Process-Product Correlations in the Texas Teacher Effectiveness Study.* Final Report No. 74–4. Austin: Research and Development Center for Teacher Education, University of Texas.

Carnegie Council on Adolescent Development (1989). *Turning Points: Preparing American Youth for the Twenty-First Century.* New York: Carnegie Foundation.

Collins, C. and Mangieri, J. N. (1992). *Teaching Thinking: An Agenda for the Twenty-first Century.* Hillsdale, NJ: Erlbaum.

deBono, E. (1970). *Lateral Thinking.* New York: Harper & Row.

Duffy, J. (1992). "Business Partnerships for a Thinking Populace." In C. Collins and J. Mangieri (Eds.) *Teaching Thinking: An Agenda for the Twenty-First Century.* Hillsdale, NJ: Erlbaum.

Eichhorn, D. (1989). *The Middle School.* New York: The Center for Applied Research in Education.

Gardner, H. and Hatch, T. (1989). "Multiple Intelligences Go to School: Educational Implications of the Theory of Multiple Intelligences," *Educational Researcher, 18* (8), 4–10.

Gough, P. (1987). "An Interview with William Glaser." *Phi Delta Kappan, 69* (7), 593–607.

Hahn, A., Dansberger, J., and Lefkowitz, B. (1987). *Dropouts in America: Enough is Known for Action.* Washington, DC: Institute for Educational Leadership.

Kletzien, L. (1991). "Strategy Use by Good and Poor Comprehenders." *Reading Research Quarterly, XXVI* (1), 70–94.

Kutscher, R. E. (1989). "Projections Summary and Emerging Issues." *Monthly Labor Review, 112* (11), 66–74.

Langer, J. and Applebee, A. N. (1987). *How Writing Shapes Thinking: A Study of Teaching and Learning.* Urbana, IL: National Council of Teachers of English.

Mangieri, J. (1991). *Personal Communication.* Fort Worth, Texas: Texas Christian University. Unpublished manuscript.

Mervar, K. and Hiebert, E. (1989, April). "Students' Self-Selection Abilities and Amount of Reading in Literature-Based and Conventional Classrooms." Paper presented at the Annual Meeting of the American Educational Research Association, San Francisco.

Morrow, L. M. (1987). "Promoting Inner-City Children's Recreational Reading." *The Reading Teacher*, 41 (6), 396–406.

Porter, A. and Brophy, J. (1988). "Synthesis of Research on Good Teaching." *Educational Leadership, 45* (8), 74–85.

Norton, D. (1990). "Teaching Multicultural Literature in the Reading Curriculum." *The Reading Teacher, 44* (1), 17–28.

Paul, W. (1989). *How to Study in College*. Boston, MA: Houghton Mifflin.

Rosenblatt, L. M. (1978). *The Reader, the Text and the Poem*. Carbondale, IL: Southern Illinois University Press.

Smith, F. (1978). *Understanding Reading*. New York: Holt, Rinehart, and Winston.

Sternberg, R.(1985). B*eyond IQ*. New York: Cambridge University Press.

Stuart, V. and Graves, D. (1987). *How to Teach Writing*. Urbana, IL: National Council of Teachers of English.

Willinsky, J. (1990). *The New Literacy*. New York: Routledge.

Zabrucky, K. and Ratner, N. H. (1989). "Effects of Reading Ability on Children's Comprehension Evaluation and Regulation." *Journal of Reading Behavior, 21*, 69–83.